FERTILE GROUND

A Pilgrimage Through Pregnancy

LAURA S. JANSSON

ANCIENT FAITH PUBLISHING
CHESTERTON, INDIANA

Published by:
    Ancient Faith Publishing
    A Division of Ancient Faith Ministries
    P.O. Box 748
    Chesterton, IN 46304

Cover and interior illustrations by Clare Freeman.

All Old Testament quotations, unless otherwise identified, are from
the Orthodox Study Bible, © 2008 by St. Athanasius Academy of
Orthodox Theology (published by Thomas Nelson, Inc., Nashville,
Tennessee) and are used by permission. New Testament quota-
tions are from the New King James Version of the Bible, © 1982 by
Thomas Nelson, Inc., and are used by permission.

ISBN: 978-1-944967-60-4

Printed in the United States of America

30 29 28 27 26 25 24 23 22 21   18 17 16 15 14 13 12 11 10 9 8 7 6 5 4 3 2

This book honors the memory of two visionaries:

my foremother in the flesh, Ruth Miriam Hone,

who saw in me a book, and

my foremother in spirit, Righteous Elizabeth,

who saw in a pregnant belly her Lord.

Contents

PART FOUR: FEARING LABOR

PART FIVE: BRAVING LABOR

PART SIX: BECOMING A PARENT

PART SEVEN: PREPARING FOR BIRTH

Prayers of a Woman with Child

Sovereign Lord Jesus Christ our God, the source of life and immortality, I thank You, for in my marriage You have made me a recipient of Your blessing and gift; for You, O Master, did say: Be fruitful and multiply and replenish the earth.

I thank You and pray: Bless this fruit of my body that was given to me by You; favor it and animate it by Your Holy Spirit, and let it grow a healthy and pure body, with well-formed limbs.

Sanctify its body, mind, heart, and vitals, and grant this infant that is to be born an intelligent soul; establish him in the fear of You.

Grant him a faithful angel, a guardian of soul and body. Protect, keep, strengthen, and shelter the child in my womb until the hour of his birth. But do not conceal him in his mother's womb; You gave him life and health.

O Lord Jesus Christ, into Your almighty and paternal hands I entrust my child. Place him on the right hand of Your grace, and through Your Holy Spirit sanctify him and renew him unto life everlasting, that he may be a communicant of Your Heavenly Kingdom. Amen.

O ALL-MERCIFUL CHRIST OUR GOD, look down and protect me, Your handmaiden, from fear and from evil spirits that seek to destroy the work of Your hands. And when my hour and time is come, deliver me by Your grace.

Look with compassionate eye and deliver me, Your handmaiden, from pain. Lighten my infirmity in the time of my travail and grant me fortitude and strength for birth-giving, and hasten it by Your almighty help. For this is Your glorious work, the power of Your omnipotence, the work of Your grace and tenderheartedness. Amen.

MY MOST GRACIOUS QUEEN, my hope, O Mother of God, the joy of those in sorrow, help me, for I am helpless. Intercede and pray your Son, Christ our God, that He lighten for me this season while I am with child, and that He ease the burden of heaviness of this unworthy handmaiden, and bestow His blessings upon the child to which I am giving birth.

For I know no other help save you, O Mother of God, that will guard and protect me and my child. For by your intercession and help, we send up glory and thanksgiving for all things unto the One God in Trinity, the Creator of all, now and ever, and unto the ages of ages. Amen.

Acknowledgments

I pinch myself to think I am so blessed as to have been the author of this book. Not many people get to see the experiences of their life culminate in such a concrete form. I owe a great debt of gratitude to those who supported, inspired, trusted, and bore with me as I undertook this humbling task.

First, to the women who have allowed me to serve their families as doula, whose bravery I carry like a secret in my heart. That they invited me into their lives at such a raw and holy time is a privilege not lost on me. Especially I thank Georgia Williams, who first asked me to stand witness, and my treasured godsib Jodi Perpetua Elliott.

I am grateful to my mentors on the journey into birth work, in particular Ida Hercules, Alex Smith, Frances Findlay, Sarah Quipp-Stenson, and Christy Feiker. In a world that considers birth little more than a necessary evil, they helped me see its transcendent and transformational possibilities.

To my fellow travelers on the Orthodox way, especially to the Magnusson, Raicu, Plested, Elliott, Redmann, Rappl, and Ghebregziabiher families: I thank you. Heartfelt gratitude to Fr. Tom Mueller and Fr. Stephen Platt for their teaching, tending, and prayer. This book would not exist if not for their generous trust.

We know that everything must shift to make room for a new being coming into the world, and many people made logistical accommodations over several years so that this project could take shape. Karen and Peter Jansson, Naomi Jansson, Tai and the Byron family, Kat and the Minto family, and Barbara and Jeffry Smith took care of my little ones so I could take care of a book. Others gave helpful counsel and feedback: Lisa Holewa, Zoe Sherman, Alessandra Rolffs, Andrew Williams, Gavin Kelly, and two who did not want to be thanked by name. I thank Katherine Hyde, John Maddex, and Nicole Roccas—collaborators at Ancient Faith—for their support.

Above all, I am deeply grateful to my family, who have borne patiently with me in love. To my parents for giving me both the physical and spiritual birth about which I write. To Melissa and Pabs Robertson, for their friendship and indomitable joy. To my children, who by teaching me to be a mother have revealed the path to my salvation. Most of all, to my husband Eric, who makes this book—and my life as it is—possible. He has graciously given me the space in which to become myself.

Introduction

To walk is to gather treasure.
—SPANISH PROVERB[1]

We make many kinds of journeys in this life. Sometimes it's a quick run to the grocery store, other times a two-week family history tour. Sometimes it's a tedious commute through traffic, others a thoughtful stroll through a labyrinth. We go on hikes, promenades, odysseys, and marathons; safaris, missions, raids, and expeditions.

Pregnancy too is a kind of journey: a purposeful one, but sometimes also slow, waddling, and laborious—more of a saunter than a sprint. And *saunter* is a good term for it. The word comes from a French phrase, *à la sainte terre*, meaning "to the holy ground." For this is a journey traversing a wide spiritual landscape. There are dizzying peaks and eerie valleys, arduous climbs and refreshing streams. Every day we draw nearer to the holy city that is our destination. There we encounter and usher into the world the divine image in a new form: our baby.

As with any epic journey, we emerge from this experience changed. Certainly, we are rounder, achier, and more sleep-deprived. But even as we grow in girth, during pregnancy we also grow spiritually. The intricate process by which God creates new life in us quite literally softens, humbles, gladdens,

11

and causes us to live for the Other. Even pregnancy's trials can be seen as a mercy, a gift, a process by which God reaches out, helping us prepare our hearts to enter the challenges of parenthood. In this way, the physical experience of walking day by day through pregnancy, one foot in front of the other, gives us the chance to become the people we will need to be. Ultimately, pregnancy can become a journey toward the Kingdom, a path to our salvation.

But looking at the culture around us, you'd never guess that pregnancy was a quest of epic proportions. Instead, it is seen in utilitarian terms: more like a quick trip to get gas than a pilgrimage. In an age when plastic-bag "wombs" can be used to bring lambs to maturity, mothers are just incubators, and pregnancy is an inconvenience only necessary in the absence of better technological solutions. At the same time, our society is very sentimental about childbearing. People want to pet us, baby us, and call us cute. The mother, as one scholar puts it, is "caught in an ever-widening gap between her idealization and denigration in contemporary culture."[2] But many of us sense that there is more to pregnancy than urine tests, multivitamin pills, and leafy greens—and, for that matter, more than rocking chairs, rosy cheeks, and rubber duckies.

This book began as a collection of ecstatic, oxytocin-fueled musings during my own first pregnancy. As I grew, birthed, and fed my baby, I felt as if the world had been blown open to me. I became fascinated with the meaning, symbolism, and poetry I discovered at the heart of the experience of making a baby. Certain themes—death and resurrection, growth and diminishment, strength and weakness—kept repeating throughout my body, my inner life, Scripture, the natural world, and the tradition of the Church. I began to see my pregnant body as theology in motion, and the journey of pregnancy as an embodiment of the soul's journey toward God.

At the same time, I struggled. I wanted to find meaning in the fight—to know that my sacrifices were worthwhile—but also to get braver. I longed to be supported, cherished, and validated in my calling. Though the path to my child's birth was one I alone could tread, I wanted to know that as a mother I was not in this by myself but was part of something bigger. As I journeyed, I felt beside me the presence of other women, not just the tens of millions around the world who were pregnant at the same time I was, but a community of birth-givers spanning time and salvation history. A whole host of path-breakers, mapmakers, Sherpas, and veteran pilgrims surrounded me. I began to see myself as one of them—as an intrepid traveler gathering her courage to complete a sacred mission.

Once I began to work as a doula, I got to accompany other women as they walked their own holy path. The term *doula*, meaning "female slave" in Greek, is a new name for an old role. A doula is a childbirth companion, supporting growing families through labor in practical, emotional, spiritual, physical, and informational (though not medical) ways. At a given birth I might be found running my client a bath, reassuring her husband or partner, helping her identify good questions to ask care providers, supporting her body in her chosen birthing position, fetching cushions for her baby's first feed, or simply holding vigil at her bedside.

Because birth, life, and God are experienced only relationally, I have chosen to populate this book with stories. Its material is informed by my own personal experience of gestating, home-birthing, and breastfeeding my four living children, as well as miscarrying a fifth, and by my fifteen years of work with other mothers. Parts of my experience are universal; everyone on earth has a mother, and everyone was born. But that doesn't mean I assume that you are just like me. As a doula I've stood witness as scores of other women brought children into the world, each one in her own way. As a childbirth educator, I've engaged with the unique questions each family faces in advance of a new arrival. I know that, even if we are headed to the same destination, your path will be different from, and every bit as valid as, mine.

Whether you are expecting your first baby or your fifth, this book is for you. It's for you whether you are delighted or mortified to be pregnant. It's for you if you end up braving a cesarean, a straightforward birth, or anything in between. And, though I have chosen to refer to all babies as "he," it's also for you whether you're expecting a boy, a girl, or multiples. ("He or she or they" proved too clunky, so I chose the singular male pronoun to help distinguish mother and baby. Please substitute your own pronouns as necessary.)

Throughout this book, there are various accounts of human physiology and medical fact. I am not a pharmacologist, a neo-natologist, a practitioner of breastfeeding medicine, or anything of the sort, but as a childbirth educator I have spent many years gleaning from research studies undertaken by those who are qualified within the relevant fields. Our human understanding of the complex mechanisms of pregnancy, birth, and lactation is curiously underresearched and continually evolving, so some of what you read here may in time prove inaccurate. In the meanwhile, I have endeavored to base all my descriptions on the best available scientific evidence.

This book is not intended to provide medical or spiritual advice, so if you have any concerns regarding what you read here, please speak with your priest or your medical care provider, who know you and your situation personally. What this book *is* intended to be is a spiritual guidebook for your pilgrim's journey. It divides the journey into stages, with one chapter for each week of your pregnancy. Each week has its own topic, which I hope will prove relevant to the specific terrain you're crossing at that time, helping you find your path and look out for the sights.

I divide the journey into stages, with each chapter forming part of a larger section. "Welcoming a New Reality" (Weeks 6 to 9) starts to wrestle with the significance of a positive pregnancy test and asks how each of us can begin to make our heart, not only our womb, a receptive place for a baby to grow. During Weeks 10 to 17, as the hesitancy of the first trimester gives way to the more self-assured second, "Being Pregnant" looks at some fundamental motifs of the experience. Next, in the conceptual heart of the journey, "Symbols of Birth" (Weeks 18 to 20) explores Christ's central metaphor for salvation, that of being "born again," and what it tells us about the significance of our actions as women bringing forth new life in the world.

On the eve of the third trimester, first we tackle some of the fears, then develop some antidotes to the fears, that many women have approaching labor, examining the purpose of these fears in our lives as Christians ("Fears about Labor," Weeks 21 to 23, and "Support for Labor," Weeks 24 to 27, respectively). In "Becoming a Parent" (Weeks 28 to 33), we cast our eyes down the road to the postpartum period, garnering from Holy Tradition some of the spiritual resources we will need to thrive on life with a tiny baby. Finally, the section called "Preparing for Birth" (Weeks 34 to 37) takes us to full term, illustrating the symbolic shape of the changes occurring in our bodies on the threshold of motherhood.

This is not a book for binge-reading, but for chewing over slowly. Not knowing at what point along the road this book would find you, I designed each chapter to stand alone, so that you'd be able to flip forward and begin reading at the week you happen to be in at the time. After that, by reading one chapter each week, you'll be accompanied all the way to the completion of your pilgrimage. If at any time your path should end unexpectedly, you will find an appendix addressing pregnancy loss at the back of the book.

Here's how I imagine you using this book, week by week. I envisage you settling in with a warm drink and maybe with a loved one, at a certain time each week. Beginning with the Prayers of a Woman with Child printed at the front of the book, I hope you'll then take your time digesting the week's chapter. Though you might only spend fifteen minutes doing this, you may notice its theme cropping up all week long. As your thoughts brew, my vision is that you'll use the discussion questions at the back of the book as a prompt for journaling or conversations. If you have a friend who's pregnant at the same time as you are, so much the better—you can undertake this journey as companions.

I pray that, with the help of this book, your pregnancy will be transformed into an act of prayer. May this *sainte terre* prove to be fertile ground for growth as you commend yourself, your baby, and "all our life unto Christ our God."

ONE

Welcoming a New Reality

Fiat

Let it be to me according to your word.
—LUKE 1:38

As we rang the doorbell my husband and I looked at each other sideways with sheepish newlywed smiles. Someone buzzed us in and, with the busy Belgrade street behind us, we navigated the fragile steps into the darkness of the Communist-era building. My knees gave way with excitement and apprehension. We were strangers in a strange land, coming for our first appointment with the obstetrician the embassy had recommended.

Just days previously we had learned that I was pregnant: our first child. We'd been too bashful to ask our go-to Serbian friends for help, so my husband had negotiated the cross-cultural purchase of a pregnancy test. Once the two lines appeared, we'd immediately set the Hallelujah Chorus blaring.

The very hour of that positive test, a whole giddy universe had begun to open before the eyes of our minds. It was a vast realm of possibility, risk, inevitability, timelessness, responsibility, and hope. It hurtled outward into the dark unknown of our married future at terrifying speed, joyously gobbling up the void as it went, like a new Big Bang. It was a moment out of time, implanted in eternity. It was *what was yet to come* and *what had already occurred*, both at once. What was going to happen had actually already happened. There isn't a tense for that, in the English language at least.

Inside the brightly lit clinic, we waited under a poster of a woman in a gauzy dress and flower crown, benignly nestling to her unthinkably pregnant belly the head of a partially dressed blond child. Finally we were ushered into the doctor's office, where a lady with neat black bangs and the requisite white coat motioned for us to sit down at her desk. Behind her, the view out the window was of the half-built basilica of St. Sava, on its way to becoming one of the biggest Orthodox churches in the world. She asked what had brought us to see her.

"We've just discovered that I am pregnant," I said, trying to control myself so that my face would not split in two. She was the first person we had graced with this preciously held news of ours, yet to my surprise her face did not even betray a professional smile. In the small pause that ensued, the ghost of a thought that we might be in the wrong place flitted past. The doctor nodded knowingly and folded her hands on the desk.

"So," she said straightforwardly, unflinching, "are you happy about this, or not?"

We had stumbled, unawares, upon the first crossroad on our own pilgrimage through pregnancy.

The implication of the doctor's question was clear. There was a decision to be made. We were now to choose between two paths, which she showed us with equal willingness. This airy room with its beautiful view and shining instruments could become the place we would visit regularly, vigilantly, even liturgically, monitoring our baby's growth and being counseled on how to calibrate every aspect of our lives toward his well-being. Or it could become the place our baby was destroyed, almost— *almost*—as if he'd never been. The degree of difference between the two paths at this point was as small as the speaking of a word, yet the choice would pivotally change the future—for us, for our family, for our friends, and even, mysteriously, for the world itself.

Perhaps the doctor's question should not have shocked or surprised me, but it did. Surely she could see the shine in our eyes. Of course, on an academic level I knew that there were any number of circumstances under which a woman would be hesitant, conflicted, upset, or devastated to be facing pregnancy, but looking over the parapet from the sheltered depths of my own happiness I could hardly glimpse those other realities.

Taken on its surface, this question—"Are you happy about this or not? Are you or are you not planning to nurture this life you have set in motion?"—was at best redundant and at worst an offense to the glassy-eyed couple. In the moment it held no more than shock value. A deeper value only became clear over time, as hourly trips to the bathroom round the clock became my way of life; as morning sickness caused me to revisit each breakfast; as my pelvis grew uncomfortably soft and rickety in preparation for letting a baby through. *Are you happy about this, or not? Are you able to embrace with humility all this brings?*

The story of this first doctor's visit is not a story about a bad question. Far from being a bad question, it is one I might ask myself daily. In fact, the obstetrician's question was a gift because it made explicit the choice I had, to embrace this pregnancy or to reject it—whether on a physical, emotional, or spiritual level, or on any level I might be tempted to. It gave me a chance at the outset of my pregnancy to respond with my own fiat, as the Holy Theotokos (Mother of God) did. *Fiat*, meaning "Let it be. Let it be to me according to your word" (Luke 1:38).

The Theotokos said yes. She chose to extend the fullness of her self as a free gift to her Lord. And she made the decision despite not knowing exactly how this would work or what lay ahead. As it turned out, what lay ahead was this: the burden of being unwed and pregnant in a culture that would seek to objectify, shame, and disown her for it. It was the work of constantly giving Jesus to the world, not keeping Him to herself but allowing *anyone* who would hear and do His Word to become His mother (Matt. 12:50).

It was the tremendous sorrow of standing under a cross while her son, the fruit of her body, died a torturous criminal's death only feet away, and not being able to save him. It was the sheer desperation, shared by grieving mothers in every age, of becoming that apparent aberration of nature, a parent who has to go on living after the death of her child. After the Resurrection, it was bearing the responsibility, after *all that*, of bringing the joy of the gospel to the world, no matter how much she would have preferred to stay in the shadows. So when we say she gave her all, it wasn't just her body she gave but the whole course of her life. She may not have known at the time of her fiat that this was what she was saying yes to, but she was.

Our own yes is not exactly like the one the Theotokos gave, because unlike us, she was saying yes to a pregnancy that had not yet begun. What we are called to affirm may also seem comparatively easy and insignificant. Yet our fiat is an icon, or image, of hers. We each face our own very real struggles that tempt us away from fully embracing the reality of pregnancy. We may have practical doubts, such as whether we can afford to provide good things for this child. There may be complicated relational questions, such as how family members will react to a new arrival. Some of us face deep emotional concerns, like those tracing back to our family of origin. For others like me the struggles are mainly physical—for instance, how we'll make it through the whole of pregnancy if we're this exhausted all the time.

In the face of whatever particular struggles we ourselves face, like the Theotokos we all ask on some level and at some point, *how can this pregnancy be?* But also like her, we are invited to make our own fiat. When I think a bit more about what this fiat is and is not, five things about it strike me as notable.

First, this fiat is not about being pumped up with delightful feelings. The Theotokos was *troubled* in her heart upon meeting the Archangel Gabriel when he came to announce to her that she would be the Mother of God. Saying yes occurs in the context of my concerns, rather than washing them all magically away. It does not mean that I should expect myself to be filled with natural joy, or beat myself up if I experience conflicted feelings— after all, self-hatred is a strange means by which to try to reach for joy. Rather, my fiat is about a decision. I have my struggles, but by God's grace I can count myself willing to face up to them with an openness to what lies ahead.

Second, a fiat is not a game plan. When the Theotokos said yes, it was with questions—questions about the mechanics and meaning of the proposal. *How can this be?* She was given an answer: "The Holy Spirit will come upon you, and the power of the Highest will overshadow you; therefore, also, that Holy One who is to be born will be called the Son of God" (Luke 1:35). It *was* an answer, the truest answer, but not a biological answer, and perhaps not the answer to the question she thought she was asking: "How can this be, since I do not know a man?" (Luke 1:34). Like me, she didn't know, or need to know, how everything would happen in order to be game for it.

The reality of a positive pregnancy test can feel a bit surreal and take some time to sink in. Fair enough. In the many centuries before the age of home pregnancy tests, which were only invented in the late 1960s, our foremothers would have reckoned more organically with their pregnancies. Evidence would come from within rather than from an objective test that could verify or deny. An intuition, a wave of nausea, an unearthly tiredness, or a menstrual period that never came would hint that a new life was present. Then a gradual accumulation of physical signs would lend that suspicion credence over the coming months: quickening (the mother's first feeling of the baby's kicks) and a growing belly. Labor and birth would be the final clincher.

Our foremothers would have had the better part of a year to become used to the idea of new life. They would have moved slowly from the theoretical into the concrete, rather than expecting themselves to internalize such a huge tectonic shift in the space of the couple of minutes it takes for the test to process. It's actually one of the blessings of pregnancy that it takes so long (though it certainly doesn't always *feel* like a blessing). Imagine if the human gestation period were short, like the opossum or the hamster at around two weeks—if, no sooner than we discovered we were pregnant, our babies were ready to be born and the first pangs of labor began! What a shock that would be to us humans, who often need time to get used to things. So my yes can be a gradual yes; my fiat may take some time to build to its full volume. For me as for the Theotokos, full *acceptance* of reality is not the same as full *knowledge* or *understanding* of reality, and that's all right. A fuller understanding will come over time.

Returning to our five traits of a fiat: Third, a fiat is not a once-and-done. The Theotokos's question was one she revisited regularly throughout Christ's life. "Why have you treated us this way [by losing us at the temple]?" (Luke 2:48)—in other words, *how can this be?* "They have no wine" (John 2:3)—the implication being, *how can this be?* And, at the foot of the Cross, no matter how much faith she had come to have, I imagine she can only have asked again in her humanity, *how can this be?*

I too will be tempted to hold my pregnancy, my child, at a distance again and again. Giving a fiat to God's plan does not mean the same question will not pop up again, sometimes in even harder forms. This *yes* I am invited to say at the beginning of pregnancy is one I will be called on to say again and again, not only throughout pregnancy but regularly in my life as a mother, too. *Yes* then becomes the cross I take up on a daily, or even during some seasons an hourly, basis.

Fourth, pronouncing a fiat is not a passive thing to do. We call this story of the conception of Christ the Annunciation, as if Gabriel's role was simply to announce to Mary what was going to happen. Of course, God, who is not bound by time, knew that the Theotokos *would* say yes, so in that sense His messenger was making an announcement. But the Theotokos was not a mild virginal pushover, acquiescing to an imposition. She had the freedom to say no, but she actively chose to offer her humanity to God's divinity for the purpose of bringing to the world the One who was saving it. Though she was certainly humble, she is also first among the saints, the leader of our Christian army in the spiritual battle against the enemy. Coming from her, *fiat* sounds more like a strong battle cry than an eye-rolling teenagery "okay, then."

In fact, looking a bit closer at the word *fiat* itself, we see more of its strength. The fourth-century Latin Vulgate translation of the Holy Scriptures, where this word appears, gives the word not only to the Theotokos but to various people throughout the Bible, including Moses, David, the devil, Paul, and most strongly of all, God Himself, at the dawn of creation. *Fiat lux,* He said: let there be light! (Gen. 1:3). Of course, far from being a surrender to any pressing outside forces, this is the ultimate act of free self-expression: the creation of something entirely new, from nothing. The Theotokos's fiat was free and uncoerced too—and so can mine be.

Finally, fiats are not just for pregnant people. Whatever our circumstances, human life offers constant opportunities to embrace God's gifts to us or to hold them at arm's length. Sometimes my heart is hard, or I consider myself too busy, or I think I know better, or I feel unworthy. When I choose to embrace the gift of pregnancy, no matter how complicated it is for me, I act as a living sign to the world. I become a model of fiat for others, just as the Theotokos is a model of fiat for me. Not only that, but I even become an example for myself. Pronouncing *fiat* is a transferable spiritual skill. Through the practice of saying yes during pregnancy, I learn to do so when God calls on me at other times of life.

Co-Creators

We are God's fellow workers.
—1 CORINTHIANS 3:9

Quiet moments were rare after my third child was born, but one Sunday morning while everyone else was at Liturgy, she and I sat in the silence, drinking one another in. Curling her elegant fingers around my thumb, I squinted to discern the swirls of her fingerprints—a tiny work of art at the end of each digit. With forensic accuracy, their unique configuration marked her for who she was: a person the likes of whom the world had never before seen. I started to wonder how those patterns got there.

Way back during pregnancy, I learned—between weeks six and thirteen, in fact—my baby's fingers and toes had developed pads. Over the course of the next month, a landscape of miniature mountain ranges had taken shape on each one. What I read suggested that those emerging patterns were slightly influenced by genetic inheritance, but much more important had been the movement of the amniotic fluid surrounding her as the pads formed. The lines I could now see had appeared as she wriggled, sloshed, reached, turned, touched, and grew during her earliest days in my womb. The dance steps of our shared life had shaped my baby's very body.

With her hand in mine, I cast my mind back. This swirl, I wondered—was it created when I bent to sign my other children's foreheads with the cross at bedtime, to weed my garden, or to kiss the icon of Christ each time I entered my church? Was the little U-turn on this finger etched in as my grandmother gave me a pat on the belly to celebrate my pregnancy, or with the steps of a sunset walk with a dear friend, or during the welcome-home hug I'd given my husband at the end of each day? This interesting spiral—did it arise from belly laughs or the quaking of tears?

The act of making a baby is sometimes called *procreation* (the Latin prefix *pro* meaning "forth"). But the phenomenon of fingerprints proves that mothers are more than procreators, merely bringing God's creation forward into a new generation. Mothering is not just something my body is used for, a passive means of production. Rather, from the beginning He entrusts me to help mold the clay from which He forms humanity. Astonishing as it seems, the Creator lets me come alongside Him, working next to Him in the dirt as His work takes form. He empowers me to be not simply a *procreator* but a *co-creator* of one of His greatest works: a human creature who uniquely bears His image and who will help write the next chapter in the story of the world's salvation history. It's a noble and high calling indeed.

Knowing how impressionable my baby is, even literally speaking, I can leverage this powerful knowledge for good. During pregnancy and parenthood, I have the chance to take the tiny new creature God has made and, by carefully curating the circumstances of my own life, attempt to protect, nurture, and shepherd it toward the loveliest self it can become.

And, boy, does my culture urge me to do so. No shortage of "expert" advice instructs pregnant women how to behave in order to maximize the chances of bearing a happy and healthy child. The tide of tips and tweaks comes from magazines, medics, matushkas, and memes. It comes from every side and involves every area of life. I'm supposed to relax but keep active. Eat more protein than I have any desire for yet not gain too much weight. Avoid sushi—so what if my mother is Japanese?

There are guidelines regarding my sexual life, my posture, my cooking, my emotions, and my working hours. That's not to mention the restrictions I place on myself based on instinct. At the movies, I turn away from gory scenes so that the baby in my womb won't "see." Walking past a construction site, I cross the street to try to shield my belly from the din of the machinery.

Yet the story of human fingerprints has something deeper to say. It seems to be a parable, a physical illustration that points the way to a bigger inner reality—because it's not only my baby's physical features but also his inner self that is being shaped by the events of his prenatal life. Right from his earliest moments, I am laying down for him experiences he will retain. Even during pregnancy I am providing, or as his mother actually *being*, the environment in which he experiences the world. I influence him by the sounds his forming ears hear through the watery drum of the womb, by the taste of the food I eat transmitted through my amniotic fluid, by the sharing of hormones that are the physical corollaries of the emotions I experience.

For every one of us, the first experiences our mothers provide are deeply formative. For some people, like the little children who quite casually share memories of their time in the womb, these impressions are ones they can keep hold of, put words to, and incorporate into their life's narrative. But for most of us they are lost from conscious memory, incorporated into our lives in ways more subtle but equally real.

Recent scientific research has confirmed the profound connection between pre-birth experiences and future health, whether physically, spiritually, behaviorally, or psychologically measured. It was discovered, for example, that a chronically stressed mother is more likely to have a child of low birth weight, a marker linked to health challenges.³ Another study found that babies whose mothers sang them lullabies in the womb cried less than those whose mothers didn't.⁴

And the impact of our maternal care extends not just to the health of our own children, but to future generations as well. Researchers in epigenetics have discovered that early life experiences work on our pre-existing genetic material, sliding the dimmer switches on our genes up or down to express or suppress their tendencies, and—most amazingly of all—that these changes themselves are then passed down within the genes of future generations. Researchers experimenting with mice have observed, for instance, that those who have been through traumatic experiences have babies that grow up to exhibit traumatized behavior, even if those babies themselves had uneventful lives.⁵

Today's nurture, it seems, becomes tomorrow's nature. It reminds me of the Old Testament Scripture in which God tells us the sins of the fathers are visited upon the children, to the third and fourth generation (Ex. 34:7). Often we read these words as a vengeful threat, but they could equally be viewed as a practical public service announcement directed at a people who did not have modern science to inform them about the impact of their parental actions.

Most of us expectant mothers wield our creative influence with great seriousness, almost as if we can't quite help it—as if it somehow flows from our nature and calling as human persons. As Metropolitan Kallistos Ware says, humans are by nature creative beings; creativity is part of what it means to be made in the image of God.⁶ Being creative, he says, means to take the raw materials God gives and shape them so that they are transformed into something new, something in which a glory that was hidden before is now revealed. We reshape, reform, fashion, and at our best transfigure, though sometimes we also disfigure and mar.

Yet while we are creators, we are also creatures. The creativity that belongs to us is only ours by virtue of God's image in us. God is the one who calls into being new things *ex nihilo,* out of nothingness and into existence—we are the ones who simply reconfigure what we already have. We may "lead" our lives, but we do not conduct, enact, or execute them. We fine-tune the details of our health with leafy greens and filtered water, but it is He who sustains us with every beat of our heart—and, starting as early as sixteen days from conception, our baby's. Again, it may be our actions that brought together sperm and egg, but He provides the spark of life, manifested in the large burst of energy that medical imaging indicates is released at the moment of conception. And when He does, the result is a new human person, rather than just soup, or a new chemical element, or a destructive implosion. Yes, the power over life and death does not belong to us.

Nevertheless, how easy it is for me to fool myself into thinking I am the one in control. The surrounding culture backs me up on this misapprehension. It's common to hear that I "create my own reality." The good in my life is a credit not to God's mercy but to my sensible decision making. Everything "wrong" with my life is seen not as being mysteriously needful for the good of my soul, but as having a cause that might have been avoided. ("Who sinned, this man or his parents?" as the disciples asked Jesus regarding the man born blind.) If I have a good-natured baby, it must be because of the sleep training schedule I'm using. If I have cancer, maybe it's because I'm holding on to anger.

So perhaps after years of carefully avoiding pregnancy, I decide I am ready for a baby and switch modes. I monitor my fertility and plan for the month, or even for the day, when my baby will be conceived. If I become pregnant, we may be inclined to think *I fulfilled my plan*. Or maybe after a long struggle and perhaps some medical assistance, I conceive a much-desired child. We may think *I finally succeeded*. Or if planning had nothing to do with it, I might be teased, *oops!*, as if I pressed the wrong button on a vending machine and ended up ordering the wrong thing. Either way, pregnancy is thought of as the result of human success or failure.

True, God seeks our cooperation, but our actions aren't the full reason pregnancies happen. New humans come into being when, working within the boundaries of their parents' free choices, the Giver of all good things makes an astonishing gift. "A man's heart plans his way"—or doesn't, as the case may be!—"but the LORD directs his steps" (Prov. 16:9).

Many things are already fixed at a very early stage of development and cannot be changed by anything anyone might do. They were fixed at fertilization, when the chromosomes from two gametes intertwined, fused together, then ripped apart, leaving precisely enough genetic material for a single person, though made from two. It is a biological process that allows for endless variations, even from the same material. He could have created anyone, but our Lord in His wisdom prepares in my womb *just* the little person I need for the working out of salvation—in me, in that person, and even in the world. After my best efforts to nurture and protect, what is returned to me is far more than anything I could have orchestrated.

Here we have a hint that the creative work of childbearing shares its shape with the creative work we do each Sunday at

Divine Liturgy. The first move, naturally, is God's. Eucharist begins with God's provision of the raw matter we work with—the grains of wheat and grapes that grow forth from the earth. We add to them the sweat of our brow as we cultivate, tend, harvest, mill, crush, ferment, knead, and bake those materials into bread and wine, then bring the fruit of our work to God, lifting it back up to Him with prayers of thanksgiving. Next God blesses the bread and wine and returns it to us, changed by the action of the Holy Spirit into His Body and Blood. Finally, we offer ourselves back to God, filled and transformed by His gifts into a life-giving and light-bearing gift for the world.

Like the Eucharist, childbearing is a collaboration between humanity and God—a process of synergy, with new energies, layers of reality, and blessings added at each turn. Here, the original material God provides is our bodies, with their eggs and sperm hiding latent inside, infused with life-giving power. Through the creative intimacy of sex, we make a self-giving offering to one another, which within the sacrament of a chaste marriage mysteriously is also an offering to God. We reconstitute and return God's raw materials, and He blesses them to become a new human life, tiny but growing furiously from the earliest moments. We are then called to offer that life up to Him, knowing that though we will do our best to sustain it, its blessing and safekeeping are in His hands. When the child is born, the gift is again returned to us in a new form: a life not just laden with the potentialities of the womb but rich with the fulfilled actuality of interpersonal relationship.

Finally, we parents understand that this gift is not for us alone but must come to fullness through being offered up and shared. As a child gains agency and independence, he is empowered to live out his own unique calling in the world. For as Metropolitan

Kallistos says, "God expects from each one of us something that He does not expect from anyone else in the entire universe. Each has a vocation of making something beautiful in her or his special way."[7]

Seeing the co-creative work of childbearing through this eucharistic lens reveals my parental role as priestly in nature. "The Eucharist is the anaphora, the 'lifting up' of our offering, and of ourselves," writes Fr. Alexander Schmemann[8]—and in the liturgy of childbearing, my baby is the living sacrifice I lift up to God. When I cooperate with the creative work of God in this way, pregnancy becomes an act of worship, transformed from a mere biological process into a sacred act. The primary creative work of these nine or ten months becomes not just taking my iron supplements and avoiding loud construction sites, but continually offering up the little one God has offered to me.

"We lift them up unto the Lord!"

Recognition

Christ within me
—ST. PATRICK'S BREASTPLATE

In a little French village stands the Church of the Resurrection, Taizé. The darkness inside is pierced only by the light of candles and the tinted sunshine that reaches in through a few small stained-glass windows. In one corner, easy to miss, I find a little treasure: a window bearing the etched inscription *Magnificat*. It is worked almost entirely in intense shades of red, and looking through its glass to the daylight outside reminds me of what life in the womb must look like to a baby.

Walking over to this window, I can make out Righteous Elizabeth, the mother of St. John the Forerunner, my patron. Her belly is rounded by two full trimesters of pregnancy, her arms open in greeting to the Theotokos. The cousins are very close, just a moment away from embrace. Their eyes meet in hopeful recognition. Their pale glass faces and hands stand out, bright light from the afternoon sun in a sea of crimson. Behind them, a black cat sits in the doorway of a tile-roofed house.

Only by coming nearer still and standing at the feet of these holy women do I see the full work of the artist. Etched into the belly of each woman is a figure, almost indistinguishable from the folds of her clothing. Inside His mother, the baby Christ stands and reaches out in a stance mirroring hers. Inside Elizabeth, a tiny Forerunner extends his arms, too, from a kneeling position. The infants' eyes are locked, like their mothers'. Their anticipated embrace is a few months rather than a few moments away, but equally tangible. The etched figures are so subtle that seeing them is less like looking through a porthole and more like sharing a secret.

The Theotokos's pregnancy is new; her belly, unlike Elizabeth's, shows only the hint of a curve. As she opens her cousin's garden gate, the world passes by in the street behind her, unaware of who is in their midst. But Elizabeth glimpses what others do not. As she sees the Theotokos approaching, we can imagine her putting down her broom and hurrying out of the house, wiping her hands as she comes down the path with a third-trimester waddle and a joyful shout. Righteous Elizabeth knows to be on the lookout; perhaps she has a bed made up and a special meal prepared for her dear cousin. She may even have heard that Mary is pregnant. Still, surely even she is not forewarned that by bringing this relative under her roof, she will also be hosting the long-awaited Messiah. Yet Elizabeth does not miss the little stowaway. She immediately recognizes Him, hidden behind the veil of His mother's flesh, greeting Him as "Lord" and His mother as "blessed" (Luke 1:45). The Forerunner also understands and communicates his prenatal veneration with a leap of joy. (It's possible, given it was Elizabeth's sixth month, that this was the first movement she felt from him—her quickening.)

Though this stained-glass window is not an icon, it is reminiscent of iconography. Its style is simple and reserved. There are no haloes, but the glass conveys in light what a halo does in pigment: the energies of God's holiness, flowing through the people portrayed. Like an icon, this window not only depicts an event (recounted in Luke 1:39–56) but also invites those who see it to participate in an inner reality—to acquire the spiritual X-ray vision of Elizabeth and John, so that we too can discover the hidden Christ within the quiet recesses of our lives. For He does not come to us as a booming voice from heaven, a lightning bolt, or a message on a blimp. But if we look for Him, He is always there to be found: at the heart of a painful situation, shining forth in the beauty of sunrise, or revealed in the simple gifts of bread and wine shared among friends on an ordinary Sunday morning. Most of all, we are called to discover Christ at the core of each human person we meet. Beggar, enemy, or immigrant: by virtue of His image in us, *all* people carry Him in the womb of their being. If souls were as transparent as stained-glass figures, we would see the Christ child etched inside each one, just as He appears inside the Theotokos in the window at Taizé.

And Orthodox iconography frequently portrays human souls in this way. Even the souls of adults appear as babies, swaddled tightly in strips of white cloth. In the icon of the Dormition of the Theotokos, for example, the body of the Mother of God lies in its resting place, but her soul appears above it as a tiny baby in swaddling clothes, encompassed by the arms of her adult Son and a host of angels. We cannot look at this image without being drawn into its greater context. The wrappings in which the soul of the Theotokos appears evoke both the swaddling clothes the infant Jesus wears in the icon of His Nativity and His winding sheet in the icon of the Myrrh-bearing Women—the sheet depicted lying stiff and empty like a chrysalis in His tomb. Putting these three icons next to one another, we understand: the swaddling clothes of the Incarnation and the discarded shroud of the Resurrection are the vesture of our own souls, too. It is the life of Christ that lies at the heart of our personhood. His image gives our souls their true humanity.

That I should bear in my heart an image of the living God is a great wonder by itself. But, because I am pregnant, the mystery reaches a layer deeper still, because I also bear in my womb another image of Him. There's body within body, each with a soul, and at the core of everything, Christ. As in the English children's party game Pass the Parcel, every layer of this mystery hides a treasure, with the grand prize nestling in the very center. When a child is born, it is as if this package is unwrapped and an entirely new form of God's image is unveiled in the world.

More than mere reproduction, birth is the dawning of a new light, a moment when divine and human touch one another. It is in essence a spiritual event—a theophany (or showing forth of God). This is why Ina May Gaskin, perhaps the world's best-known midwife, calls birth a sacrament: "I think that a midwife must be religious," she writes, "because the energy she is dealing with is Holy. . . . The midwife's job is to do her best to bring both the mother and the child through their passage alive and well and to see that the sacrament of birth is kept Holy."[9]

As a doula, I get to witness such theophanies on a regular basis. When I am called to a birth, it's almost always in the middle of the night, when the roads are dark and deserted. Under the cover of prayer and a full tank of gas, I am not afraid, but I wonder that the marvelous secret I'm in on is unfolding unbeknown to the sleeping world.

At first I usually find the expectant mother at home, even if she plans to move to a medical facility when labor is more advanced. I have usually asked the family to leave their door on the latch so that I can creep in with a minimum of fuss, entering the home as reverently as I would a little church (which is just what St. John Chrysostom says a household is). Sometimes a pet comes to greet me, but it's strangely uncommon even for a watchdog to bark.

I lay my bags down as soundlessly as I can, my ears straining to ascertain in which room the laboring woman is. I follow the sounds of her breath, as intimate and rhythmical as Liturgy. There is often a trail of candlelight, brightening as I approach her bedroom. Peering in, I see her. There she kneels, shiny with the sweat of self-sacrifice, working to bring a new child of God into the world. The privilege of being invited to share this holy section of space-time is not lost on me. "But why is it granted to me?" I want to exclaim with Righteous Elizabeth. And with the infant John, I want to jump for joy.

What would it look like if we were to approach our pregnancies with this same veneration? What would be different if we regarded our little ones as images of God being revealed in the world? Could we learn to approach our pregnancies with prayerful wonder? Could we use every one of those millions of times a day when our thoughts turn to pregnancy to thank God for this new theophany? How would it be if in these weeks we stopped to honor our babies' reality as frequently as we used the bathroom? Imagine if, when going to bed, we recognized them by making the sign of the cross not just over ourselves but over our bellies, too.

When I was pregnant with my fourth child, each night after our family prayer time I would stay behind a few minutes longer in the icon corner to intone the Prayers of a Woman with Child (printed in the front of this book). Many times tears came to my eyes as I prayed specifically for the "body, mind, heart, and vitals" of the baby I was expecting. "Into Your almighty and paternal hands do I entrust my child," I chanted. When that baby was born, it felt like meeting an old friend, because

I had already begun to know and recognize her as God's image through prayer.

In this way, over the course of pregnancy and family life, the full personhood of our babies will come gradually into clearer focus. God willing, they will eventually become grown people with whom we can connect deeply, go see movies and share lively dinner-table conversation. For now, "deep calls unto deep" (Ps. 41/42:7) in an encounter that is resounding but rather unspecific.

However, God's recognition of our little ones is highly personal right from the start. "My bone," writes the Psalmist (138/139:15–16), "made in secret, was not hidden from You. . . . Your eyes saw me when I was unformed." Even the hairs of the scalp, which already have their own unique pattern at just sixteen weeks' gestation, are all numbered (Matt. 10:30; Luke 12:7). And so from the One who sees His own image where others see only the folds of a skirt, let us learn to recognize in our little ones the sanctity that is theirs from the start.

Hospitality

Let all guests who arrive be received as Christ, because
He will say, "I came as a guest, and you took Me in."
—THE RULE OF ST. BENEDICT[10]

A few hours after we were married, my husband and I waved our happy guests goodbye and zoomed off in our getaway car with cans clattering. The nearby bed-and-breakfast which held a reservation for the new Mr. and Mrs. Jansson called those thrilling names from across the English hills.

But, far from the celebratory welcome we'd long anticipated, we arrived to find the eighteenth-century house dark and shut. There was no answer at the door, no note waiting. We called forlornly through the letterbox. The prospect of homelessness on our wedding night gave us the boldness of desperation, and finally we tried the front door. It was a foot thick and very heavy, but unlocked. Like thieves we let ourselves in, unsure whether to attempt silence or conspicuousness as we stumbled down the hall. February draughts stirring in the gloom directed us to an empty bedroom which we hoped might be ours. Plopping our bags down, we made ourselves as comfortable as we knew how to be, but slept with the uneasy rest of trespassers.

We all have stories of being the awkward guest in someone else's space. These moments are mundane but deeply unsettling. They rock our sense of being at home in the world. On honeymoon, among flocks of partying friends, indeed in our own skin, we may feel dislocated, adrift, alone. These experiences point to a deep truth we had hoped to forget: that as human persons we are strangers in a strange land. We're not really from around here. We belong safely in Eden, our true motherland, but must make our own way in the world outside until that day we can settle in "a better, that is, a heavenly *country*" (Heb. 11:16). "For here we have no continuing city, but we seek the one to come" (Heb. 13:14).

Christ, the most fully human of us all, faced the force of this struggle. He left His Father's mansion and came to stay with humanity. He by whom the Earth was made did not have a permanent dwelling-place in it, but merely "pitched His tent among us" (the literal meaning of John 1:14). He spent His childhood as a refugee in Egypt and His adulthood as a homeless itinerant, traveling on foot with a motley band of friends and relying on the goodness of strangers for bread and board. His earthly life was bookended by His birth on the floor of a stable and His criminal's death on a cross.

In the face of our universal human loneliness, good hospitality is a taste of heaven on earth. A simple glass of water, offered and received with love, can be healing, holy. It's as if, in the face of their existential estrangement, host and guest together add a small stone to the rickety bridge between earth and heaven. And no wonder: the welcome of a human host gives a taste of the welcome of God, the True Host. He is the One who welcomes each of us into the creation He made. He's the One who, when we return to Him having squandered our inheritance like the prodigal son, sees us approaching from afar. Though we still stink of the pigsty, He dashes down the road, welcoming us home with an exuberance of hugs and kisses (Luke 15:11–32). And He's also the One who eagerly extends to us the hospitality of the Kingdom that is to come.

And so the Scriptures invite us to extend this divine generosity to others. "The resident alien who dwells among you shall be to you as one born among you, and you shall love him as yourself; for you were resident aliens in the land of Egypt," it says in Leviticus (19:34). In the New Testament, St. Paul instructs us to practice hospitality (Rom. 12:13). From start to finish, Scripture presents hospitality not as a leisure activity but as fundamental to our life of faith, for receiving God cannot be separated from receiving others. When I host those in need, I entertain angels (Heb. 13:2) or even Christ Himself (Matt. 25:35). In opening my house to others, I make myself His home (Heb. 3:6).

Pregnancy calls me to live out this vocation by offering the welcome of paradise to the little one in my womb. He is like a guest lodging for a season in the innermost chambers of my body. At a cost to myself, I share with him my food, time, and space. Of course, doing so is part of the pregnancy package, and once I sign up I don't get to choose my terms. But I do have a choice to make. In what manner will I receive my guest? Will I settle for being the miserly mistress of a boardinghouse who provides every bodily need but in a perfunctory spirit? Or can I throw open the doors of my heart to this little one? What does giving him good hospitality entail?

When I close my eyes and imagine good hospitality, I tend to see an image from a home furnishings catalog: a pristine dinner party lubricated with wine, attended by an eclectic collection of young professionals. After polishing off the third course, they have pushed back their chairs and seem to be toasting a promotion or planning next year's cruise. The hostess stands laughing on one side, and neither she nor any of her guests appears to be suffering from morning sickness, first-trimester exhaustion, or for that matter allergies, head lice, a bad haircut—really any form of suffering. If there is any grit to the scene, it is invisible in the glow of the perfectly arranged candles.

This might seem to be the kind of impeccable reception I offer my little houseguest. Inside my womb, the environment is comfortable, with dim lights and soft background music. The thermostat is always set just right. The bathroom is completely private and never occupied. My guest knows no hunger nor thirst: all bodily needs are met before they arise. He is always held and rocked personally to sleep, and is asked to leave only once he's ready. Such luxury! Not even an army of architects, interior designers, and personal chefs could rival it. It's like the primal childhood home of our fondest reminiscences, to which we can only strive to return. As such the womb is the archetype, standard, or symbol of hospitality.

But if I am to live up to this standard and give my child perfect hospitality, it seems I have a little tidying up to do over the next seven months. I may have high hopes of fixing certain things before I become a parent: perhaps my diet, prayer rule, or finances. Maybe I feel I can't have this baby until I've rectified a certain relationship, dealt with piles of paperwork, or come to terms with a previous traumatic birth experience. But whatever I do to put it in order, my house won't be fully ready. I cannot, and do not need to, make myself into a "qualified" person by my own power. By blessing me with a pregnancy, God has made it evident that He already considers me prepared enough to receive this guest. It isn't a perfect hostess my little one needs, but *me*.

In any case, catalog-worthy perfection is probably not quite what St. Paul had in mind when he instructed Christians to practice hospitality. The Greek word he used is *philoxenia*, literally translated as "stranger-love." Our English word *hospitality* also comes from the Latin *hospes*, meaning "alien, foreigner, exile," someone far from home.

And this is more like what I actually have to offer during pregnancy. I host my growing baby not like a dinner party guest, but more like a refugee bunking with me for a season. I don't get to stuff clutter into the closet or sweep the dust under the carpet before he comes. And that's because as a mother I don't just open my home to my child: I become that home. The welcome I offer may be ragged, complicated, and intimate, but it's real: not an interruption to my life, but an invitation to share it. Ultimately, it's this kind of deep, scruffy hospitality that meets the real needs of my guest. Participation, not perfection, is what makes him welcome.

It isn't always easy to share at this depth. True hospitality requires that guest and host make themselves vulnerable to one another. A guest puts himself at the mercy of his host for his safety and sustenance, but the host, too, risks having her generosity abused or rejected. So to open my door to a guest, no matter how tiny, opens me to the possibility of loss. Even as I begin to love the one growing in me, I know that I am going to lose him someday—God willing, when he reaches independence and leaves my home, but perhaps much sooner than that, maybe even during pregnancy. While he is yet unborn, I choose to embrace my child—to become subject to him even as he is subject to me—though all the while I'm unsure how long he will remain under my roof.

Nevertheless, it's worth the risk because of how deeply formative human experience shows this deep kind of hospitality to be. Many psychologists testify to the lasting effects in people's lives of their mother's feelings toward them as they grew in the womb. Working with clients, they discover that being an unwanted child can leave people with the sense of being under threat or worthless, even into adulthood.[11] By lowering the fortifications of my heart and throwing wide the gates to let my little guest in, I can protect him from that danger. This doesn't mean blithely denying any ambivalence I may feel about pregnancy—on the contrary, it means resolving to face and address it bravely and shamelessly.

The Fathers of the Church agree that the spirit of a host's welcome is all-important: St. Peter instructed Christians to offer hospitality to one another "without grumbling" (1 Pet. 4:9). Evagrius Ponticus exhorted his fellow monks, "Let us not welcome our brothers as if we were doing them a favor, but . . . as though we were indebted to them by a loan."[12] Saint Benedict advised those following his Rule, "Let all guests who arrive be received as Christ, because He will say, 'I came as a guest, and you took Me in'."[13] I also have the chance to receive my baby in the womb as if I were receiving our Lord, the archetypal stranger, so that my child will be able to say to me, "I was a stranger, and you made me welcome." In this way, these months in the womb can provide him a first taste of the warmth and welcome of divine Life.

TWO

Experiencing Pregnancy

Self-Denial

He must increase, but I must decrease.
—JOHN 3:30

Julia the Pregnant Bookkeeper was a new recruit at the organization I worked for straight out of college. In our small, open-plan office, all Julia's coworkers were close witnesses to the struggles of her pregnancy. As the weeks passed, her workday became a constant choreography of movement between our single-stall bathroom, the convenience store downstairs, and the nap station formerly known as her desk. The quiet sterility of the room was often punctuated by the sounds of her bodily needs: expressive crunching and satisfaction when her snacks came out, vociferous objections to the smell of other people's food at lunchtime, and loud sighs, belches, and complaints at random intervals. To me, for whom motherhood was a world I could not imagine inhabiting, she seemed so intolerably full of herself.

Having now experienced five pregnancies of my own, I'd view Julia differently. During these months, an enormous work is wrought inside us, and it is natural to turn inward toward it. Our physical needs become very direct and urgent. The changes to our baseline bodily functions are dramatic and remarkable, at least as viewed from the inside. As we learn to accommodate pregnancy, those around us must learn to accommodate us. Yet if we're demanding, it's because another person's needs are expressed through our bodies. If we require additional help, it's only because we have turned our lives over to the service of another. If we're full of someone, it may be our babies, not ourselves. In this way, pregnancy blurs the line between self-centeredness and self-denial.

Balancing the needs of our growing babies, those around us, and ourselves is one great struggle, or *ascesis*, of pregnancy. This Greek word, used by the Church to refer to the practices of abstinence that are a vital part of our life of faith, literally means "exercise" or "training." Like Roman soldiers seeking to better their performance in battle by engaging in acts of self-denial, we Orthodox Christians fast strictly before Divine Liturgy, abstain from animal products during fasting periods, give alms, undertake works of charity, and submit to the guidance of spiritual fathers or mothers. Additionally, our monastics—who could be regarded as professional ascetics—practice prayer of the hours throughout each day and night, sexual abstinence, and further dietary restrictions.

Pregnancy, it might be said, makes of us professional ascetics, too. Though the motherly path is not identical to that of the monastics, it travels toward holiness along a parallel road. Like theirs, our life is about turning away from ourselves and toward the other. On the way, we give up our ability to sleep through the night, interrupted not by the call of the bells waking us for a service but by a kick in the ribs or the limitations of a cramped bladder. Our old wardrobe is given up and our body image shifts, not under black robes but in clothing with bigger and stretchier waistbands. Our eating and drinking habits are altered not by a rule of our community but by nausea and never-ending hunger. We fast not from animal products but from fasting itself, giving up our usual spiritual practices in order to provide full nourishment for our growing baby. Our independence is limited not under a formal hierarchy but because we simply can't reach to tie our own shoes. We refrain from some worldly activities not because we have renounced them forever but because they are too tiring, or suboptimal for our baby's growth. The new guides we look to are midwives and obstetricians rather than an abbess. We give up not our homes in favor of a monastic cell but the very space inside our own bodies. We join a new community, not of monastics but of mothers.

With all this self-giving, sometimes pregnancy feels like surrendering *everything*. I can go away resentful and complaining, or sad, as the rich young ruler did when Christ asked him to give away all he had (Matt. 19:21). The world around us certainly takes a dim view of the restrictions that are part of human life. Limitations are seen as *limiting*, that is, negative. We are encouraged to tolerate "no limits," to break through the glass ceiling, to push past the barriers, to live an unbounded life. Seen from that perspective, our constraints are nothing but pesky flies in the ointment of infinity. Embracing them, as monastics or pregnant women do, is countercultural—nothing short of foolishness.

Through the eyes of the Scriptures, our boundaries look quite different. Finiteness is seen as part of being human, the creature of a Creator. The Garden where we were placed by God at the advent of our existence was custom-made as the place best suited for our living and thriving. One of its main features was the wall surrounding it, marking it out as our home.

Those who've visited a walled garden know how it can feel: protected, peaceful, and orderly in the best possible way. There are paths for exploration. The sun shines over the walls, and the rain still falls inside, but predators are kept at bay. Within Eden's walls life must have been much like that. We had everything we needed, and our freedom was total—so total that we were even free to reject the confines themselves. We did not hesitate to exercise our liberty to live according to a pattern other than the one God had put in place. We ate fruit from the one tree we had been told it would be better for us not to try.

This meant choosing to go it alone outside the walls of the Garden. We quickly discovered what God had tried to protect us from. Outside the Garden in the wild world, we are exposed. The walls no longer protect us from shame, so we cover ourselves with leaves. The walls no longer shelter us from spiritual hazards; now we must battle them constantly. Where all creatures were once united in a community of peace, now man, woman, and serpent are pitted against each other. As we look back over our shoulder, the walls of the Garden no longer appear so confining.

Like Adam and Eve, each of us is painfully aware of our limitations as human beings. Every tick of the clock, every wave of tiredness, every homeless person we pass, every elbow in the crowd reminds us that we live a finite life. Our time, energy, patience, money, power, and relationships are exhaustible resources (and don't we know it in the first trimester). Yet for us as for Adam and Eve in the walled garden, the defined parameters of our lives have purpose and value. They help to keep us safe and sane, comfortable in the knowledge that we are creatures, not Creator. The limitations God calls us to live by do not entrench our finiteness but show us how to use it to best effect. His boundaries describe, not deprive: they map out for us the path to a good life.

Christian asceticism is the practice of embracing our human identity as finite creatures. Rather than acting upon our every whim, we practice self-denial through following a way not our own. So as not to be full of ourselves, we empty ourselves. But in our self-emptying, we seek not to become nothing, as a Buddhist does, but to unite ourselves to the One who is "all in all" (1 Cor. 15:28)—not to negate our lives but to fulfill them. We empty ourselves (in Greek, *kenosis*) in order to become full of God (*theosis*). We lose our lives in order to save them (Matt. 16:25). We cease to play God, overthrowing a despotic impostor king to make room for the true King who serves His people with tender love.

Saint John the Forerunner describes this dynamic when he says of Christ, "He must increase, but I must decrease" (John 3:30). In pregnancy, my life becomes a symbol of this paradox. As my belly starts to round out, in a sense I increase. But in another sense I decrease, the space in my body being taken up by another in me, leaving less room for my own organs. My child increases; I decrease. And so it is with the inner life. It is the decrease of myself—my egoistic, false, self-serving self—that makes room for the increase in me of Christ, my true Life. If I allow it, pregnancy can work this in me as I learn once more to live for the Other.

But to see the humility childbearing brings as a blessing is not to say that being humble ever becomes much fun. So what is there in it for us? What is good about self-denial at this time? Why would God, who loves us so dearly, make ascetic struggle so inherent to the continuation of humanity? Why would He allow a mother's path toward salvation to pass through such difficult terrain? Without trying to guess the mind of God, I can share what I have noticed of the mercies hidden in the heart of the travail.

It seems to me that the self-giving of childbearing is excellent training for life as a parent. The call for ascesis is not over when the baby is out; on the contrary, it is magnified. The needs of our newborn child are no longer under cover of our own bodily needs, to which we quite naturally attend, but belong to someone with a distinct existence for whom we must put aside our own way. Imagine if nature required us to tend a newborn who eats, poops, and sleeps around the clock without any preceding training in shallower water! Parenthood is a voyage into the deep sea of self-offering, and pregnancy is God's way of easing us in at the edge.

Our ascetic struggles during pregnancy are also of benefit to the world. The people around us have abundant chances to serve us for the good of their own souls. The need for others' self-giving service in pregnancy is like a chain, starting with the neediest and most vulnerable—the tiny baby—and linking through the mother to the supporters on whom she relies. It is the responsibility of the stronger members to tend and serve those further down the line. Every time they come to our aid, even as simply as opening a door for us or brewing us a cup of tea, these people are taking an opportunity to work out their own salvation. But our struggles are even a benefit to those we may never meet, for pregnancy, the phenomenon itself, is a witness to the world of the possibility of self-giving love. Even if in our own eyes our efforts are weak, by God's grace we are a walking example of this love in action. I only wish I'd noticed this in the days I shared an office with Julia.

❧ WEEK 11 ❧

Death

*We are . . . always carrying about in the body
the dying of the Lord Jesus, that the life of Jesus
also may be manifested in our body.*
—2 CORINTHIANS 4:8–10

When I was pregnant with my fourth child, our priest gave the Sunday school class I was teaching a tour of the liturgical objects that are usually hidden away behind the iconostasis. Holding up a silk-lined rectangular cloth, the priest explained this was an antimension—meaning "in place of the table." On this cloth, the eucharistic Gifts of bread and wine are placed for consecration. The antimension, he told the children, has been consecrated like an altar—and he showed us the place where a bishop had signed it to indicate his blessing for Liturgy to take place. Without this antimension, said the priest, our community would not be able to celebrate the Eucharist.

He began to unfold the layers, each one revealing more detail of the cloth's design. We could see Christ's body, laid out before the Theotokos and the Myrrh-bearing Women and overlooked by angels. In the corners were the four evangelists, carefully drawn, and in the middle a little lump where the fabric wouldn't lie quite flat. That, explained our priest, was the spot where the relics of a saint were sewn inside.

Standing among the children of my Sunday school class with another child growing inside, it struck me: this is an apt metaphor for our experience of carrying a baby. Like the antimension, pregnancy is essential to the functioning and continuation of our human community. It can be beautiful, but sewn into its very fiber is death. Because right from the start, becoming pregnant faces me with the truth of human mortality. Having sprung from nothing a matter of weeks ago, the new life I'm just beginning to come to terms with could equally rapidly be overtaken by death; the incidence of miscarriage, I read, stands at around twenty percent of all pregnancies, and eighty percent of these occur in this first trimester.* And if I have lost a baby before or have fertility concerns, the shadow of miscarriage looms still larger than its statistical likelihood.

This awareness of death seeps through and colors other areas of my life that don't seem to have anything to do with pregnancy. Wherever I turn, the demise of the natural world is ever present. News events are filled with calamity and destruction that touch me to new depths. The older generations of my family appear to teeter perilously close to the edge of mortality. Even the "less significant" deaths I'm exposed to on a regular basis—a bird that has flown into a window or a squirrel killed by a car—become infused with extra meaning and weight.

Pregnancy also brings into focus the prospect of my own physical death, often for the first time. As my appointment with the birthing room ticks daily nearer, I'm reminded of the other great solitary work of life that cannot be delegated or dodged. But though this ancient fear sits always at the back of my mind, I don't speak of it: that would seem a little melodramatic. These days, I'm told, dying in the act of bringing a child into the world is less likely than being struck by lightning in the course of a lifetime—at least if I am so fortunate as to give birth in a wealthy

---

* See the Appendix to this book, written for those who suffer a pregnancy loss.

country. Yet, small as the chance is, insufficient time has elapsed in the history of humanity to dispel it from my modern mind.

And despite advances in medical technology, recent statistics increasingly make the link between fertility and mortality look tragically pertinent, at least in the US. The risk of dying from pregnancy-related complications here remains low in absolute terms (around 28 per 100,000 live births) but it has risen steadily since 1982, doubling just between 1990 and 2013, even as it halved during about the same period in the world as a whole. African American women are four times more likely to die than white women. And, because of underreporting, the Centers for Disease Control and Prevention estimate that our actual situation is two to three times worse than statistics show.

Even taking the numbers at face value, forty-nine other countries now have lower maternal mortality rates than the US, including best-scoring Belarus (at 1 per 100,000) as well as Iran, Libya, Turkey, and Bulgaria. Birth is still safer in the US than in many places. Developing countries account for 99% of maternal deaths globally. In Sierra Leone a staggering 1100 mothers die per 100,000 births. Still, our own figures are shockingly poor considering the dollars we spend. US healthcare expenditure is the highest in the world, and more money goes toward maternal health than any other category.

What am I to make of these harsh realities? The mortality that is my constant companion during pregnancy and birth: is it a friend or a foe? As with the antimension, could there be any holiness hidden in the folds of its dark engulfing skirts?

Contemporary culture's answer to these questions is schizophrenic. On one hand, demise and decay are seen as feeding evolutionary progress and, as such, considered natural and good. Death is to be welcomed and even facilitated when we no longer see clearly the purpose of our existence. In fact, we seem to be rather entertained by it: the average episode of one popular series contains 172 deaths.

Yet our cartoonish fascination shows not that we are at peace with our mortality but that we are enthralled by its fear. We need to objectify it as a caricature in order to keep its reality at arm's length. And, for the most part, we're pretty successful at doing so. Most deaths (like births) once occurred in bedrooms but now happen in hospitals. Bodies are kept in funeral home fridges rather than in living rooms. Even at an open-casket funeral where death looks us in the face, the deceased is carefully made up and coiffed in an effort to disguise the pale stiffness and disfigurement of a body from which the life has departed.

In pregnancy, too, the force of death remains taboo. Many of the women I work with confess that they are afraid of dying in childbirth, but feel unable to confide in their dearest ones. The one-dimensional chipper spirit of parenting books and congratulations cards seems to insist that we "express only a blossoming sense of joy and anticipation, even as the person we have thought ourselves to be is transfigured and reborn," as one author puts it.[14] "Many cultures pair birth with death and treat women's fertility as the gateway to both states. But our culture, by insisting on revealing only the life-affirming aspect of pregnancy and birth, seem[s] to make the darkness more palpable."[15]

We Christians can certainly agree that death is a horror. "As the separation of body and soul," writes Metropolitan Kallistos Ware, "death is . . . a violent affront against the wholeness of our human nature"[16]—and never more so than when a woman's life ends in its very prime, on the cusp of being offered to a new generation. With Christ Himself, we weep at the grave, and we do our best to thwart its attempts on us (John 11:35). We cannot call our fallen friends to rise, as He could, but we can take action to prevent those maternal deaths that are preventable—which, according to some authorities, means almost all of them.[17]

On a societal level, we can look determinedly at the causes of our rising maternal death rates, asking complex questions about the role of technology, conflicts of interest within the medical-industrial complex, and the place and value of women in our society. We can begin to address the injustice that means that so many more mothers die in some communities than in others. On a personal level, we can make careful decisions about our maternity care—for example, about which healthcare providers and institutions we'll entrust with our safety during labor. Often, these are precisely the decisions we are making at this stage of pregnancy.

But if maternal mortality were somehow eliminated world-wide overnight, death would still remain integral to the journey to parenthood. Even if I thrive physically during my childbearing, I must die a multitude of little deaths as I am transformed from a maiden into a mother. I leave behind the lightness of girlhood to embrace a more grounded life. I surrender the illusion of myself as a self-sufficient bootstrap-puller in exchange for deeper connection and interdependence. My priorities and interests shift. Not all my friendships accompany me through these parted waters. My whole self-concept must undergo a metamorphosis. As one new mother put it, "I had to sign [something] the other day, and I was surprised that I still had the same name."[18] Or, in the words of a Beriba proverb, "A pregnant woman is a dying person."[19]

If death is an inextricable part of pregnancy, then a sufficient response to it cannot stop at horror, denial, and prevention.

Rather than trying to rip this strange thread from the tapestry, we need to find a way to work it into the beauty of the design. Our physiology itself illustrates that this is possible. According to scientists, human bodies are in a perpetual state of death. Our cells perish and are replaced with such frequency that it takes only about a month and a half for the entire outer layer of our bodies, the epidermis, to be replaced through new growth. If cells do not die when they are supposed to, as happens with cancer, the health of the overall body is jeopardized. The death of the individual cells is what allows the whole body to remain alive and be renewed.

We see life-giving death unfolding in the world around us, too. In winter, plants that have exhausted their energy on growth concede to the cold. Their leaves and stalks brown, shrivel, and fall to the ground. In the Midwest, snow smothers them several feet deep, veiling their demise so that when it recedes as the weather warms, the ground emerges shockingly bare. It appears that everything is dead, that this was the winter that finally killed off the garden once and for all. But the sleep of the season allows these plants to recover from their summer efforts. Their tender roots have not been killed. They are simply regathering strength, ready to come back with force in spring to astonish us with a green resurrection before our eyes.

This pattern of regeneration through demise is the context in which our own deaths take place. Saint Paul describes it as like a seed, which does not come to life unless it dies (1 Cor. 15:36). We pregnant ones are also this seed, swelling to the point of bursting with the new life inside, shedding the hull of our old selves and making way for newness. But the epitome of this process is the saving death of our Lord. Christ, who unites humanity and Godhead in Himself, took humankind to the grave when He embraced death on the Cross; but because Life itself could not perish, He rose, bringing us out on the other side, into the light of Life with Him.

The death of our bodies, then, is no true death: it is merely a rest awaiting resurrection. It is not to be feared, for "neither death nor life . . . shall be able to separate us from the love of God" (Rom. 8:38–39). Neither is the demise of the old selves we outgrow a tragedy. It is in fact to be embraced, for by losing our transient life we lay hold of Life with Christ (Matt. 16:25). The only death that is truly fearsome is the death of the soul—that is, alienation from God, the source of our being. By reminding us where our true Life lies, the awareness of our mortality becomes a door not into despair, gloom, and paralysis but into great joy.

Within our Orthodox faith, the remembrance of death is considered a fruitful spiritual discipline—St. John Climacus puts it as step six on his *Ladder of Divine Ascent*. Pregnancy provides a special opportunity to grow into this practice. Every time my high-maintenance body expresses one of its needs, I can stop to recall that it will perish; that the bones I can feel under my skin are part of a skeleton that will one day lie in the ground; that the breath currently feeding both me and my baby with oxygen will cease. And by sharing the early news of my pregnancy with those who will undertake to pray with me, rather than waiting until later when the risk of miscarriage eases, I can transform the chance of death into the chance to deepen the supportive relationships that are going to be my lifeline no matter what happens to my baby.

In ways like this, it's possible to discover the meaning of the antimension in our own lives. The eucharistic Gifts rest on a cloth embedded with bones: the greatest of our joys sit atop a bed of peril. The cup we pray to have removed from us is also the Fountain of Immortality. Death is sewn into the very fabric of our lives as expectant mothers; yet it's this that helps make us a suitable altar, a holy place to celebrate the life-giving love of God.

❧ WEEK 12 ❧

Weakness

*And He said to me, "My grace is sufficient for you,
for My strength is made perfect in weakness."*
—2 CORINTHIANS 12:9

Most of my phone calls from clients come between about one and four AM, and this one was no exception. From Leah's relaxed tone I could tell this was still early labor. Contractions were spaced luxuriantly far apart, and she was able to talk right through the sensations with no trouble. Nevertheless, this was her second baby, and second babies come notoriously quickly. I jumped out of bed, grabbed my bag of doula tricks, and zoomed off into the night.

I found Leah at home, by now a little further on her journey. She was in lovely spirits, but intermittent tightenings were beginning to stop her in her tracks. Every few minutes her breath would catch and she would hang from her husband's shoulders, swaying her way through the next sixty seconds before the banter resumed.

The rhythm of her labor was hypnotic, with contractions and rests and breaths and hours swelling up and melting away again and again. Now with each labored breath came a vocalization, a firm low *ah* sound. Her husband's chest proved too lofty, so she followed her body's lead to stand beside the bed, leaning with her fists sunk into the mattress, lifting one heel then the other off the ground. When each contraction passed, she flopped contentedly forward, letting the nest of pillows in front of her take the weight of her full belly and head. Breaks were shorter, and there was no more joking or chatting. No energy for that—we were having a baby.

Soon after checking in at the birth center, Leah's labor entered a new phase. Now she wanted to be down as low as her body could go. She was on her hands and knees on the floor mat, circling lower and lower, around and around. The loud noises from deep in her throat told us that she was working at full capacity. Occasionally she called out for God's mercy. Contractions were long now, about ninety seconds, and when each one was over she melted under the force of gravity, her face sunk into the mat and her knees wide. She was gone in a far-off underground world, and firm touch was the only language that could communicate across the gulf.

Leah's moment of victory came only half an hour later. Her baby girl was born into the gloved and waiting hands of the two midwives who had cared for her throughout pregnancy. Grandma brought the baby's big brother in from the waiting room to meet her, in his pajamas and bedhead. Outside the window, commuters passed in cars, oblivious to the everyday miracle that had just occurred on the seventh floor.

This birth story, like every birth story, could be seen as a tale of a woman brought low: riches to rags. Certainly, at the end when the baby arrives the riches reappear, but labor itself is more about the rags. The work of labor brings us to our knees. We prostrate ourselves over and over with each contraction like a slo-mo version of Lenten prayers. As hours pass, the relentlessly rising intensity transforms us slowly from upright bipedal creatures, *homo erectus,* into more primitive quadruped mammals—as if in a backwards illustration of Darwinian evolution.

Mentally, as well, we are brought low by the continual return of these surges, grinding us down like crashing waves gradually eroding a stone cliff. Where we were self-possessed, we now beg for help. Where we once had strong opinions, we no longer care about our modesty or preferences as long as we can be finished. Over time we move out of our usual rational mode of operation and into a more primitive state of mind, from strength and composure to what might be called weakness.

But we don't have to wait for birth to experience the weakness of childbearing; we've had a strong taste of it already. Pregnancy weakens us to the physical core. We buckle under the weight of the utter exhaustion of the first trimester. The influence of increasing levels of the hormone relaxin makes our pelvic ligaments soften, creating an expansive passage for our baby's birth but also quite literally making us come loose at the hinges. Our minds too may feel soft, rounded, and squashy where they were once firm and defined and hard. Our thinking is a degree less efficient and sure. We may suffer deep doubts about our own abilities to give birth or to be a mother.

It is hard to live a weakened life. Vulnerability is so despised in our society. When we wish to convey disrespect for something we call it a "sign of weakness," as if that were a bad thing. We take weakness itself as a sign of weakness, so to speak. As women who've trained ourselves for years to be independent and self-sufficient, we may find pregnancy a grinding gear change. Now, our main achievements, such as keeping our growing baby alive another day, are mostly invisible and unacclaimed. We are loath to admit to being diminished, for fear of evoking notions of "the weaker sex." It's as if one slip-up from us might singlehandedly reverse all our sisters' precarious and hard-won victories.

How did we get ourselves into this predicament? How have

we become so dead-set against our human vulnerability—and even against ourselves when we accidentally display it? It's understandable, really. A weak object is one that is brittle and could easily be shattered, crushed, or broken. We do not want to break. From our experience in the world, we know that breaking hurts. We have loved and been rejected. We have exposed our true hearts only to be mocked. We have been kicked when we were down. We have relied on others who have failed us. We have reached for help, only to receive a slap on the hand. In some of these experiences we have felt perilously close to total obliteration. Now, we would rather protect ourselves with a hard and impermeable exoskeleton than risk suffering such injuries at the hands of our fellow sinners again.

Understandable as it is, our disdain for weakness does not serve us long-term. We can only get away with hiding in an imaginary fortress temporarily. In the end, life brings to all of us a circumstance that reveals our neediness, whether that is serious illness, old age, bereavement, or—yes—pregnancy.

Christ Himself shows us the way to embrace vulnerability even when it's terrifying. By taking on our humanity, He who is the Resurrection and the Life voluntarily became subject to death, as well as to rejection, humiliation, and all the things we fear most. "We do not have a High Priest who cannot sympathize with our weaknesses," writes the author of the Epistle to the Hebrews (4:15), but one who embraces our weakness so fully that He takes it on as His own.

We can use the vulnerability of pregnancy as an impetus to follow His example and grow deeper into an acceptance of the weakness that is part of our humanity. Doing this can in fact benefit us in several ways. As St. Isaac the Syrian says, "Blessed is the person who knows his own weakness because awareness of this becomes for him the foundation and the beginning of all that is good and beautiful."[20]

First, the weakness of pregnancy keeps us rightly oriented to our Creator. Our vulnerability is a symbol of our universal human reliance on Him, reminding us moment by moment to look to Him to save us. Like St. Paul's "thorn in the flesh" (2 Cor. 12:7), our weakness continually jabs us in the ribs, to keep us from boasting in our own power and to dispose us to receive Him. Imagine what unrealistic expectations of ourselves we would develop if pregnancy brought us only the jaw-dropping power to produce life without any attendant trials! We would be tempted to forget our need for God and worship ourselves as some kind of fertility goddesses. The unglamorous life of a spit-up–covered, sleep-deprived parent would then come as an even ruder shock than it already does. Rather, "the Lord is near those who are brokenhearted, and He will save the humble in spirit" (Ps. 33/34:19); it is when our hearts are tenderized by pummeling that they are soft enough to soak up His love.

Second, the experience of weakness keeps us rightly oriented to our fellow human beings. Being brought low helps us number ourselves among "the least of these" (Matt. 25:40): those who are hungry, thirsty, strangers, naked, sick, or in prison. It helps us to grow in compassion and solidarity for those who suffer and to learn to serve Christ in them. Our hearts are moved when we learn of the plight of others who must bear the same indignities that we bear but who are also homeless, or incarcerated and shackled for childbirth, or bringing their babies into the world in the midst of war.

But being rightly oriented to our fellow human beings means not only extending compassion to others—it also means being willing to be on the receiving end of others' help. This is often harder than it looks; receiving often seems to require more humility than giving. I remember that as a toddler one of my children was determined that she could take care of everything all alone. Even if her sweet stubby fingers took fifteen minutes to zip a coat, she would push away any helping hands, insisting "Self! Self!" Sometimes we are that toddler too. But just as we are working out our salvation through service to other people, likewise our neediness offers them an occasion to which they may rise. These weeks give us the opportunity to practice graciously accepting the help we're offered, allowing our reliance on our fellow human beings to be a reflection of our reliance on God.

Strength

I make humans. What's your superpower?
—T-SHIRT SLOGAN

"Whorehen I am weak, then I am strong" (2 Cor. 12:10). This week brings us to the second half of St. Paul's dichotomy. In the New Testament, *strength* is conveyed by several Greek words, each with its own emphasis. Here St. Paul refers to *dynamis*, meaning potency or ability—the root of the English words *dynamic* and *dynamite*. Then there's *exousia*, the kind of power that is wielded, as in a monarch's reign. We also have *kratos*, which could be translated as *might*—as in God's title Pantokrator, All-Powerful. Finally there's *ischyros*, the word from the Trisagion hymn, which can be translated Holy *Strong*.

It's our *dynamis*—that is, sheer bottled potential—that finds new expression in childbearing. As this second trimester dawns, most (though certainly not all) of us start to enjoy an experience of such strength. Newfound vigor replaces the need for toothpicks to prop our eyelids open. Any nausea tends to pass. Increased blood volume and oilier skin lend that healthy glow everybody talks about. Now bigger than any bodybuilder's bicep, the womb's myometrium takes over from the gluteal group as our strongest muscle. People may notice in us a gently emerging but powerful new beauty that had been latent and is now revealed. Our bodies are running full tilt on the task they were designed for. We're finally starting to experience physically what we've known academically: that pregnancy is not an illness but a sign of great health. It's as if nature is showering us with compliments: "Look how young and fecund you are! Your body is full of genius. You have received favor from the Almighty; blessed are you among women!"

But the vigor of the second trimester is a dim shadow of the strength that culminates in us at the time of birthing. Even more than pregnancy itself, a satisfying birth experience has the potential to leave us feeling utterly victorious. During the birth of my second child, I remember prowling up and down our hallway on all fours in the middle of the night, roaring like a lion, baying like a wolf. I had been brought low by labor, yes, but I had also been taken up. Each contraction brought a tremendous power sweeping through me like a wind, whirling me to the heavens, grounding me to the earth, and transforming me into a full version of myself. The mother-force was irresistible, invincible. My strong pain was undone by a total exhilaration that I wouldn't have traded for the world. I've never felt mightier since.

After labors like that one, we women are transformed by a new respect for our own capabilities. "I never was much good at athletics," we might say, "but now I've found my sport." As we face future challenges, our memory of birth is a constant source of strength, demonstrating that if we can do that, we can do anything. Even as elderly women, recounting the detail of our birth stories will light up our faces as brightly as when our babies were a week old.

Of course, not all the births women experience are satisfying. Not everyone enters motherhood with a sense of strength. Many in fact emerge feeling profoundly traumatized and stripped of power, like the nobodies of their own birth stories. Their agency, autonomy, and even their humanity have apparently been snatched away by events or people beyond their control.

Does telling these survivors they are strong make a mockery of what they have suffered? I hope not. For as a doula, I am witness that the conditions of straightforward, happy birth are not the only ones under which childbearing women show their resilience. I have watched women in all circumstances become impossible forces of physical fortitude and mental endurance— not only *even* when, but *especially* when they are called on to withstand great trials. And often other birth partners share my views. Many a woman's husband or partner will say afterward with a shake of the head, "I had no idea she was that strong. I'm really not sure I could do what she did."

The faces of so many women come to mind—each one a victor worthy of a place in the history books. I assisted one mother who, after three days of labor, consented to a Cesarean she hadn't planned, and still found the strength to insist on breastfeeding her baby on the operating table even while surgeons sewed her belly closed. Another woman's partner was incarcerated, so she had to use one of his daily permitted five-minute phone slots to communicate the news that she was laboring—then, after a long and silent twenty-four hours, a second to tell him that their baby was born and healthy.

I remember one mother haunted by past sexual abuse who summoned unthinkable courage to give her baby safe passage through the same flesh that had been violated. How could I forget?—the woman whose beloved husband, deployed and at risk of death in a conflict zone, could only attend their baby's birth via video link. Or the first-time mother who managed to push her baby out without a contraction simply because her baby was in danger. And how about the one whose photo appeared in the news, proudly clutching the baby she had birthed above rising flood waters in the branches of a tree?[21]

What are we to make of the contrast between what an observer would say of these women's strength and what they might say of themselves? The Greek terms we explored and their differing connotations may shed some light on the apparent contradiction. Perhaps when we feel weak and defeated, it's because the unfolding events of birth have called on us to surrender the exousia, or authority, we customarily have over our bodies and lives. Having chosen to endow care providers with responsibility for our well-being so that we can focus on the task at hand, we become subject to things beyond our control: the actions of those around us and the happenstance of unforeseen events. But even when our exousia ebbs, we are not rendered powerless, because another kind of strength remains. This is the dynamis— the inherent potency—which awes doulas and husbands, and it can never be taken away.

Because our dynamis is not dependent on outside circumstances, childbearing can neither "empower" nor "disempower" us. In fact, nothing can—for our power is a fundamental part of who we are. The dynamis of pregnancy and birth-giving consists in the very nature of our womanhood, which contains the seed of life. While labor is a prime outlet for womanly dynamis, each of us manifests this mysterious force in our own particular way, whether our baby is born under operating room lights or in a mountain stream, whether we are mother to many nations or unable to conceive.

Yet we are only free to experience the fullness of our dynamis when others treat us in a way that also honors our exousia. As studies reveal, the most satisfying birth experiences are those in which we feel respected by our caregivers and fully participant in what happens to us, rather than those that are pain-free or that go exactly to plan.[22] Our dynamis can find its expression in any circumstance, but its full brightness shines forth when those around us support and confirm it.

What does it look like when a society truly values the dynamis of birthing women? The Aztecs of Mexico in the fourteenth to sixteenth centuries provide an example of one such culture. When an Aztec woman birthed safely, she was hailed as a soldier returning victorious from battle, and her new baby was greeted with a war cry. Midwives paid her homage with a speech:

> *My beloved maiden, brave woman . . . thou hast labored, thou hast become an eagle warrior, thou hast become an ocelot warrior, thou hast raised up, thou hast taken to the shield . . . thou hast encountered . . . now our lord hath placed thee upon the eagle warrior reed mat, upon the ocelot warrior reed mat. Thou hast returned from battle, my beloved maiden, brave woman: be welcome.*[23]

If a woman died in childbirth, her midwives' custom was to take shields and carry her away, but young warrior men would follow the procession and engage the mourners in a skirmish, trying to steal the woman's body as a totem. If the warriors could get a section of hair or a finger—specifically the middle finger!—they would insert it in their own shields to make them valiant in battle. I wonder how different things would be if we too honored the new mothers of our society as victors emerging from a rite of passage completely transformed and ennobled.

But though Aztec culture seems far removed from our own understanding of the world, an association between battle and birth isn't entirely alien to the tradition of our faith. The prophet Isaiah writes, "The LORD shall go forth like a mighty man; / He shall stir up *His* zeal like a man of war. / He shall cry out, yes, shout aloud; / He shall prevail against His enemies."

The passage goes straight on, giving the warrior-Lord these words: "'I have held My peace a long time, / I have been still and restrained Myself. / *Now* I will cry like a woman in labor, / I will pant and gasp at once'" (42:13–14, NKJV).

One moment Isaiah compares God to a battle hero; the next, to a birthing woman. By pairing battle and birth in this way, the prophet allows us to see the commonalities that make them, in their small way, an imitation of God's own victorious love. Birth and battle, he shows us, share a common cry, the shedding of blood, courage in the face of danger, pain, and the perpetuation of life—some of the themes, too, of our Lord's definitive rite of passage into Hades. At His Passion, He too gives life by squaring up to death with a shout of victory: "It is finished" (John 19:30)—only His work enlivens not just a single child or single nation, but the whole cosmos. Isaiah's implication is that, when we are trying to comprehend the might of God's love, childbirth is as good a parallel as any the womanly experience has to offer.

It may, in fact, be the best that human experience has to offer. It is the birth-giving of the Theotokos, after all, that makes her the model for all Christians, whether male or female. As Orthodox writer Frederica Mathewes-Green writes, Mary, in becoming the dwelling-place of God, proved to be "our best example of heroism in the battle against sin,"[24] deserving of her venerable titles Champion Leader and Captain, Queen of War.[25] But quintessentially strong as she is, even the Mother of God is not the source of her own might. One icon depicts her in chainmail and a helmet, yet as her weapon she wields not a sword but the cross. She is powerful only by virtue of having been overshadowed by "the power of the Highest" (Luke 1:35).

We live in a cultural environment that urges us to "look within" to find the strength we need, but for us, as for the

Theotokos, our power comes only by virtue of an overshadowing. As even the secular writer Sheryl Feldman puts it, "There is a power that comes to women when they give birth. They don't ask for it, it simply invades them. Accumulates like clouds on the horizon and passes through, carrying the child with it."[26] This power has its source in God, whose "'strength is made perfect in weakness'" (2 Cor. 12:9) and whose dynamis is Christ crucified (1 Cor. 1:23–24). He Himself, not our own middle finger, is our "strength" and "shield" (Ps. 28:7 NKJV).

The reality of this is often played out very concretely in the moments just before birth. For most of us, the baby comes only at the point when we declare, "I can't do this!" Giving up is so reliable an indicator that birth is near as to be practically its own stage of labor. True power appears in us only when we come to the *end* of our strength, when the circumstances no longer allow us a false sense of our own abilities. On our own steam, bringing a child out of our bodies and into the world proves entirely "impossible, but with God all things are possible" (Matt. 19:26).

But we are enriched rather than belittled by this reliance on God for our strength. To think we'd have to conjure for ourselves the tremendous resilience required for pregnancy, birth, and parenting would be paralyzing, but the knowledge that our power flows from Him is a great relief. It's okay if we don't already possess the strength we'll need; like the spring in our second-trimester step, it will come to us unbidden when the time comes. By this experience of His overshadowing power, we are emboldened and fortified for the warrior's work ahead.

Links

A cornucopia full of fruits in all stages of development resembles the course of human marriage: it contains the old, young and middle-aged, children who have already been born and babies still unborn; its fruits follow one another and appear like the continuous succession of humankind.
—ST. EPHREM THE SYRIAN[27]

Belly buttons are pretty fascinating, as any preschooler knows. Your average three-year-old, when she's not busy twiddling her outie, is likely at a table somewhere, crayon in fist, embellishing her drawings of everyone from bishops to playmates with navels. A couple of years and several developmental stages may pass before her figures get clothing or fingers, but belly buttons feature right from the start.

Into adolescence and adulthood she will hardly give them another thought until, during the weeks of pregnancy, her own navel jumps out and grabs her attention once more. Her belly grows under her very nose, concave shapes waxing convex as birth approaches. ("When the belly button pops," as the adage puts it, "the baby's done.") This navel-gazing may find an inner expression as she becomes more pensive and withdrawn, searching her soul in anticipation of motherhood. Deep questions and longings stir inside her about the future of herself, her family, and the world.

But expectant mothers and preschoolers are not the world's only belly button enthusiasts; in fact, they are among surprising company. Perhaps the most dedicated members of the club are the Byzantine monastics for whom navel-gazing is more than an amusing pastime: quite literally, it is a spiritual practice. First described by St. Symeon the New Theologian,[28] *omphaloskepsis*, as it's known, is a psychosomatic method for use with the Jesus Prayer. As he prays—"Lord Jesus Christ, Son of God, have mercy on me, a sinner"—the adherent slows and synchronizes his breath, his chin tucked to his chest and his gaze turned toward his belly button.

This practice proved very contentious in the fourteenth century, but the Church Fathers evidently considered it worth defending. Our bodies, they affirmed, can serve as a dynamic aid to prayer, and the humble belly button has a unique role in this regard. As a spot at the core of the body, the symbolic navel—in Greek, *bembix* or "whirlpool"; in Anglo-Saxon, *nafe* meaning "the hub of a wheel"—can help us cast our mind's eye toward the true center of our being. There, in what the Church Fathers term "the heart" or *nous,* we encounter the Living God.

The Fathers' observation that things get personal and intimate inside our navels is one with which modern science would concur. Here in the twenty-first century, North Carolina State University's Belly Button Biodiversity Project (I'm not kidding) discovered that each person's navel shelters its own thriving and distinctive ecosystem. Among sixty belly buttons, over 2,300 microbial species were identified, the vast majority of which showed up in just a single navel. Researchers found Japanese soil bacteria on a man who'd never been to Japan, microbes associated with hostile deep sea environments, and over a thousand organisms totally novel to science. Yet, amid the diversity they also uncovered some commonalities. No one species was found in every navel, but most belly buttons contained vast colonies of one of the eight dominant kinds.[29]

Whether looked at playfully, prayerfully, or scientifically, the human navel represents a portal to the intimate recesses of personhood. It symbolizes both what we have in common as human mammals and what distinguishes us as unique people. It reminds us that, at our core, we are all conjoined. A belly button is, after all, a scar at the site where each of us was once linked to another person, belly to belly, by a physical cord. Stretching between our tummy and the placenta embedded in our mother's womb, this cord does its job for a time, then is severed at birth. Its stump shrivels and drops off, leaving the belly button as its only trace.

This is the inheritance of human interconnection that we now pass to the little ones within our wombs. And it's at this point in their development, week fourteen of pregnancy, that the umbilical tie joining us to them comes into its own. Let's consider the physical purpose this tie serves, in hopes that its spiritual significance will also emerge.

In the very early weeks, a baby's nutrients come directly from his mother's uterus, where his delicate organs form in a deoxygenated environment free from the danger of destabilizing free radicals. The umbilical cord forms by week seven in preparation for the switch to a new aerobic metabolism requiring oxygenated blood. For a couple of weeks the two nutritional systems overlap while the mother's placenta matures fully. But it's not until twelve weeks that blood flow through the cord is fully established, and not until fourteen weeks that the changeover becomes complete. Now, the baby's red blood cells can circulate out of his body through the cord and into the nourishing placenta, making a U-turn within the very vascular capillaries whose lining is bathed in his mother's blood. Astonishingly enough, this exchange between them takes place without their blood ever mingling.

The umbilical cord itself is springy, translucent, coiled, and tough enough that birth attendants invited to cut it are often surprised by the elbow grease required. It's long, too: about as long as the baby at birth. Inside it are hardworking blood vessels which at term will carry a quarter-liter of blood every minute. Insulating and protecting these vessels is Wharton's jelly, a mucusy tissue containing undifferentiated stem cells with healing properties. Its gelatinous texture keeps the cord slippery and slack enough to preserve blood flow even if the baby somersaults into a tangle. Thanks to this padding, babies who are born wrapped in their cord (as a third of all babies are) can simply be unwound. Even if the cord is around the neck, the baby remains safe while oxygen is flowing from the placenta rather than through the airways.

At birth, the cord remains a bulging shiny blue, pulsating with the baby's heartbeat. As mother and baby greet one another, the portion of the baby's blood stored in the placenta—about thirty percent—gradually pumps back to its rightful home in his little body. As the baby begins to breathe independently and the cord's job is complete, its structure starts to collapse, taking it slowly to a limp and empty white. Within about five minutes, the cord has naturally clamped itself and can be cut.

Tough and pulsating, healing and protective, the umbilical cord is a symbol of the living link that is forming between us and our babies. Like the heartstrings that grow stronger each day, the cord ensures that our babies belong to us, and we belong to them. But it also reminds us of other, invisible bonds that solidify and transform during these days.

A woman and the father of her child become united not just

by a mutual agreement but by a shared lineage as they bring the child into the world. Their baby is a common relative who brings their separate family trees together as one. "Here at last is bone of my bone," they may say not only of each other, as Adam did of Eve; in unison they may also say this of the child they share. But it's not just his parents: the coming of a child has a web of consequences for all his relatives' pre-existing bonds. Depending on how his particular family is peopled, he may transform an only child into a sibling, a youngest child into a middle child, parents into grandparents, in-laws into blood relatives. The baby is less of a new *addition* than a new point on a mathematical shape which changes the relationships between all the other vertices. Family-making is more akin to geometry than to arithmetic.[30]

The net of umbilical bonds proliferating in all directions not only takes in our relationships within the present world, but also casts out into the past and the future. By having a child, we add a new umbilical link in the chain of human life. We extend by a whole generation the human family that began in the belly of our first mother, Eve, and continues to our children's children. We see this in Christ's two genealogies, found in the Gospels of Matthew (1:1–17) and Luke (3:23–38). They each take a different tack, illuminating and completing one another. Saint Matthew roots Christ's lineage in Abraham and David through Joseph's line, emphasizing Jesus' credentials as the Jewish Messiah who comes to fulfill the Scriptures. Saint Luke's account works backward from Christ, but after David and Abraham goes further, all the way back to "Adam, the son of God," framing Christ not just as the fulfilment of the Jewish scriptures but as the heart of humanity itself.

Like Christ, each one of us is here as the result of a chain of "begats." Testimony to this is written into our very bodies. From a newborn's shriveled brown cord stump to the creased slit of an elderly person's belly, our navels remind us of our gut-level connection with the ones who came before us. Every belly button we see on the beach testifies: each person has a mother, two grandmothers, eight great-grandmothers—a birth story, a family tree. Some of the characters are known to us—those ancestors with colorful stories that have been passed down—but many are unknown. Plenty, like the prostitutes, thieves, murderers, and idolaters of Christ's lineage, might even be considered a blot on our pedigree. Yet each one has been absolutely vital to creating the world as we know it: a single degree of deviation high up in the chain would have yielded an entirely different result. We need every one of our foremothers; we are them.

Just as our foremothers helped form our current circumstances, we also are busy writing the future. We may feel insignificant in the span of history, yet like the obscure characters from Christ's genealogy whose names we struggle to pronounce, we have no idea who is coming down the line. For those women carrying a girl, the future is nested inside the present in a quite literal sense. Even before birth, all the eggs a female baby will ever have are stored in her ovaries. They are not ripe yet; one or so will mature during each of the approximately 450 fertile cycles in her adult life. Nevertheless, during this early part of the second trimester, they are proliferating in her, peaking at around seven million (of which the best 400,000 will remain at the time of puberty). In a mother's womb, her baby's womb carries the seeds of her own grandchildren.

This is seen in the beautiful icon of the foremothers of Christ, where four generations are pictured nestling into each other across space-time in a simultaneous embrace, each one spiritually and physically vital to the continuation of her line. Maria, the great-grandmother of Christ, towers over her descendants at the back, her hand on the shoulder of her daughter Anna, seated in front of her. Though Anna's face is that of an elderly woman, she appears smaller than her mother. In her lap is nestled her daughter, the Mother of God, a little smaller still yet also fully grown. Finally, on a cushion in the lap of the Theotokos we find the infant Christ.

Seen next to one another in this way, the generations we normally consider far removed from one another—between a person and his great-grandmother—seem to shrink, compressing into insignificance the gulf separating us from them. Indeed, if we assume an average number of years per generation, we are only about seventy-six generations removed from Christ's foremothers—the same exact number there were between Him and Adam, according to St. Luke's Gospel. These women are a bridge between Scripture and modernity, promise and fulfillment, Old Testament and New; and we too are bringing about a new spiritual era by ushering a new child of God into the world.

In doing so, we lean heavily not just on our foremothers and forefathers in the flesh, who passed us their genes, but also on our spiritual forebears, by whose fidelity our faith came to us. These may be devoted mothers of our family tree who told their young ones simple stories of God's love at the hearthside; brave martyrs throughout the ages who would rather give their lives than renounce their faith and who are now crowned in the Kingdom; or godmothers whose secret prayers sustained us through turbulent times as young adults. We are called to take our place in their ranks, keeping the flame of faith alive for our spiritual descendants, who in ways now unknown to us will participate in the salvation of the world.

In the end, the umbilical bonds of love reveal the ecstatic

oneness of all, past and future, spiritual and physical. "You are all one in Christ Jesus," writes St. Paul (Gal. 3:28)—or, as James Joyce puts it more cryptically in *Ulysses*, "The cords of all link back, strandentwining cable of all flesh. That is why mystic monks. Will you be as gods? Gaze in your *omphalos* [belly button]."[31] *All* flesh, he says: this mystical reality somehow encompasses the whole of creation (because, after all, hammerhead sharks have belly buttons, too).

So we dare to hope that the healing cords that once linked all creatures, now cut by sin, will one day be restored, and every living thing will again be linked by love as immediate as that now pulsing between us and our babies. While we wait for that day, the humble navel remains an eschatological symbol, in its comical way pointing us to the Kingdom of heaven.

Trinity

The child is a bridge connecting mother to father, so the three become one flesh, as when two cities divided by a river are joined by a bridge. And here that bridge is formed from the substance of each!
—ST. JOHN CHRYSOSTOM[32]

Pregnancy is the icon of human connectedness.
—FREDERICA MATHEWES-GREEN[33]

It was perhaps the strangest feeling I've ever had. The head of my first baby had just been born. After months of wondering what it would look like, his pale doughy face with its scant fringe of brown hair was right there to be seen. Yet his whole body, with its attendant newborn needs— needs for food, breath, love, sleep, and fresh diapers, which would soon make themselves unambiguously felt—had not yet been revealed in the world.

While I waited through two minutes of eternity for the con- traction that would unveil him fully, I felt the familiar sensation of my son's feet kicking inside the top of my womb. But now for the first time, I could also feel him on the outside, flexing his neck with indisputable agency as he wriggled toward the light. He was an individual, but still part of me. I was a mother but not yet a mother; one yet more-than-one. That moment held two realities in mysterious tension: he and I were at the same time an interconnected unit and distinct beings.

In the coming days, as this child settled into our family, the fulcrum shifted a little, and the balance of our unity and distinctiveness settled on a new point, skewed toward his independence. I no longer had to do his breathing and digestion for him, but we still needed one another. As much as he required my milk, I needed him to take it. This was a matter not just of emotional desire but of raw physical necessity. If he slept a little longer than my body expected, my full breasts would suddenly bloom forth into pain-veined melons, until he helped me by feeding.

Time unfolded, and my rhythms necessarily conformed to his, not just by duty but by natural consequence. When he so much as stirred I would respond with an urgency that came from deep in my body. We hardly left the house. Our life became a bright circling cloud of feeding, burping, bathing, changing, admiring, resting, crying, pacing. It was an entirely shared life, one in which I was my*self* but definitely not my *own*. I was living what scholar Lisa Baraitser calls the maternal condition of "being singular and multiple simultaneously."[34]

As Christians, we put our faith in a God who is both one and more-than-one. We worship the Holy Trinity: Father, Son, and Holy Spirit. The Godhead is unity-in-diversity, a single divine reality with three instances of divine life, equal persons sharing a single essence. As such, God is "not just a unit but a union, not just unity but community."[35] Within the divine life, the self is found and fulfilled only in the love of another. This reality is seen at every stage in God's revelation to the world, even back to the creation of the universe, when He spoke in the first person plural, saying, "Let Us make man in Our image" (Gen. 1:26). At the baptism of Christ, however, "the Trinity was made manifest. For," we sing to Christ in the Theophany troparion, "the voice of the Father bore witness to You, calling You His Beloved Son, and the Spirit in the form of a dove confirmed the truth of His Word."

To plumb the depths of the mysterious doctrine of the Trinity is impossible. The Matins service of Pentecost itself refers to it as a "strange teaching"; St. Gregory of Nyssa calls it "riddles."[36] Yet, as Metropolitan Kallistos Ware reminds us, mystery isn't just something hidden: by nature, it's also something partly disclosed.[37] Like a veil, mystery simultaneously obscures and invites us to discover what it cloaks. We want to approach, to discover more. So the Holy Trinity is not some incomprehensible enigma to be swallowed but a dynamic experience of divine life that continually draws us in.

That the Godhead is a mystery to participate in is clear from Scripture. Though the word Trinity is not found there, the Bible's three most explicit Trinitarian formulations all appear in service of the worshipping practice of the Church. In Matthew's Gospel (28:19) the resurrected Christ instructs His disciples to baptize "in the name of the Father and of the Son and of the Holy Spirit." Saint Paul ends his second epistle to the church at Corinth (13:14) with the Trinitarian blessing our own churches use to this day: "The grace of the Lord Jesus Christ, and the love of God, and the communion of the Holy Spirit *be* with you all. Amen." And when greeting the Christians of Asia Minor at the start of his first epistle (1:2), St. Peter defines the Church with reference to the three divine Persons she worships. As our tradition attests, it's within a community of faith that the life of the Holy Trinity is expressed.

Pregnancy can form one such community. For an expectant mother is not merely herself but an encounter, a gathering. A pregnant body is a place where "two or three [if she is carrying twins] are gathered together" (Matt. 18:20). When they meet in the Lord's name, His presence "there in the midst of them" is revealed, imitating—however imperfectly—the shape of God. In this way, those whom pregnancy assembles into a unity of self-giving love are transformed into a living icon of the Holy Trinity. Despite being tired, sore, overwhelmed, grumpy, weak, fatally flawed—despite everything, in motherhood we can somehow mirror the triune God to the world. What a great mystery! What a high calling!

Saint Augustine cautions us against taking Trinitarian parallels to family life too far. Those who conceive of mother, father, and child as a "completed" image of God in three Persons he considers almost comically misled. To think of a human father standing in for the Father, a child for the Son, and a mother for the Holy Spirit is "so absurd, nay indeed so false, that it is most easy to refute it. For I pass over such a thing, as to think the Holy Spirit to be the mother of the Son of God, and the wife of the Father."[38] Certainly, we wouldn't want to make direct correlations between particular human roles and divine realities, and even a loose human analogy for the divine life of the Godhead will be a dim shadow of its fullness. Yet Christ was optimistic about humanity's potential for mirroring the life of God: for example, he prayed "that they all may be one, as you, Father, *are* in me, and I in You; that they also may be one in Us" (John 17:21). This both emboldens us to look for commonalities between Trinitarian and family life, and cautions us not to push the analogy too far.

To spot the parallels, let's place our own lives side by side with Andrei Rublev's icon, the Hospitality of Abraham, some version of which can be seen in nearly every Orthodox church. This icon brings to life the story from Genesis 18—19 of the three strangers who came unannounced to visit our holy father and mother, Abraham and Sarah, as they camped by the oak of Mamre. The arrival of the three visitors is described as an appearance of God (Gen. 18:1), of "the Lord" (Gen. 18:22), and the Church has come to understand them as mysteriously pointing to the Persons of the Holy Trinity—although without forgetting that the Father and the Holy Spirit cannot truly be depicted in human form.

We see the figures seated together at a table, their wings tucked behind them and their haloed heads inclined toward one another. Each one holds a staff demonstrating His own authority. Their faces are exactly alike; their clothing shares a color palette. The central figure is dressed in the colors in which Christ is traditionally robed: red overlaid with blue. Following His gaze, our eyes are left with nowhere to stop, as the communication between the persons proceeds in a never-ending loop. An imaginary line encompassing the shoulders of the figures also makes a geometric circle. On the table in front of the three is a chalice, a form echoed in the shape made by the legs of the figures on the left and right. Their feet point to the final space at the table, which remains conspicuously open and inviting.

The *distinctness* of the three divine Persons revealed in this icon certainly finds a sort of parallel in our experience of pregnancy. Just as the three figures are distinctively dressed, a mother and her baby are distinguishable one from the other. Quickening, which marks the first flutters of the baby's movements that she can feel, may occur around week fifteen, especially if she has been pregnant before, and from this time on, the otherness of her baby will never be far from her mind. She may be sitting still at a concert and feel him keeping the beat of the music; she may even be kicked awake from sleep. Around the clock, these sensations will remind her that she is not her baby and he isn't her.

The *unity* of the Godhead shown in Rublev's Trinity icon also finds some analogy in our human motherhood. Of course, unlike the Persons of the Godhead, a mother never shares full oneness with her child. Nevertheless, as we stand with swelling bellies, gazing on the three figures in the icon, the circular movement of their reciprocity speaks deeply to us. Their openness to one another moves us. We experience anew the truth that God is not just a self-contained unit but a relational being. We awaken to the beauty of the fact that there can be no *I* without *Thou*. We remember that we too are ourselves only in the context of one another's love.

Theologians have given the enticing circular movement of the three Persons the name *perichoresis*, a word that is difficult to translate without losing any of its many meanings. One scholar, Julian Stead, has listed the different connotations of *perichoresis* as various Church Fathers used the term.[39] When we consider each Father's usage in turn, it's apparent that every one of the meanings Stead identifies has some corollary in the experience of childbearing.

For St. Macarius of Egypt, Stead says, *perichoresis* means "to encircle or encompass." This encompassing appears in the Rublev icon in the rounded shoulders of the three figures as they sit in their circle. The encompassing aspect of pregnancy is most striking when we consider that a woman may bear a son—that her female body can walk around with a big bundle of Y chromosomes in it. Her flesh seems to incorporate more than is possible—or, to mimic the Akathist Hymn to the Theotokos, to be more spacious than itself. Yet her baby also somehow encircles her. Pregnancy can be engulfing, consuming all her waking thoughts, every drop of her energy. Especially if she usually thrives on quiet time alone, such a thorough invasion of her "personal space" may make her claustrophobic in her own body. (Others seem to exacerbate this, treating her as if her body is somehow public property, even reaching out to touch her belly in a way they never would have done before.) After her baby's birth she belongs so much to her baby that she sometimes wonders if she no longer belongs to herself.

Saint Maximos the Confessor, Stead says, uses *perichoresis* to speak of "rotation," "reciprocity of action." The circular movement of our eyes as we engage with the Rublev icon brings to mind a baby's spiraling path through his mother's pelvis at birth. The uterus has muscle fibers that run top to bottom and side to side, and a third layer wrapped in the shape of a whirlpool; the coordinated contractions of these three muscle groups steer the baby around and down, helping him turn to navigate the bony landmarks of his mother's pelvis. She, too, accommodates his body with a rotating motion, instinctively rocking her pelvis back and forth, around and around, to help ease him down. So mother and baby participate reciprocally in the circular dance of birth.

Stead says that in the writings of Pseudo-Cyril and St. John of Damascus *perichoresis* connotes "coinherence, interpenetration." Studies show that substances from a mother penetrate rapidly to her baby in the womb: for example, food flavors are shared through amniotic fluid, so that babies can recognize them after birth.[40] Almost all drugs taken by a pregnant mother are also administered to her baby. Happily, this means a mother can take steroids to help her baby's lungs mature quickly when he or she will need to be born early; unfortunately, it also means the opioids commonly used to relieve labor pain can cause babies to need reviving at birth. It's not just a one-way street, though: material also passes in the other direction, from baby to mother. In the phenomenon known as microchimerism (named after the chimera, the hybrid creature of Greek mythology), unborn children leave a genetic calling card in their mother's bodies, their foreign cells remaining and multiplying there for decades. Like the hues of the Trinity icon, where the dominant colors of each figure's robe are picked up in smaller details of the others', a mother's brain may contain immune cells from all her babies, even if she miscarried them so early she never knew she was pregnant.

Finally, for St. Gregory the Theologian, Stead says, *perichoresis* means "to interchange, reciprocate." In the icon, the persons are not just locked in a staring competition but are engaged in mutual exchange. Likewise, my baby and I are engaged in a dynamic conversation, exemplified by the role of the placenta, starting around six weeks of pregnancy. It is my child's organ, essentially functioning as his lungs, digestive system, and kidneys, but fused to *my* womb. His blood does not mix with my own—in fact, we may have entirely different blood types which mustn't mix—but it passes so very close that I share my oxygen and nutrients by diffusion across the interface. Antibodies to illnesses I have fought teach my baby how to deal with life on the outside. I may think of my placenta as providing him a service—I give him nutrients and oxygen, and he sends me back his waste. But in fact the placenta's porous interface allows him to serve me, too. For instance, when I get hurt, unique fetal stem cells migrate from his body into my bloodstream, rushing to the injury site to help it recover. Even on a physical level, the ministry of a mother and her child is truly reciprocal.

These definitions cannot exhaust the meaning of Trinity, but they reveal something of the shape of God's life so that we can spot it where it appears on a tiny scale in our own family lives. May the encircling, rotating, interpenetrating, reciprocal love that arises as we become mothers carry us another step forward into the unfathomable love of Father, Son, and Holy Spirit.

Unknown

Your eyes saw me when I was unformed.
—PSALM 138(139):16

I recall the ultrasound that gave my husband and me the initial glimpse of our first child: my head propped in the crook of my elbow, a cold squirt of gel on my exposed belly, the hard pressure of the instrument into my skin, a figure in black and white emerging from static on the screen. This figure looked hardly human, an alien life form with an implausibly big head and eye sockets too widely spaced. But as we watched, the image stirred. In a single, smooth, and undeniably deliberate motion, that big head turned to the side. A hand came up to the face, and a pulsing movement began. Our son was sucking his thumb. The personhood of the one we were examining suddenly leapt into focus. It was a coordinated act of individuality and will at only fifteen weeks of pregnancy.

Probably all parents consider their child exceptional (and they're right!), but this was no display of precociousness on my baby's part. What we witnessed was just another moment in the life of the womb. It was I, not my child, who reached a new developmental milestone that day. I took a step toward knowing him as a person. The kernel of instinctual knowledge that had started to grow somewhere inside me even before my pregnancy was confirmed suddenly blossomed forth in the light of new information provided by the ultrasound. Out of the black-and-white static void in my mind, a sense of who he was started to form.

From the chaotic waters on the face of the deep, a shape arose.

As time passed, further "data" came out. A few seconds after we saw him go for his thumb, we discovered that he was male. Some weeks more and I felt him flutter inside me, at first only here or there, but eventually so often that I could anticipate his busier times of day. I developed a sense, somehow, of the sort of person he was. His birth opened up whole new swathes of information about him: his looks, quirks, and characteristics, but most importantly the sheer fact that he was a real-life bona fide human being—a realization that had been strangely elusive until he actually arrived. As he learned to express himself through actions and words and relationships, we came to know him better and better. Now that baby is a teenager, and we still learn new things about him each day.

Parenthood, we might say, is a journey from the unknown to the known. My relationship with my child begins when I'm unaware that conception has even taken place and proceeds to as full a kinship as may be possible in this world. The process of discovery becomes supercharged around the current stage of pregnancy, when many care providers offer ultrasound exams, amniocentesis, and blood tests that seem to promise moments of epiphany. Technology transforms this period into a sort of informational springtime. I can choose to find out my baby's sex, as well as the probability that he has any of a variety of syndromes and anomalies. I can even pay to have a recreational 4D ultrasound, with keepsake printouts or footage to take home. Ultrasound devices have become cheap enough that I can buy myself one and do a DIY checkup whenever curiosity strikes.

We humans aren't very comfortable with not-knowing. Fear of the unknown is regarded by some psychologists as the basic fear, the root from which all our other fears originate.

Even from childhood, the universal robber of our nightmares emerges from the darkness, clothed in black, his face covered. He's frightening because the truth of his identity is hidden. Our culture has a particularly strong case of this. If there is a scientific quandary, it must be solved. If there is an unexplored species, planet, or tribe, we must discover it. If we're on the beach, we are more comfortable seeing a mostly naked woman than a mostly veiled one. We appreciate the pristine not for its own virtues but as something one can be the first to plunder.

Even for those who have had a baby before, pregnancy introduces many new unknowns to pique our discomfort or fear. Am I doing the right things? Is my child growing with a healthy body and a typical brain? What will giving birth feel like? Will my body be forever altered? When will my baby be born? Will he and I survive? Who will this child be? How will this new person fit in with the rest of the family? Will I make a good parent? How can I bring a child into this harsh, changeable, and confusing world? What will society look like when he's grown?

There are positive aspects to our desire to know. From Homer to Harry Potter, heroes' tales throughout history tell of the primal quest to find something lost or uncover something hidden. The desire to conquer the unknown is also foundational to the spiritual life. We seek to unlock the mysteries of the universe, those hidden treasures to which Christ points. Our Christian faith moves us from mystery to intimacy, from an unknowable transcendent God to One who has a face, a name, a birthday, and a hometown. As the One St. John the Evangelist calls the *exegesis* of the Father (John 1:18), Jesus of Nazareth makes the unapproachable God seen.

And if our God is one who is known, He is also One who seeks to know. He reaches out not just to humanity in general but to each of us as a unique person, and He knows us with great specificity, even down to the number of hairs on our heads (Matt. 10:30; Luke 12:7). "Before I formed you in the womb, I knew you," He calls to us and our children, "and before you were born, I sanctified you" (Jer. 1:5).

This total intimacy is the divine goal I reach toward as I seek out knowledge of the infant in my womb. Every notch deeper my knowledge gets is a step toward a future in which "I shall know just as I also am known" (1 Cor. 13:12). It's as if at my ultrasound appointment I'm saying to my baby what the Psalmist says to God: "My heart speaks to You; my face seeks You; / Your face . . . I will seek" (Ps. 26/27:8).

Of course, not everyone considers my baby a person to seek out. In the words of St. Paul (2 Cor. 6:9), though he is known, he is regarded as unknown—as "a bundle of cells" or "the products of conception" rather than as a son, sibling, or grandchild. In this context, an ultrasound scan functions not just as a checkup on the functioning of various biological systems but as a plea for affirmation. By posting my fuzzy black-and-white printouts on my fridge or social media, perhaps I am seeking worldly validation of the relationship I have begun to feel stirring in my heart. Perhaps the quest to discover all I can about my child before he is born is not only understandable, but even a divine and redemptive task.

But how do I get true knowledge? For it's not the same as mere information. There is a difference between knowing something and knowing *about* it. Even obtaining my baby's full genetic code before birth would not be the same as meeting and getting to know him. True knowledge comes only through relationship. This is why St. Isaac the Syrian says, "Knowledge is the infancy of love," the seed of love, the beginning of love.[41] He's debunking the myth that love is blind. In fact, the opposite is true: the deepest love clearly sees and accepts the reality of the beloved one. If we know truly, we also love fully. This pairing of knowledge and relationship is the same understanding that underlies the biblical use of the verb "to know" to indicate sex. When Adam "knew" his wife, for instance, the result was Cain (Gen. 4:1). This greatest act of intimacy humans can share is the benchmark or symbol of true knowing.

Deep knowledge cannot be rushed. There may be moments when the process gets a turbo boost, but it's important to remember that true knowing comes only with time. Like a bride anticipating her wedding night, during pregnancy I may look forward to, even idolize, certain future moments where I believe my beloved will be decisively revealed to me—be that an ultrasound appointment or maybe the birth itself. How much easier, I think, it will be for me to love the one whom I have seen than it is now, when I have not seen (1 John 4:20)! But, as any married person knows, people don't wake up the morning after their wedding with every marital enigma solved and no questions remaining. Birth is neither the first nor the final stop on the road to knowledge of my child. Instead, it's the unfolding of a new layer of a mystery.

Neither can true knowledge be gained by force. Parents who walk away disappointed after their "gender-reveal" ultrasound appointment because their baby's legs were crossed at the wrong moment know this all too well. For as Fr. Dumitru Staniloae writes:

You cannot know your neighbor in a personal way only on your own initiative, or by an aggressive expedition. In order to know him he must reveal himself, on his own initiative; he does this in proportion to the

*lack of your aggression to know him. How much more so with God, the
Supreme Person and one who isn't clothed in a visible body; man cannot
know Him unless He reveals Himself.*[42]

When I do try to take knowledge by force, there are often terrible consequences. Amniocentesis, a prenatal test in which
a syringe is inserted through the abdominal wall and into the
womb, puncturing the bag of waters in order to remove a sam-
ple of amniotic fluid for genetic investigation, carries a small
miscarriage risk. If I have few risk factors at play, this may well
mean the test is statistically more likely to cause my baby to die
than it is to identify a chromosomal irregularity. Even ultrasound, which is used on practically all babies born in industrialized nations today, is known to heat and modify body tissue—which is why it is used therapeutically, for example to treat
muscle injury. Though the best available evidence indicates
ultrasound does nothing to reduce rates of stillbirth,[43] its use in
pregnancy remains routine.

A third caution concerning knowledge is that I must take
care not to make it an idol. Full and perfect knowledge of anything is not possible in this world. There is so much that cannot
be explained even about relatively simple things like rocks or
earthworms; how much harder it is to plumb the depths of a
human soul! Even couples who have been married for decades
will say that a perfect meeting of the minds still eludes them.
With so many years of comfort and familiarity under their
belts, it becomes clear that they can never attain perfect knowledge: within each partner's soul is such a universe, it proves
impossible to explore its limits even in a lifetime. Likewise
with the child I carry: over time I may come to know him
as only a mother can, but even into old age parts of him will

remain undiscovered, and perhaps even inaccessible—except of course to God. This side of heaven, the veils that separate us from others persist.

And this realization takes the pressure off. I can go easy on myself if at this point things still feel surreal, if I haven't yet come to terms with pregnancy as fully as I'd like and my baby still feels more like a fuzzy concept than a person. I can allow the process of knowing to unfold at its own pace, much as our foremothers did before the advent of ultrasound technology. Even without technological assistance, throughout pregnancy they still came to know their babies, whether this one was a hic-cupper or that one was quiet after breakfast. Who knows, maybe they were even more in touch with their babies because their information came not from a phone call with the doctor's office but from within. Maybe the veils between ourselves and the full truth of reality can have a positive function after all.

The value of veils is confirmed within the tradition of the Orthodox faith, where they are found everywhere one might look. In monasteries and churches, many women cover their heads with a scarf. During services, the clergy and altar serv-ers cloak their regular clothes with vestments; after baptism the newly illumined is robed in white. Our altar is set behind the iconostasis, shielding it from view when the royal doors are shut. A cloth called the *aer* veils the chalice and diskos used for the Holy Mysteries. Incense clouds the air. The songs of the people veil some of the prayers said quietly by the priest as the Liturgy unfolds. Even the church building itself is a kind of veil, setting the life of the church apart from the life of the out-side world.

When veiling is such a source of disquiet in wider society, why does the Church hold it so dear? I'd like to suggest two useful functions veils can serve. First, by obscuring, a veil prompts questions about what lies underneath. It simultaneously covers and invites us to *dis*-cover what it cloaks. And sometimes the veiling itself, not the unveiling, does the disclosing. Andrew Williams' example of an invisible man is helpful here. I can't see the man at all, but by throwing a sheet over him, I could make his location and shape known. The sheet creates an icon, or image, of the man himself.[44]

My womb is like a sheet thrown over the "invisible man" inside. Pregnancy both hides and, if I pay attention, reveals the new person who is coming into the world. Rather than being impatient for a sharper insight, I can practice contentment with the manner of knowing currently accessible to me: the instinctive, prayerful whisperings of a still small voice which some experienced mothers say cannot be felt so intimately once the baby is born. I don't now possess face-to-face knowledge concerning my child, but that should not cheapen the knowledge I do have or cause me to abandon the quest for it.

Second, a veil provides protection. It shields something special or sacred from public view. Clothing, for instance, protects our bodies both from the elements—the sun and wind and rain that might burn and chafe and soak us—and from the gaze of others. The Church dedicates a whole feast day to the Protection of the Mother of God, which she is seen to bestow on us by the covering of her veil. Because the word for "veil" has a rich meaning, connoting a cloak or shroud as well as protection or intercession both in Russian and in Greek, the name of the feast is variously translated "The Veil," "The Protection," and "The Intercession of the Theotokos." Likewise, the veil of flesh cloaking my baby mercifully provides a buffer between his translucent skin and the harsh outside world, until the day he is strong enough to live without that protection. If this shielding also keeps him hidden from me, so be it. I wouldn't want it any other way.

Naming

You know the name and age of each,
even from his mother's womb.
—ANAPHORA OF ST. BASIL

rucks don't *usually* make me laugh out loud; however, I can't help but snicker to see the logo of a certain local relocation firm. On its vehicles is emblazoned the name: Hernia Movers. I scrunch my nose and peer into the cab, hoping the company name—presumably called after its founders—won't prove medically prophetic for the poor driver inside.

Even the name of a company is significant; how much more so that of a new human! By this stage of pregnancy an ultrasound can uncover my baby's sex, and his father and I may start thinking about what to call him. It's a challenge both exhilarating and intimidating: one with decisive and lasting impacts, from what it is we'll shout as we call our toddler away from the playground to the search terms his descendants will use when they undertake genealogical research in three centuries' time.

A whole raft of research confirms that a person's name plays an oddly central role in the overall story of his or her life. One study discovered that people were disproportionately likely to be in a romantic relationship with someone whose first or last name resembled theirs.[45] Another indicated that people are more likely to choose a profession with a name like their own (Denise the dentist, for instance).[46]

The Church honors the gravity of the parental task of naming with prayers read by a family's priest on their baby's eighth day. Depending on local tradition, the priest comes to the home or hospital, or the baby is brought to church by the parents, god-parents, or midwife. The priest makes the sign of the cross over the baby, using for the first time the name of "the servant" or "the handmaid of God." This same formulation will be used in the church throughout the child's life, echoed at his baptism, communion, betrothal, and funeral. The eighth-day prayers ask that just as the child is now recognized by name, the name of God also "may remain unrejected by him." Ultimately, the service looks forward to that time when the child "may receive the blessedness of the elect in [God's] Kingdom." Right from the child's first days we see that his name has a role in his salvation as a human person.

If a name is so important, then how do we go about choosing? On one hand, it is a completely free decision. In the second biblical creation narrative, the man's first task was naming the animals, and the text emphasizes the agency that belonged to him. God "brought them to Adam to see what he would call them. Thus *whatever* Adam called each living creature, that was its name" (Gen. 2:19, emphasis mine). He was to determine what each species God had *called into being* should *be called*, so it could be differentiated from the others.

In our society parents often go about choosing a name with the creative exuberance of Adam, essentially calling our children "Whatever." Names rise and fall in the rankings like pop songs, with novel ones riding into being on a tide of popularity. Some parents choose names that feature in current events, celebrity families, or hit shows, and these eventually become the elderly persons' names of their generation. Others create entirely new names, for example out of syllables from other family monikers.

Assuming I'm not in a country like Iceland, where at the time of writing, babies' names are selected from a pre-approved governmental list, I'm at liberty to use my full creativity. Yet even a culture where choice is king places some limits on our options. The United States doesn't have an approved list, but we still seem to want veto power over our citizens' names. This became clear from one news story in which a New Jersey store refused a request by the parents of three-year-old Adolf Hitler Campbell to make a cake decorated with his name. Amid the ensuing media attention they lost custody of all the children in the family. Commentators called the Campbells' choice of name for their child tantamount to abuse.

In a society which protects a parental right to choose even the most offensive names, why should an "Adolf Hitler Campbell" give us such pause? What exactly is it that makes a name synonymous with Nazism so clearly bad for a child and bad for society? Consider roll call at this boy's school: day by day, a name synonymous with the worst human atrocities becomes normalized.

At the other end of the spiritual spectrum from Adolf Hitler, the associative power of names is also the reason the Jesus Prayer, at its heart a simple recitation of Christ's name, is so beloved of Orthodox Christians. By saying His name we invoke His presence. These examples show, and even the most ardent free speech advocates have to admit, that a name is more than an arbitrary collection of syllables. It's an attempt to capture the substance of the reality of a whole person in just a couple of words. It's an invocation of the spirit the name represents, or as Fr. Thomas Hopko says, "a presence and a power of the reality of that which is named."[47]

When I name my child, then, it is not within a vacuum but within a profound matrix of meaning. Naming is not a utilitarian task but a sacred charge, part of the process of co-creating with God a new human life. Like an iconographer crafting a divine image, who by tradition inscribes the icon's name when every other detail is complete, my naming completes the holy work of pregnancy and birth.

And meaning is the difference between Adam's job and ours. The creatures he named were without precedent, and none of the syllables he uttered when he saw them evoked pre-existing realities. On the other hand, almost any moniker I might choose for my child will be associated with someone else who has the same name. Even an entirely new name has syllables with their own connotations. The naming of a child thus resembles more closely Adam's naming of the woman. Her name wasn't just "whatever he called it," as the animals' were: it was more like Christ's name, or indeed Hitler's name, in that it signified something. "So Adam called his wife's name Life, because she was the mother of all living" (Gen. 3:20).

Like Eve's, many names in Scripture appear next to the word "because." Jacob receives the name Israel, meaning "one who struggles with God," because "you have prevailed with God and with men" (Gen. 32:28). Samuel gets a name meaning "God has heard," says his mother, "because I asked for him from the Lord God Sabaoth" (1 Kingdoms 1:20).

Similarly, any name I choose for my baby has a *because*: perhaps simply because it sounds pretty to me, because he just looked like a Jehoshaphat, or because it keeps a family name in use. But within Christianity I have bigger *becauses* at my disposal. I have the chance to take a name that ties my child not just to my sense of personal taste or the family of which he's already part, but to a web of holiness incorporating the salvation history of the whole world.

I can do this by choosing the name of a holy person from the tradition. By choosing a saint's name, I can give my child a model of victorious struggle to keep ever before his eyes right from the outset. The saint for whom he's named becomes a dear friend, and when I call my child's name, it's as if I invoke the saint too, asking for the prayers of one already in the company of God. Using the name becomes like asking a blessing on the child, praying for his salvation. Some parents select a saint already beloved to them; others wait to see on whose feast the child's birth or eighth day falls and choose from among the saints commemorated that day. Sometimes a saint unexpectedly makes his or her special care for a child known. In some traditions the child's godparents choose a name, or he is called after a member of their family.

But naming a child with reference to saints and godparents and calendars in this way may seem to limit our creative freedom. In a consumer society, we usually resent any lack of choice, and *self*-limitation is seen as practically inexcusable. But throughout history given names have often been determined by a cultural formula, for example where convention held that a child be named after a certain relative, or after their place in the birth order: Quentin for a fifth child, Sextus for a sixth, Septimus for a seventh, and so on. The parents of Holy Scripture, too, often had no choice at all. Saint John the Forerunner was given his name by the Archangel Gabriel during a visit to John's father while he served in the temple. Zacharias was struck dumb and wasn't going to be allowed to name anyone anything at all until the day he scribbled "His name is John" on a writing tablet (Luke 1:60). The Mother of God, too, was told what her son's name would be (Luke 1:31).

But perhaps limitations are an inherent part of the process

of delineating something as being itself. Even the transcendent Godhead is content to limit Himself to a name. Before Moses' encounter with Him, God was simply known as *El Shaddai*, the Most High, the Almighty. The definite article—*the*—indicates a certain distance. But when Moses met God in the burning bush, he asked what to say when people wondered who it was that had sent him to free the Israelites, and God answered, saying, "'I AM the Existing One. . . . Thus you shall say to the children of Israel: "The Existing One sent me to you"'" (Ex. 3:14). God was certainly saying more than just "Me: I sent you." Through a little wordplay He was revealing Himself as the eternal One, with His people from the beginning and forever. It was hardly a chummy pet name: Jewish tradition held that the I AM was to be spoken only once a year, and only in the temple by the high priest, who was to whisper it in the Holy of Holies under the cover of loud song. Yet the disclosure of His name was something of a mutual revelation that made both God and His people more clearly seen: "'This is my name forever, and My memorial to all generations. . . . I have surely looked upon you and all the things that happened to you in Egypt'" (Ex. 3:15–16).

But with the Incarnation of the Word of God, the transcendent God whose name could not be spoken submitted to being named by a human parent, perhaps even nicknamed by his friends. We know Christ as *Jesus* from the Greek, but His contemporaries would have called Him the Aramaic *Yeshua*, the same as our name Joshua. The *because* of His name was this: it meant "God rescues."

There was a Joshua, son of Eliezer, in Joseph's line (Luke 3:29), but the Joshua more strongly evoked is another—a holy forefather of Judaism, Joshua son of Nun, who succeeded Moses as leader of Israel. Moses had led the people out of slavery, but it was Joshua under whose staff the people passed through the parted waters of the river Jordan and into Canaan (Josh. 3:16–17). Sounds rather like Christ, doesn't it? By entering the waters of the Jordan, He too brings His people, baptized into His death in those same waters, out of slavery to sin into the Promised Land of resurrection in God's Kingdom. God's rescue mission to the people of Israel alluded to in the meaning of Joshua's name was completed in the person of Yeshua the Savior. His name weaves Him inextricably into the human story.

So we see that by revealing His names, God has revealed Himself to humanity with increasing intimacy over time. Now we not only dare to speak His name but hold it very dear, as the "name which is above every name" (Phil. 2:9). When my child gets a name, it facilitates our personal relationship in this same way. He and I take a step further out of the unknown, that dark land we explored last week, and into the light of knowledge of one another.

We also experience the intimacy of names by negative example, as when a person suffering from dementia forgets the names of her relatives. This is a deeply estranging experience. I may believe I am still dear to her, but I have no way of being sure when she has forgotten even my name.

Conversely, our deepest experience of being known is when we are brought into God's "Memory Eternal," when at the end of our season on earth we may find our names written in the Book of Life (Rev. 20:12–15). At this time it is said God gives us a new name, a name that reflects the reality of our deepest selves, perfectly known and loved by Him. "To him who overcomes . . . I will give him a white stone, and on the stone a new name written which no one knows except him who receives *it*" (Rev. 2:17). It's a name so personal as to be exclusive between ourselves and God, like a secret term of endearment between spouses that would never be used in public.

Here we see the teleological flavor of our earthly names. They denote what we currently are, but by failing to capture the fullness of reality, they also point forward to what we shall become. Throughout Scripture and in the life of the Church, many figures receive a new name when a new spiritual reality becomes manifest in them. Abram and Sarai become Abraham and Sarah, the Father of Many and the Princess of Many (Gen. 17:5, 15). Simon becomes Peter, the Rock on which the Church is built (Matt. 16:18). Saul is renamed Paul after his encounter with the Lord on the way to Damascus (Acts 13:9). Within this same tradition monastics also take a new name upon their tonsuring.

This is a tradition into which I as a parent also enter. For it's not only I who give my child a name—he gives me a new name too. It's the one name at once most universal and most deeply personal: at first just "ma," one of the few syllables his little mouth can form, then "Mama," "Mom," or some version of his own. Like any name change, this one can take some time to get used to. One woman describes giving birth with the support of her mother. "Let's lift Mum onto the delivery table," said the obstetrician. The woman recalls wondering why they would do that to her mother when she herself was having the baby. She wasn't yet thinking of herself as Mum.[48] Once I grow into it, though, this change reflects that my personhood has been transformed through the assimilation of a new identity like Sarah or Paul.

As I become a mother, this new identity becomes an inseparable part of the context for my life and faith. The new creature I find myself becoming is the one who is being saved, indeed the only one now who can be saved. I wonder what name, by God's grace, I will find written on that white stone. It will be more than "Mama," surely, yet something of "Mama" will appear there. As I grapple with potential names for my baby, may I also grapple with my own new name. In embracing it I inch ever closer to what I shall be: my truest self, known and loved in the Kingdom of God.

THREE

Exploring Birth in Symbols

Light

The true Light . . . gives light to every man
coming into the world.
—JOHN 1:9

With this chapter we begin a little series on the deep symbolism of birth. Over the next three weeks we'll reflect on the central parable Christ uses to teach us about salvation. Entering into the love of God, He says, requires being born a second time. "'Unless one is born again, he cannot see the kingdom'" (John 3:3).

The words "born again" carry heavy cultural baggage, and often I'm tempted to let them pass me by. But being pregnant, my ears tend to prick up at any mention of birth. It's as if I am able like Nicodemus to hear Christ's words for the first time, and their curious directness strikes me. I too need some clarification: "'How can a man be born when he is old? Can he enter a second time into his mother's womb and be born?'" (John 3:4). The birth Christ is talking of, He says, is a spiritual birth through baptism. But why did Jesus choose the language of childbirth to speak of salvation? What do physical and spiritual birth have in common? What is it about being born that aptly illustrates being born *again?* Remaining with these questions over the coming weeks, I find that holding birth and salvation side by side as Christ did gives me a richer understanding of each one in view of the other.

THE PLAY OF LIGHT is often very special at the birth of a child. Warm water casts its rippling reflection on the ceiling; oil glistens; perspiration glows; day dawns on a woman getting ready to have her baby. Many times I've turned to a laboring mama between her contractions: "Look!" I whisper, gesturing to the window as the first light creeps into the room. "The sun's rising on your baby's birth-day."

Like cats seeking out the privacy of a warm linen closet to have their kittens, most women begin labor under cover of darkness. They instinctively choose to preserve the murk of night, with electric lights dimmed or off. Physiologically speaking, this aids the flow of labor. Oxytocin needs to synthesize with melatonin, the nighttime hormone, to produce the contractions that will lead to birth. Melatonin receptors in the uterus have been proliferating over the final weeks of pregnancy, so at the time of birth the womb is primed to be especially sensitive to lighting fluctuations.

While darkness helps, overly bright lighting, especially from artificial sources, can be an impediment, because it inhibits melatonin release. Unfortunately, this phenomenon makes institutional conditions particularly unfavorable for birth, so sometimes a client will ask me to switch the room lights back down after each medical procedure; other times a client adds an eye mask to her hospital bag. Women birthing at home usually have more control over their environment, and dancing candlelight or a fire in the hearth are often seen. Sometimes a woman chooses complete darkness, and some midwives carry a miner's headlamp for working under such conditions.

Equally, the light at a birth affects the one being born. Imagine: from the beginning he has been growing enfolded by warm shadows. Ever since sixteen weeks of pregnancy, when he began to respond to the light filtering through his sealed eyelids, the world has appeared subdued and dim. Even when he first opened his eyes around twenty-eight weeks, what he saw was still diffused through flesh. If someone held a flashlight up to the walls of his space, its reddish glow was something fascinating to reach for rather than a glaring invasion.

At the moment of his birth, he emerges, blinking, into an entirely new world. It is not like reaching the light at the end of a tunnel, because he wasn't aware this passage had an end. It's perhaps more like suddenly stumbling out of a dark cave into daylight. Garish white brightness surrounds him, and everything appears in sharp relief. As his eyes adjust, things he had previously only glimpsed shadows of are now displayed in unimaginable fullness before his eyes.

Being born is, amongst other things, an experience of *coming into the light*.

I'm certainly not the first one to think of it this way. Radiance and childbirth have been conceptual twins throughout the history of human thought. For instance, the Roman goddesses of childbirth, Juno and Diana, thought to protect laboring women, also bear the epithet Lucina: "bringer of light." Their Greek equivalent, Eileithyia, often appears carrying a torch. The long-held association between the moon and female fertility is another example. A belief that a full moon brings babies persists, despite studies indicating that there's no correlation. And the modern Spanish term for giving birth is *dar a luz*, meaning literally "to give to light."

To bring our children into the light is to induct them into the beauty of our world, to share with them something we treasure. The light is so dear to us—so "gladsome," as we sing at Vespers. In the depths of winter, when daylight hours are short and it's grey and overcast, how we long to be visited by brightness! On the coldest days, we cherish the sun as it glistens brightly off the snow like the twinkle of an eye. In the evenings, lights welcome us home, shining cheerily in the windows through wind and rain.

In the warmer months, the sunrise reflected over water gives a double illumination, making us happy to see another day. As we cherish the last few moments of sunlight in the evening, the dying light reveals gorgeous strata of lavender, rose, peach, and buttercup. There's the gleam reflecting off the face of one greatly beloved, revealing every crease and hue and pore and expression and making his heart accessible to us. And who can forget the beauty of Pascha night: after circling the church three times in the darkness, we enter to find the air inside luminous with incense and alleluias.

This is the glorious world into which we bring our sons and daughters: the world of campfires, Christmas tree lights, meteors, lighthouses, dinner candles, and gemstones. This is the luminosity that meets them on their birth-days. These are the brilliant mysteries they behold with their fresh newborn eyes. This is the tide of impressions they must learn to process. No wonder they stare so intently!

Why is it, we might muse, that light so stirs our souls as well as our eyes? Stunning as it is, it seems to be an image, somehow, of a deeper beauty. In the life of Christ, earthly light appears many times as a symbol of spiritual light. When He heals the man born blind (John 9), for instance, both the man's eyes and his heart are illumined. The man receives his sight, but also the insight that Christ is God's Son and that the fullness of his own life will be found in following Him. Physical darkness likewise serves as an image of spiritual darkness. The cosmic tragedy of the Crucifixion is shown in the shadow that covered the earth from the sixth hour to the ninth (Mark 15:33).

And what is this spiritual light that the earthly light can only hint at? It isn't the light of a star burning in space, or a lamp that enlightens only by burning up what is already there, but the Uncreated Light, a brightness that existed even before created light and darkness were separated. It's the same light in which God appeared to Moses on Mount Sinai, in a bush burning without being consumed (Ex. 3). It's the pillar of fire in the darkness by which God led the people of Israel to their freedom (Ex. 13:21).

It's the "brightness of His glory" (Heb. 1:3) in the person of Christ, "the Sun of Righteousness" (Mal. 4:2), who said, "'I am the light of the world'" (John 8:12). It's the luminescence shining from our Lord's very garments at the Transfiguration, which "became shining, exceedingly white, like snow, such as no launderer on earth can whiten them" (Mark 9:3). It's Christ descending into the abyss on Holy Saturday, shattering the darkness of Hades with the brilliance of His life-giving love. It's the radiance of the "Orient from on High"[49]—that is, the one from the east, the rising one, the dawn of paradise—who enlightens human hearts. Like the dawn, it's a light that visits our darkness and makes us get up: "Awake, you who sleep, / Arise from the dead, / And Christ will give you light" (Eph. 5:14). It's the shining of saints who are so inhabited by holiness that their faces visibly radiate His glory.[50] It's the glory that rubs off on the angels, like the one announcing the Resurrection whose "countenance was like lightning" (Matt. 28:3). It's the warm illumination of heaven, where the city of God has no need for street lamps, because He is the light (Rev. 21:23).

In a few months, my baby will make the foundational step on

his earthly path toward the heavenly radiance. His journey out of the darkness of the womb will be the first (physical) birth that makes his second (spiritual) birth possible. But it will also be something more: a prophetic act, symbolizing the movement of the human soul toward the Uncreated Light. The journey out of the womb provides an image of spiritual enlightenment: "The people who sat in darkness have seen a great light, / And upon those who sat in the region and shadow of death / Light has dawned" (Matt. 4:16, quoting Is. 9:2). Perhaps this is an aspect of what Christ meant by being "born again": God's children must come into the divine light just as human children are first illumined by the sun's light at birth.

God's warm brightness will always rest on my child, no matter which way he chooses as his life unfolds. Whether it's acknowledged or not, God's radiant love illumines the whole of humanity: "He makes His sun rise on the evil and on the good" (Matt. 5:45). Like a blind person with a migraine who becomes averse to light she cannot perceive (which can happen!), even one who doesn't know the light continues to experience its effects. Yet I have the opportunity to direct my child actively along the illumined path. My bones and muscles and sinews will guide his body into the earthly light; in the same way, my heart can point his heart to the light of heaven. After the enlightenment of his birth-day, I can help him come to the enlightenment of baptism, the enlightenment of the Holy Mysteries, the enlightenment of a life of prayer, and finally, the enlightenment of death into the Kingdom, so that his whole life is a progression toward unity with God.

The illumined path on which I ask my child to join me is not always easy. For him as for me, the same light that warms, enlightens, beautifies, and purifies can also be blinding, singeing, exposing, and consuming. In the moments following birth, he will grimace as his eyes are flooded with light, and throughout his first months, he'll continue to be quickly overwhelmed, even to the point of sleep or tears, as he learns to take in all he sees.

It's the same way when we encounter the divine light. After coming down from his meeting with God on Mount Sinai, Moses had to veil his shining face so as not to terrify his people (Ex. 34). Saint Paul was temporarily blinded after coming across the risen Jesus on the road to Damascus (Acts 9). And the eyes of St. Seraphim of Sarov were so bright with holiness that his visitor Motovilov could not bear to look him in the face. In our own lives, the divine radiance brings to light the darkest corners of our souls, allowing what was hidden to be seen and judged justly in the light of God's love. This may be exactly what we need, but it can prove deeply uncomfortable.

Still, I bring my child to the divine light because I know it's only there that languishing souls find their salvation. After birth, then, the next step of the journey is clear. At the age of forty days or so, according to the wisdom of the Church, I can bring him to baptism, otherwise known as Holy Illumination. This beautiful service is packed with the symbolism of light. "You are enlightened," the priest will declare to the freshly baptized child; then his whole body will be anointed with oil. Only those of us living in the age of electric lighting could miss the ancient association oil has to light. Of course, it causes things to gleam brilliantly but, added to lamps, it also provided the main light source after nightfall during every century before the twentieth. Toward the end of the baptismal service, the baby is given a new white gown. "Grant unto me a robe of light, O most merciful Christ our God, who clothe Yourself with light as with a garment," the chanter or choir will sing as my baby is dressed.

But the symbolism of light isn't confined only to the day of baptism. I participate in it every time I stop to light a beeswax candle on the way into church, or indeed, a tea light on the kitchen counter. If I melt down under the influence of pregnancy hormones, or hear some sobering news, I can pause to kindle a little flame. This does more than just make my worship pretty. My candle stands as a sign of my burning love for God, the casting open of my heart to receive the divine light, the ardor I aspire to. I may have trouble keeping prayer alive in my heart for more than a few moments at a time, but a candle burns without faltering from the time its wick is touched with flame to when it sputters out in the sand. If I keep a vigil lamp in the prayer corner, the flame needn't go out at all. Its little light stands as a visible call to prayer at the center of my home.

As we prepare to usher our children into both the earthly and the heavenly light, let us allow ourselves to enter more fully into light too. Let's throw ourselves open to the radiance of His love so that no dark corner remains. Let us be born once more into His bright glory.

☙ WEEK 19 ☙

Waters

If you pass through water, I am with you; and the rivers shall not overflow you. . . . For I am the Lord your God, the Holy One of Israel, who saves you.
—ISAIAH 43:2—3

In the sitcom version of birth, a round-bellied woman is shopping with a nervous man when suddenly she clutches her bottom, gasping, "Honey, I think my water just broke!" Their bugged-out eyes lock, then drop to the floor, where a puddle spreads at their feet. He freezes; they screech off in the car. A scene change and a few expletives later the baby is born out from under an immaculately clean hospital sheet.

There's a grain of truth to the comical stereotype. It can be pretty dramatic when a woman's amniotic sac releases, along with the liter of fluid it contains. But only one labor in ten actually begins with the water breaking. If it's left alone, the amniotic sac generally remains intact throughout most of labor, until the mother's cervix is almost fully open and the membrane bag bulges down into the birth canal in front of her baby's head. Then, *ping!* the laboring mama feels an abrupt release of pressure, accompanied by a burst of liquid.

Now her baby's head is applied directly to her cervix, and without the cushioning of fluid, the intensity of labor usually increases. As his head triggers muscles deep inside her pelvis, she may feel a reflexive urge to bear down and push him out. But even though the bag has now burst, because the fluid is continually renewed right up to the last moments of pregnancy, he'll likely still be born with a sizeable gush. If he inhales any fluid with his first breaths it won't harm him, as it will simply be absorbed along with the other fluid in his lungs as his body systems transform in the minutes after birth.

Very occasionally, about once in every 80,000 births, a baby's water bag remains intact throughout labor and he's born "en caul." It's an astonishing sight: a newborn in a translucent balloon, a passing visitor from a watery world. His eyes closed, his lungs still full of liquid, and his body folded tight, he barely seems to know he's been born. Only when the birth attendants peel the gloopy sac away from his face and the first hit of air meets his skin is his transformation into an air-breathing land-lubber set in motion.

En caul births were once invested with great spiritual meaning, though their precise significance varied across the centuries and continents.[51] A child born in the caul was considered variously to be destined for a happy life, death by hanging, or the monastic life. The membranes themselves were the subject of some veneration, often reflected in the names by which they were known: in Germany, *Muttergottestüchlein*, meaning "the Mother of God's hanky"; in Scotland, *haly how*, or "holy cap." Following birth, an empty sac would be either carefully disposed of to prevent its use in sorcery, or dried and preserved as a harbinger of blessing. Such a keepsake would be used as a love charm or a medical remedy, or tucked under the pillow of a deathbed to ease the passage into new life. But most commonly it was thought to protect its owner from drowning, making it a particularly coveted possession among sailors. The preserved amniotic membranes might be passed down as an heirloom, or they could be sold, with examples appearing in the classified ads of British newspapers even into the twentieth century.

Our culture no longer attaches any value to the bag of waters that is a child's first home, and it is disposed of as medical waste. But the waters of birth deserve some recognition. They are not just pickle juice, preserving a baby until he's ready: they actually make an important contribution to his development. First, the fluid maintains consistent conditions, both in temperature and in pressure. It cushions both a baby and his mama should her tummy get bumped. When the contractions of labor come, pressure is spread throughout her womb to protect him and his oxygen supply.

Second, amniotic fluid acts as a medium for development, providing both space to move so that muscles can grow and also a substance to fill a baby's forming respiratory and digestive tracts. With its help, he learns to swallow, urinate, and expand his lungs in preparation for breathing. The thriving ecosystem of microbes and amino acids in the waters both helps initiate the colonization of his gut with healthy bacteria and inhibits the growth of harmful bacteria. Finally, the amniotic fluid teaches him about the outside world, conveying the taste of his mother's food and sharing a scent with the Bartholin's glands of her breasts, so that when he is learning to feed he can head for something familiar-smelling.

As well as their physiological usefulness, the fluids of birth also remain deeply symbolic. No matter when the amniotic sac happens to break, the voyage from womb to world represents a passage through the waters. Our whole life, it could be said, belongs to this pattern. From the fluid of the womb to the deep and chaotic waters of death, human life is a voyage at sea. We function almost as aquatic creatures: our very bodies consist mostly of water, which needs constant replenishment to maintain our health. So we dedicate vast amounts of time and energy daily to fetching, purifying, and distributing this precious liquid.

Our settlements are established around its sources. In the form of rivers, lakes, and seas, water divides the land into territories, yet by flowing from place to place, touching everything, it also unites the world. And this characteristic makes water a great means of communication. It can find its way from place to place, bringing with it anything from a message in a bottle to a huge cargo vessel on the St. Lawrence Seaway.

The arc of human salvation is similarly delineated by water. In the creation narratives, it is the foundational element that sprang forth, irrigating the face of the whole earth (Gen. 2:6) and summoning forth swarms of life (Gen. 1:20). It demarcates the heavenly home, with the tributaries of Eden's river flowing forth to encircle the land (Gen. 2:10–14). A river also bounded the land flowing with milk and honey, so that by crossing the Jordan the people of God entered the promised land (Josh. 1:2). At the other end of the Bible, the heavenly city of God is also characterized by its river. From the throne of God flows a stream of water irrigating the tree of life, which is the healing of nations (Rev. 22:1–2). According to Scripture, then, water is both our origin and our destiny. The flowing river of the water of life reconnects us with the paradise we lost, tracing back to its source in the Garden and flowing on ahead to the city of God.

We might say life is water and water is life, but equally, it represents death. Dirty water kills people, including about 5,000 of the world's children every day. Even clean and pure water can be a danger: too much of it, and we are swept away under its tremendous weight. A single tsunami or flood can inundate a whole city or island. For air-breathing creatures, of course, the danger is particularly acute. Our oxygen-loving lungs quickly forget the waterlogged ways of uterine life and with a single gasp become sodden, so that we drown in too much of a good thing. So to birth our babies through the waters is to induct them into a life which even from our first breath threatens us with death.

When Christ submits to baptism by John the Forerunner at the start of His ministry, this is the stormy torrent He enters. By being baptized, He is immersing Himself fully in our humanity. He chooses to assume human flesh, undertaking our universal passage from waters through waters to waters. He makes Himself one of us, plunging into our sorrows and pain, and at last accompanying us even into the swirling abyss of Hades.

This also is the meaning of our own baptism. God willing, about thirty-six weeks from now—that is, a full pregnancy's length hence—I will be bringing my child to church aged forty days. It's an occasion to look forward to with great joy, just as much as his birth-day. Yet white lace and sweet smiles are not the whole story. The epistle we hear in the baptismal service leaves us in no doubt: "Do you not know," St. Paul asks, "that as many of us as were baptized into Christ Jesus were baptized into his death?" (Rom. 6:3).

If this epistle reading seems familiar, it's probably because it also appears in the service of Holy Saturday, where its full meaning is teased out within a rich liturgical context. At this point in the Church calendar, we are midway between Christ's death and His Resurrection. He is yet in Hades, and over a series of Old Testament readings, it becomes clear exactly what it is He's doing down there.

Several readings in, we recount the Israelites' crossing of the Red Sea, of God freeing His people from a life of slavery in Egypt by a passage through the waters. For the Israelites, these are waters of liberation, parting to usher them into a new life, but for their enemies they become waters of death, overtaking and drowning even the greatest army. At the end, when the Israelites are safely ashore, this long and sober tale bursts forth into the song of Moses, the prophet-leader who as a baby was rescued from among the reeds of the river in Egypt. He whose very name means "drawn from the water," because he was rescued from the Nile, rejoices that all God's people have been brought up from the deep: "For Pharaoh's horses went with his chariots and horsemen into the sea, and the Lord brought back the waters of the sea upon them. But the children of Israel walked on dry ground in the midst of the sea" (Ex. 15:19). Standing there listening on the eve of Pascha, we tremble, knowing that a rescue operation of which the Red Sea crossing is only a shadow is being wrought for us by Christ in the depths at this very moment. Our praises and Moses' entwine as we interrupt his song with the refrain, "For gloriously has He been glorified!"

Now many more readings follow, and it is almost time to recount Christ's Resurrection. But immediately before the Gospel, we hear St. Paul's words, reminding us that our baptism calls us to let our old self die as we pursue with Christ the way of self-giving love. Looking beyond death, St. Paul goes on, "We were buried with Him through baptism into death, that just as Christ was raised from the dead by the glory of the Father, even so we also should walk in newness of life" (Rom. 6:4). Our immersion in the waters of Christ's death is also our participation in His Resurrection. When we go down with Him into the swirling deep, it's our sins, not we, that are drowned. Death becomes the means by which we are rescued, restored not just to our old life but to a greater one.

Saint Paul called the Red Sea crossing a "baptism" into Moses

(1 Cor. 10:2), showing us that the Exodus story belongs to a baptismal archetype which finds its meaning in the death and Resurrection of Christ. Likewise we could consider birth part of this archetype and our babies' passage through the waters of birth an amniotic baptism. For everyone the seas must part, as they did for the Israelites fleeing Pharaoh's armies, with the protective waters rising up on the right and the left. As on the other side of the Red Sea, God's people become the "special people" of the Covenant; we cross the torrent to become the apple of our parents' eye.

And we hear the baptismal theme reverberating through the whole scriptural tradition. As the primordial waters of chaos were divided into those above and below the heavens, God divides the amniotic waters to allow a new creation to emerge. Like Noah, each of us coming into the world rides out the flood in a safe vessel until we land on dry ground. As with Joseph or Jeremiah, we emerge from our hiding place in a deep cistern. Like Jonah, we all must be cast up from the deep and onto the shore. With those baptized by John the Forerunner, we are submerged by the rapids before we emerge into new life. As Christ, coming out of the waters of the Jordan, was confirmed as God's Son by the appearance of the Holy Spirit, the breath of God, so we pass through the waters of birth to receive breath for the first time. As He did for Peter walking on the stormy sea, like a midwife Christ catches us by the hand and fishes us from the waters.

Understanding birth as a passage through waters helps us unpack some of the symbolic fullness of Christ's saying that we must be "born again" to enter the Kingdom. The new human's voyage through the amniotic waters and into life in the world is an embodiment and prefiguration of his baptismal movement through the waters of Christ's death, toward the wellsprings of salvation.

Pascha

If we died with Him, we shall also live with Him.
—2 TIMOTHY 2:11

If you listen to enough women tell their birth stories, eventually you'll hear someone describe labor as a painless experience. As she describes them, contractions (or, as she might prefer to call them, *rushes, expansions, pressure waves*) were seriously intense, sure, but not painful. Sometimes we'll learn of a mother who had her baby on the toilet without knowing she was in labor. Occasionally someone even says that birth filled her with the most exquisite sensual ecstasy.

Still, it's an inescapable fact: the vast majority of women experience labor as a great struggle—as transcendent, transformative, and satisfying, perhaps, but also as life-changingly, world-rockingly painful. Like the Cross of Christ, this is pain that shifts the parameters. Afterward, we must rethink everything in the light of an experience we never dreamed was possible.

A woman in labor may writhe, rock, stamp, and pace. She may sweat, bleed, and vomit. She may pant, gasp, groan, bellow, holler, and scream. She may grind her teeth, scrunch her eyelids, clench her hands, furrow her brow, tighten her shoulders, and need to be reminded to release the tension over and over as it reappears. At the height of labor, she may announce that this is crazy and impossible and that she will never, ever, in a million years, do it *ever* again.

But an hour later, her husband leans down to kiss and congratulate her as she gazes beatifically at her rosy baby nestling in her arms, and she starts musing about their *next* child. As great as her anguish was, it has been subsumed in a delight that is just as grippingly and completely real. Her eyes are no longer clamped shut, but wide open and beaming with transcendent love. No more does she raise her voice in alarm, but coos softly to her new beloved. The sweat has been mopped from her brow, and all that remains of her exertion is a glow on her cheeks. She radiates the utter joy of one for whom Pascha is real, whom the angel of death has passed by. She has been reborn.

The great joyful transformation that childbirth brings is exactly the motif Christ employs in His parable of the birthing woman.

> *"Most assuredly, I say to you that you will weep and lament, but the world will rejoice; and you will be sorrowful, but your sorrow will be turned into joy. A woman, when she is in labor, has sorrow because her hour has come; but as soon as she has given birth to the child, she no longer remembers the anguish, for joy that a human being has been born into the world. Therefore you now have sorrow; but I will see you again and your heart will rejoice, and your joy no one will take from you." (John 16:20–22)*

At first sight, Christ appears to be giving His disciples a simple heads-up: at His death they will experience an all-consuming grief, like the anguish of a laboring woman; yet just as her lamentation is replaced by joy when her baby comes, so too their rejoicing will fully overshadow their sorrow.

Yet this isn't a simple pep talk about the stages of the grieving process. The laboring woman in the parable doesn't stand only for the disciples—there's also a second layer to the illustration in which she represents Christ Himself. The clue is in the phrase *her hour*, her decisive moment. Outside this parable, Christ is the only person in the Gospels ever to be said to have *His hour*, and that's His death. So in this parable Christ is foretelling the mystery of His Passion: how the crisis of His death will be subsumed into the joyful victory of His Resurrection.

Childbirth and the Passion, He says, share the same Paschal shape, with labor standing for crucifixion and birth standing for resurrection. Both Christ and the birthing mother bring forth new life, but through pain and sacrifice. Our species is perpetuated only on the brink of annihilation. It's striking that Christ chose to describe Himself using such an explicitly feminine metaphor. He must have had some experience with the "women's business" of birth, perhaps by hearing the sounds of labor coming from neighbors' houses in the course of everyday village life, and known it to be an apt comparison.

But this parable of the Passion is not just a story of before and after: first the sorrow, then the joy. Instead, Christ emphasizes that the joy weaves itself into the fabric of the sorrow, incorporating and transforming it from the inside so that the two become one. We can see this by looking carefully again at the wording of the text. In some versions the laboring woman is said to *forget* her pain when her baby comes, but the better translation tells us she "no longer remembers it" (*ouketi mnemoneuei*). What may seem like a quibble about biblical translation is actually an important distinction. The Greek words do not imply that the woman's pain has vanished from her memory, but simply that she stops thinking and talking about it after the birth. Christ portrays her not as a ditzy amnesiac but as someone who has undergone a deep transformation. Her misery hasn't vaporized and been replaced; instead, it has been "turned"—or we might say, transfigured, subsumed—into delight.

The multipurpose verb *genesetai* that describes the turning confirms this. Having employed the word in one place to describe how the sorrow transforms into joy ("to come to pass, to be made manifest, to become"), Christ uses it again a sentence later to describe the mother's action in bringing her baby into the world ("to give birth, to bring forth"). By placing these two uses side by side, Christ tells us that just as a baby comes forth from his mother, joy is born from pain. Joy is blissful not despite the adversity, but because of it. Resurrection comes not just after death, but *through* it.

And this description resonates much better with the actual experience of childbearing. It's too facile to say I "forget" my pain. Rather, what I experience in labor remains uniquely vivid in my memory for the rest of my life, providing a pivotal reference for all subsequent experiences. If I feel safe and well-supported, I remember the struggle to give birth as a huge obstacle I overcame, and if I can do that, I can do *any*thing. On the other hand, if I am disrespected or coerced, the struggle can become a weight under which I am crushed and powerless.

Neither does my postpartum body allow me to forget the pain of labor, because afterpains resurrect it every time I put my baby to the breast. For the first week or so, when my baby latches on, the flow of oxytocin that brings my milk causes a sudden contraction that feels just like labor. These contractions fill a good purpose—in the hour after birth, they shear the placenta away from the wall of my uterus, then over the coming month they stem the flow of blood from the wound the placenta leaves behind and bring my uterus gradually back to its pre-pregnancy size. But they can certainly be intense (especially if I've had another baby before, as the contractions seem to become stronger with each birth).

At other times, the "little Passion" of motherhood is less physical and more existential. In the doorway of the nursery, Death hangs out with Life as we tuck our little ones in bed, reminding us that swaddling clothes and burial shrouds can be cut from the same cloth. It watches from the shadows as we push our laughing nurslings on creaky swings, carefully chop jumbo grapes to feed our toddlers, and watch our older children casually climb tall trees. It smirks at the final throes as our old identity gives up the ghost to be reborn in a new, more interdependent form. Death's comical sidekick, Entropy, follows us around on the endless circuit of dishes, diaper changes, and laundry, mischievously undoing our work as quickly as we can get it done. Sweetness and Sorrow dance together, weaving in and out of one another's space, breathing the same air.

The Church Fathers knew the feeling well. They describe the unity of brightness and mourning as *penthos*, which might be translated "joyful sorrow" or "bright sadness." Of course, we mothers do not have a monopoly on life's bright sadness. The Paschal mystery stands at the heart of our universal human experience. The joy of resurrection and the sorrow of death cannot be separated but always appear in the light of one another. "All living is a kind of dying," writes Metropolitan Kallistos Ware; "all dying is also a kind of living."[52] "I die daily," agrees St. Paul (1 Cor. 15:31). "The time of death is every moment," T. S. Eliot concurs.[53] Or, as the hymn declares, "behold, through the *cross* joy has come into all the world."

Yet, although the Paschal mystery is certainly not closed to those who are not mothers, childbirth may provide a unique entry point into its reality. Christ takes birth as His central metaphor for salvation, calling the process of our redemption *being born again*. Our first birth shows us an image of our second birth. This metaphor draws an even closer comparison than did the parable of the laboring woman between the work of child-birth and the work of Christ's Passion. As birthgivers, we are given to be a living symbol of Pascha—ambassadors of the Res-urrection in the world. "Here am I and the children whom the LORD has given me! / *We* are for signs and wonders in Israel / from the LORD of hosts" (Is. 8:18, NKJV).

But we are signs not in the cheaper sense of being just copy-cats; in a deeply mysterious way, by giving birth we actually "partake of Christ's sufferings" (1 Peter 4:13). Our own trials combine with His saving Passion to constitute the sacrifice of the world offered up to God across time and space. What St. Paul said to the church at Colossae, we can boldly say to the chil-dren in our bellies: "I now rejoice in my sufferings for you, and fill up in my flesh what is lacking in the afflictions of Christ" (Col. 1:24). For all human affliction is one with the sufferings of the Lord on the Cross. As St. Gregory the Great commented on this passage, "If our torments were not also his own suffer-ing, there is no way the converted and afflicted Paul would have said [this]."[54] Paul means, of course, not that Christ's offering of Himself was imperfect in any way, but that our own offerings can be united to His. The crucified One is beside us in our pain and takes us with Him to His glory.

This makes everything look rather different. The Labor and Delivery wing of the local hospital becomes the site of holy mysteries, a place to approach with awe and trembling. A grow-ing belly becomes like the cave of Jerusalem, a place where the eternal victory of life over death is being waged in quiet secrecy. Each contraction of labor has a deep-rooted saving purpose, not just for a woman and her baby but also for the world, mystically raising up every person who is homeless, lonely, imprisoned, and hungry. The birthing stool, like a little cross, is a throne of hard-won glory.

Perhaps this is what the Holy Apostle Paul meant by that rather cryptic statement in one of his letters: he says women "will be saved in childbearing, if they continue in faith, love, and holiness, with self-control" (1 Tim. 2:15). Often we take him to mean that the pain of birth is the price we pay to compensate God for the sin of Eve, a very feminine punishment for a very feminine crime. He's not saying that women are saved *by* childbearing, as if babies were collectible box tops that could be exchanged for free entry on Ladies' Night in heaven. No: women, like men, are saved by Christ—each one of us in the circumstances of our own unique life. Rather, Paul says it is *possible* for us to find our salvation *in* and *through* our maternal experience. Could it be that he means to express the same things we ourselves have found to be true: that, for those who choose to take it, childbearing can become a door into the heart of God's self-sacrificial and saving love?

Might it be that, by bestowing on us the ability to give birth, God invites us to share in the great mystery of Pascha?

FOUR

Fearing Labor

✖ WEEK 21 ✖

Control

The LORD will fight for you; you only need to be still.
—EXODUS 14:14 (NIV)

It's a fearsome business, having babies. Even seasoned mothers approach childbirth with a healthy dose of trepidation. As birth educator Pam England puts it, "worry is the work of pregnancy."[55] Yet we know "God has not given us a spirit of fear, but of power and of love and of a sound mind" (2 Tim. 1:7); so, rather than leaving our apprehensions to grow unacknowledged in the darkness, over the next three weeks, let's bring them into the light of day, asking ourselves why they are so integral to the experience of becoming a mother and whether they might offer an opportunity for growth.

OFTEN WHEN I'M WORKING with a client preparing for birth and we start to get really comfortable with each other, she'll start airing her worries about labor. "I'm scared I'll lose it," she may say. "I don't want to be *that person* who cusses her baby into the world." Or, "I'm terrified of pooping in front of everybody." "What if I don't make it to the hospital on time?" "I don't want my husband to see me that way." "I'm worried I'll be robbed of power over my body by a pushy physician." The most fearsome thoughts of all are equally common but less often verbalized: "Oh God, don't let us die." Tracing each one of these concerns back to its root, we see they all arise from a single origin: the fear of events so unpredictable and powerful, they rip away the sense that we are in command of our own lives.

In a consumer economy, the feeling of losing control is unfamiliar and debilitating. We're taught that we're managers of our world, capable of producing any outcome we desire. We choose what suits us from among the infinite options on the restaurant menu of life, and we are perfect judges of what's best. Relative to our ancestors, we are unhindered by the realities of nature or custom. We're no longer born into a familial profession but can shape our lives into whatever form we fancy. Our daily activities aren't limited by the availability of light, because electrical power has put the might of the sun under our command. We use plastics and pills to control the number and timing of our children. Where there's uncertainty or risk, we mitigate it with insurance we can buy for a premium. An undesired outcome in our lives indicates some failure on our part to prevent it. No wonder pregnant women are anxious about finding themselves subject to forces they can't control.

On one level, the fears my clients express are easily dispensed with. To each concern there could be a chipper retort. "*Most* women poop during pushing, actually, without even noticing. Nurses take it as a happy sign a baby's descending, not as a personal insult!" "The swearing thing is an urban myth. A lot of the time labor makes women especially sweet and thankful to the people around them." "If you're going to be uncomfortable with the people around you, there's an easy solution—reconsider whom you're inviting to your birth." "Even if the hospital is an hour away, a first-time mama can leave the house pushing and still make it in plenty of time." As for the fear of death, "Haven't you heard of statistical probability?"

But if I recited these points to an anxious client, I'd expect to see her eyes roll. While such retorts are factually true, they're unsatisfying. Even the finest appeals to rationality do not dispense with our fearful preoccupations, because they come not from a place of logic, but from somewhere deeper. They arise in the stories woven right into our identity as women: from painful personal experience, from sensationalized media reports, or from legends of birth lodged in our cultural memory. Mathematically, the things we dread are unlikely to happen, but intuitively, we understand they could. And so the best way to answer our concerns is not to brush them away with reasoned refutations but to engage them as a phenomenon—not to question whether our fears are likely to come true, but to ask what truth they already hold. What are they telling us about ourselves? What response are they calling us to?

There is in fact a spectrum of possible responses. At one end I might react by making a point of being flexible. When friends, colleagues, or fellow laundromat customers ask about my plans for birth, I say, "I'm going to go with the flow, just wait and see what happens." What I'm not saying is, "I'm not going to tell you because I don't want to have to eat my words. I would like to think things can happen in a fairly straightforward way, but apparently I have no idea how it's going to go, so I guess I'll just put myself in the hands of the professionals and be ready for whatever they say is necessary. I'm scared stiff, frankly, after the stories I've heard, but God knows I'm determined to stay as relaxed as I can."

There are lots of admirable things about this approach. Not least, it's a humble acknowledgment of life's true unpredictability. Even if my worst fears don't materialize, *something* is bound to happen that could not have been anticipated or controlled. I may give birth to a redhead in a family of brunettes, or end up thriving without the epidural I planned; my baby may come so smoothly there's no time to get in the birth pool, or I may need the Cesarean I'd wanted to avoid. It's almost as if some element of surprise is part of the design—as if rolling with a loss of control is a necessary skill for birth.

A second advantage is that this approach appears spiritually wise, at least at first glance. *Go with the flow* is the secular version of the counsel of St. Symeon the New Theologian: "Do not worry what will come next: you will discover it when it comes." With the words *go with the flow* I signal to myself and the world that I refuse to heed the fears that would lead me to exert a death grip on every circumstance. Though I am tempted to play God, tinkering my way toward omnipotence, I open myself to the truth of my human vulnerability. As a creature, I accept that I cannot control, know, or solve everything. I surrender.

Surrender is a prominent word in many birth preparation books. It's useful because it describes the only strategy that seems to work to manage labor's strong sensations. Like huge waves, contractions flood in, recede, and return with increasing force. With each one, my job is to dive deep, riding it out from down below. I let go, and it carries me along. I am toppled, tossed, and tumbled until I gasp for air. At the peak of the storm, when the waves are highest, I cry out that I have reached my limits. I can go no more. "Lord, save me!" I shout with Peter (Matt. 14:30). Experienced birth attendants know from the testimony of a hundred births that these words are in fact a likely indication that my baby will be along shortly. But I'm not wrong to say I can't do it. I cannot give birth on my *own* power, but only by aligning myself with a greater power coursing through me. It is God who is the Giver of Life.

Surrender requires trust, and many birth educators emphasize

the safety of yielding to these natural forces. If human reproduction didn't work, they argue, our species would have died
out long ago. As childbirth has become medicalized over the
past century and a half, we have forgotten that it's a body function every bit as routine as digestion. Rather, we think of it as a
series of accidents waiting to happen. Of course, these voices say,
childbearing is not without its risks, but life isn't either. We can
trust birth: it's as safe as life gets.

As Christians we'd agree that we're "fearfully and wonder-
fully made" (Ps. 138/139:14 NKJV). There's a great wisdom in our
birthing bodies which is a gift of the Creator. But when I plan to
go with the flow, *whose* flow am I talking about? Do I mean going
with the physiological flow of labor in my body, the workflow of
a busy doctor, or the flow of God's energies in the world? These
flows can be quite different from one another. Surrendering to
a stream of birthing hormones is not the same as surrendering
to God's will—after all, many mothers whose babies are born by
Cesarean see God's hand powerfully at work in their birth story.
Equally, surrender does not mean consenting to whatever care
plan is proposed: I cannot let myself off so lightly, but am called
to share in making these weighty ethical decisions. I'd like to
be able to surrender to God's flow, but it's not always clear what
that means when I'm in a stressful and unfamiliar medical situation. The complex meaning of surrender and flow makes it hard
to hear what this approach is suggesting we should do with our
fears of losing control.

At the other end of the spectrum from *go with the flow*, some
birth educators commend what I'll call the birth plan approach.
With this approach, I engage with maternity healthcare primarily as a consumer service. During pregnancy I research the risks
and benefits of different procedures that might be suggested

during labor. Then I formulate a plan and make a written guide to my preferences for the medical management of my baby's birth. I may seek out a provider who I know will support my plan, or rely on the fact that even if I am cared for by people I've never met before, I won't need to articulate my wishes in the heat of the moment but can simply hand them a sheet of paper. I may or may not expect things to proceed as described, but I'm assured that everyone knows my preferences without asking.

This approach also has its merits. It rightly acknowledges that the stakes are high. Labor is not just a single day in a woman's life, but a crowning event in her personal history. It's a cornerstone of her future emotional, physical, spiritual, mental, and sexual well-being. It's a prism through which she will see all her relationships—with her children, her mate, God, and herself. If she feels at peace about her baby's birth, it becomes an inner resource on which she can draw during the trickiest of days, but if it leaves her troubled, it is an additional obstacle she must overcome at an already challenging time. The birth plan approach recognizes that it's worth investing time and effort to plan for such a formative event.

This has some far-reaching implications. When I consider myself a partner in decisions about my medical care, it changes my whole way of thinking and talking about things: for example, I start to speak of myself, not my care provider, as the one who "delivers" my baby. (Delivery is for pizza, as doulas like to say.) I no longer talk of what birth positions a hospital "allows" or how overdue they'll "let" me go. Medical advice becomes an important consideration, but not the only consideration, in my choices. I view physicians not as spiritual authorities but as highly trained regular human beings, doing their best to navigate a normal day at work. Any recommendation they make is based on a number of factors: the well-being of my baby and me is a vital one, but there will be many others that might not be immediately apparent, such as hospital protocols, the workload of the day, and the risk of litigation. This usually leaves me plenty of scope for asking care providers questions about their suggestions, adding my own insights, weighing things up with prayer, and taking responsibility for deciding what to do. In the end, I may give consent for the proposed treatment, decline in favor of waiting, or discover an alternative that wasn't among the options presented.

From an Orthodox Christian perspective, the birth plan approach makes some good sense, too. We worship at the throne of God, not at the altar of modern medicine. Our obedience is reserved for those whose authority arises from centuries of Church tradition, not from any credentials the most esteemed med school could confer. As a temple of the Holy Spirit, what I do with my body really matters (1 Cor. 6:19). Rather than checking it in at the hospital door, I must share moral responsibility for its tending and care.

This approach also shares the emphasis on consent that is such a big deal in our own tradition. The Church takes care to emphasize that Christ made His sacrifice of His own free will, rather than out of any compulsion (in contrast to some ideas that later emerged of a wrathful God *having* to punish sin, as if it were stronger than He). This is seen at the anaphora of both our main liturgies. Saint Basil's Liturgy refers to Christ's "voluntary, ever-memorable and life-creating death"; St. John Chrysostom's stresses that He "was given up, or rather gave Himself up, for the life of the world." As imitators of Christ, we have a human will all our own, and we get to employ it in our lives. Sometimes we are subject to the counsel of others, or circumstances limit our choices—but we are never slaves to fate. At every point we have the freedom to choose a spirit of acceptance and thanksgiving that transcends our circumstances. Otherwise, Ss. Paul and Silas would never have sung in prison nor the New Martyr Elizabeth in the mineshaft.

The birth plan approach to labor affirms our human freedom, but it too has limitations. Not least, where the rubber meets the road, birth plans turn out to be of limited practical use. Studies have demonstrated that births where women express most satisfaction are not only the ones where things go precisely to plan.[56] The key element that makes for a gratifying birth, researchers find, is being treated with kindness and dignity in one's time of need. Even a woman whose birth is complicated and hard can regard her experience as positive if her wishes are heard and honored.

We might reasonably expect that making a birth plan would allow our wishes to be heard and honored. Unfortunately not. Studies indicate that women with birth plans stating they want to avoid certain interventions are as likely to receive them as other women birthing in the same facility.[57] We might also expect that a birth plan could help improve the quality of our communication with healthcare professionals, but again the evidence is that many women who have birth plans are treated with skepticism or even mocking hostility.[58]

Though both of these contrasting approaches have some merits, neither one is a full fix to the problem of control in labor, for life is not ordered by human management but shaped by God's grace. As it is written, "*You* are He who drew me from the womb" (Ps. 21/22:10, emphasis added): it is neither we who "deliver" our babies, nor our healthcare providers, nor the labor process, but God Himself. He is the "physician of our souls and bodies" who attends every labor and gently receives all the world's babies into His pierced hands. If He could be said to be "in control," it is not as a business executive but as a servant King who grants His creatures such radical freedom that He submits to die at their hands. When our fears about losing control in labor remind us that we are not the masters of our world, we know that we are not alone: even God, in a sense, was not the master of the world He made. In the moments in which we experience our powerlessness, He is God with Us. Therefore, though my baby's birth may be beyond my full control, I am assured that my co-suffering God is working to bring good from this and every situation. "'For I know the [birth] plans I have for you," declares the LORD, "plans to prosper you and not to harm you, plans to give you hope and a future'" (Jer. 29:11 NIV).

Pain

Now I suffer; however, another will suffer for me,
because I suffer for him.
—ST. FELICITY, AS SHE GAVE BIRTH IN PRISON
AWAITING MARTYRDOM

The writer Virginia Woolf lamented "the poverty of the language" of physical pain.[59] Words cannot really reach into the heart of the experience of pain and capture it for others to grasp. But this doesn't stop them from trying. When we're pregnant, everybody and her neighbor wants to tell us about the trials of childbirth. Even over bagels at church fellowship hour, we get it: *Care for an alarming birth story with your tea?*

The intensity of labor has been a subject of perplexity and fascination since the human story began. According to Scripture, it originates in the Fall of humankind when God tells the man, the woman, and the serpent the consequences of what they have done. Each will have to bear the burden in a particular way. "To the woman [God] said, 'I will greatly multiply your pain and your groaning, and in pain shall you bring forth children'" (Gen. 3:16). A proper understanding of this so-called "curse" rests heavily on the word *pain*. And the Hebrew term is difficult to translate. It conveys not just what we'd call pain, but also struggle, work, toil. This resonates, because even women who've experienced pain-free birth agree it involved a lot of work.

But the toil is not uniquely given to the woman. God uses the identical word when He tells the man, "'Cursed is the ground in your labors. In *toil* you shall eat from it all the days of your life'" (Gen. 3:17). Elsewhere in the Old Testament the term *toil* has a positive connotation as the kind of labor that yields hard-earned fruit (e.g. Prov. 5:10). The apocryphal view is that God's pronouncement to the woman shows His intent to make her suffer, extracting the proverbial pound of flesh as payment for her transgression. But under examination the Hebrew text leaves room for the possibility that the struggle of childbearing fulfills the good purpose of a loving God who is much more recognizable to our Orthodox faith.

What advantages could labor pain possibly provide? According to the history of medical pain management, none. And a brief survey of the development of medications for labor pain illustrates the lengths humans have gone to eliminate it. For millennia, our foremothers coped with labor using only natural methods: rocking, swaying, breathing, and moaning their way to parenthood. It wasn't that they had no pain relief to resort to, but the solutions came from everyday experience. The companionship and touch of other women was vital. Moving around was better than lying down, and a doorway to press back against felt good. A nice warm bath, an herbal remedy prepared from the garden, or a glass of home brew could help, too.

The introduction of inhalation anesthesia to the birthing room in the nineteenth century was a game-changer, providing a quick narcotic effect on the central nervous system while the user stayed conscious. Its use was swiftly normalized after Queen Victoria received chloroform during the birth of her eighth child in 1853. Pain started to seem like an optional part of childbearing. Why wouldn't women bypass it if they could? Some families found out why not: the line between an effective dose of chloroform and a deadly one was fine. While it was being discerned, many women paid the ultimate price.

The endeavor to dispense with the pain of labor reached a new milestone in the nineteen-teens when chloroform was replaced by a medication called *twilight sleep*. Developed by a German physician, this treatment was an injectable combination of morphine and scopolamine. It left many women with no memory of giving birth. Some new mothers told stories of waking up to be introduced to a pretty baby and wondering when their own labors would start. Others became frenzied and were blindfolded and shackled in canvas beds. Still, women's magazines in the USA touted twilight sleep as offering pain-free birth, and many wealthy women traveled to Germany to have their babies under its effects. To some, access to twilight sleep was synonymous with women's rights; others viewed it as an attempt to sidestep the so-called Curse of Eve and an affront to the will of God.

Meanwhile the side effects on babies became glaring. Many newborns struggled to breathe and could not be resuscitated. In months, the use of this method faded out entirely. Though twilight sleep had a short-lived history, it changed the public view of birth, which had always been seen as the business of women in the family home. Now it was a medical event whose discomforts were to be managed by hospital physicians.

As twilight sleep fell out of favor, a more promising technique was being developed. It gained momentum in the 1970s and is now used by around sixty percent of women giving birth in the USA: the epidural. Inserted through the skin of the birthing woman's back, a small tube administers a combination of medications (usually a local anesthetic and an opioid) into the outermost part of her spinal canal, leaving her in her right mind but without any sensation below the chest. This allows a mother having a Cesarean, for example, to remain conscious to meet her baby.

As a doula I've seen many an epidural provide huge relief and a sense of control to women who just moments previously had felt deluged by the intensity of labor. On the face of it, the epidural looks like medical history's answer to Eve's dilemma. Could it be that humanity has now dispensed with the toil God warned would be part of childbirth, without any adverse consequences?

Sadly not. Undoubtedly getting an epidural is more humane than twilight sleep, and less deadly than chloroform, but it's not without its own serious potential side effects. An epidural is part of a package of treatments that connects the user to various bags, poles, and monitors with at least five tubes, bands, and wires. Even a "good epidural," which enables the mother to participate somewhat actively in the process of birth, confines her to bed. Gravity cannot help her bring her baby down, and he is more likely to settle in a tricky back-to-back position. Accordingly, pushing takes on average two to three hours longer. Three times as many women receive Pitocin, a drug that hastens labor but risks distressing the baby. The likelihood of an instrumental birth (where forceps or suction is used to pull a baby out) doubles. Severe perineal tears are more common. An epidural, it seems, can take away the pain of contractions, but it can't remove the struggle of childbearing.

Such a catalog of the side effects of epidurals may lead us to investigate other options. The main alternative is drugs from the heroin family—opioid medications such as Demerol, Stadol, or Fentanyl. (The latter is the drug implicated in the opioid epidemic now causing increasing numbers of overdose deaths.)

A single quick-acting dose is injected into a muscle, a vein, or the spinal column. Unlike with an epidural, it's the mind rather than the body that becomes numb. Opioids make users drowsy, dreamy, and sometimes nauseous. As some of my clients have said, "The epidural took the pain away from me, but the opioid took me away from the pain." And like any medication a pregnant woman receives, opioids reach the baby. If he is born before they wear off, he may need to be resuscitated with Narcan to reverse the effects of overdose.

I wish I could describe other readily available, less risky pain medications, but sadly this concludes our brief tour of the options.** At this point many women are surprised that in the twenty-first century, there would not be more choices, or better choices, for labor pain relief. Even with the best drugs, toil-free birth remains out of our reach. Every procedure that addresses one problem creates another of its own. A medication that takes away a mother's physical pain might lead to mental anguish or to a struggle for her baby. An operation that saves a mother from hours of difficult work requires months of painful recovery. As in a game of whack-a-mole, every time technology bops the struggle on its head, it rears up in another spot. Modern medicine has lulled us into a false sense of security if we think the struggle of childbirth is a matter of consumer choice, a box we can check or uncheck on the birth plan.

Why would our loving God permit this? How could He whose abundant mercy meets us daily allow that humanity be perpetuated only through pain? Why would the "Treasury of Blessings" turn to us in our moment of need with a curse? These questions can only be answered with other questions. Is the pain

---

** A few other possibilities that exist in theory, like nitrous oxide or water injections into the back, are unavailable in most US hospitals.

of birth really a curse? Do women actually experience it this way? What is giving birth actually like?

Ask ten mothers to describe how labor feels, and we'll get ten different answers, but there seems to be a consensus that a contraction is like a very strong menstrual cramp. Over the course of about a minute, its power builds, then passes away entirely. One thing is for sure: while it's there, the feeling is utterly commanding. It's not possible simply to ignore it and carry on with other things. Yet a woman may describe the feeling as "positive pain," such that she can distinguish between normal intensity and something that "feels wrong" if a complication arises.

Despite what we hear of watermelons and small holes, the pain of a straightforward labor is somehow different from the pain of injury. Such a sensation tells us not that our bodies are being hurt, but that they're operating at capacity. It's a muscular pain: the exercising of the largest muscle in the body, the full-term uterus. It's a growing pain: the widening of our cervix to a huge ten centimeters. It is an accomplishment in the making—a challenge rather than a threat.[60] In this, it bears less affinity with breaking a bone or tearing a ligament than with climbing a mountain or eating a spicy curry. It's also distinct from suffering. Some women birth with great pain without considering themselves as having suffered because mentally they welcomed each sensation; others feel no pain on account of having been anesthetized, yet their experience causes great anguish.

If birthing pain feels like "positive" pain, what is it adding? What could the benefits be? Let's talk about three major blessings it can confer. First, pain helps us prepare for a successful birth. As "God's megaphone" (to use C. S. Lewis's term),[61] pain gets us to stop what we are doing and seek out the resources we need to carry us and our babies safely through. One such resource is social support. Psychologists have confirmed that the companionship we seek out in times of pain actually reduces our physical symptoms.[62] In turn, those who witness our struggle—like the husbands or partners, mothers, sisters, friends, midwives, and doulas most of us choose to surround us as we birth—respond with sympathy and are more likely to help us in future. Indeed, it's these relationships, forged in the fire of trial, that we lean on so heavily during the raw and needy weeks of early motherhood. Pain, one of the building blocks of intimacy, draws together a protective community surrounding the vulnerable new person who is coming into the world.

Pain also prompts us to gather nutritional resources that might be needed for future difficult events. Researchers have found that after enduring discomfort people tend to "reward" themselves by choosing more calorie-rich foods.[63] During labor, some women want to eat; some find food does not go down well; others benefit from a jolt of energy, perhaps a honey stick or sports drink, at a strategic moment. But after giving birth, almost every mother is ravenously hungry. Even the most unappetizing hospital tray or greasiest takeaway becomes a lavish feast. The toil of birth has primed them to seek daily calories at precisely the time they start to need them to make breastmilk—which takes about 500 additional calories a day.

A final resource pain prompts us to seek out is a supportive environment. People in pain tend to withdraw to a dark, quiet place where there are fewer other stimuli and we can focus our energy on coping with the sensations at hand. The intensity of our contractions therefore brings us to the shelter of a safe place to birth our babies—for our foremothers, a firelit cave away from the claws of predators; for us, the hospital or the birthing center, or a cozy corner of the home. Without these feelings to bring us to a halt, our babies would come as we continued our normal activities—in the elevator or the drugstore. Our discomfort helps ensure our babies enter the world with warmth and dignity, born not onto asphalt or linoleum or dirt, but into welcoming skilled hands.

Second, pain is a great teacher. Imagine for a moment living without it. A handful of people in this world, born with a rare gene mutation that makes them impervious to physical discomfort, can explain just what that would be like. Deprived of their body's pain signals, these people must rely on other senses to warn them about the risk of injury; by the time they smell burning flesh, it's already too late. Labor pain, too, serves as a coach instructing us how to give birth safely and effectively. It makes us swivel, rock, and bend, experimenting to find the postures and positions that ease our baby down and into the world. Once his head comes low enough to trigger nerves near the rectum, no one needs to count to ten or yell at us to push: the pressure shows us exactly what to do. Upon feeling the burning sensation of crowning, we instinctively hold back, slowing the birth of the head so that our tissues can stretch without injury. And as it teaches us how to birth, pain also teaches us about ourselves. Once we've come through on the other side, we look back knowing we are capable of great things, which makes us more confident stewards of the vulnerable new life we have brought into the world.

Third, pain can add meaning and beauty to our lives. Across every age and culture, pleasure and pain appear as twins ever in each other's presence. According to the ancient Chinese formula for contentment, "To be dry and thirsty in a hot and dusty land and to feel great drops of rain on my bare skin—ah, is this not happiness! To have an itch in a private part of my body and finally to escape from my friends and go to a hiding place where I can scratch—ah, is this not happiness!"[64]

The pattern of labor likewise places pain right next to pleasure. Contractions come in a pulsing rhythm, so that after one passes the next few minutes are spent in complete comfort—and not just comfort but bliss, as one look at the face of a woman resting between contractions will indicate. The hypnotic pattern of pressure and release, pressure and release, whirls her away into a galaxy of feel-good hormones where the air is too thin for fears to grow. The stronger the sensations become, the more the endorphins flow, so that the challenge is transfigured into its own solution. The moment when we are biochemically most primed to relish the beauty of the universe is the exact time we are given a tiny, exquisite new creature to love and serve. One woman puts it colorfully: "You don't have to be an unusually brave person to give birth without drugs. I'm something of a [coward] myself, but childbirth is a drug in itself. It changes your consciousness just like it stretches your skin. It all takes care of itself and just happens."[65]

Considering all the gestures of divine mercy we find peppered throughout the intense experience of childbirth, the "curse" model of birthpangs doesn't really work. It simply doesn't seem to fit with women's experience. So, circling around to the Genesis passage with which our present chapter began, how are we to understand the implications of the Fall for Eve? What are we to make of God's words, "I will greatly multiply your pain and your groaning"?

It may help to remind ourselves that within Orthodox theology, the departure from Eden is understood as a result of rather than a punishment for the sin of our first parents. They were sent from the Garden not because they were no longer wanted,

154

but because they had chosen to live separately from the presence of God and to follow their own incompatible path. Among the many tragic ramifications of their decision to exclude themselves from Life was death. No longer would they live eternally in His love. Logistically speaking, they would need to reproduce if their race were not to die with them.

Contemplating this, St. Gregory of Nyssa includes among his features of fallen life not just things like old age, memory lapse, and dirt (yes, dirt!), but also gestation.[66] Such an understanding represents the insight of only one of the Fathers. It is far from universal in Orthodox theology and needs to be contemplated together with God's commandment to humankind, given before the Fall, to be fruitful and multiply. However, as pregnant women we experience our fruitfulness only within a fallen world in which death is a daily reality, and it is useful to consider with St. Gregory that it may be not just the *pain* of birth but human reproduction itself that is a consequence of the Fall.

At any rate, reproduction opens us to pain: the growing pains of birth and parenting, of growth by division, of the separation whereby one body becomes two. But this doesn't mean childbearing is evil; not at all. Childbearing, pain and all, may be God's beautiful way to make the best of a sorry situation—a mercy He extends to allow humanity to continue in spite of death. Even God's Plan B, if such it is, offers us a beautiful taste of His life.

Note that with C. S. Lewis, "I am not arguing that pain is not painful. Pain hurts."[67] Neither am I saying we need not hope for the day when "there shall be no more pain" (Rev. 21:4). But we need to know that the toil of labor is something we are able to withstand, even somehow to benefit from. God reaches out to save us not just *from* our labor pain, but *within* it.

And so, in place of a curse model of birthpangs, I'd propose an *economia* model. It's as if our birthpangs are a merciful dispensation that offers a solution to a compromised situation in the fallen world. Under this model, the pain of labor appears as a gift—a dark and strange gift, but a gift nonetheless. Similar to the Church's permission to remarry or an exemption from fasting rules on health grounds, the pain of childbirth is a gift we'd prefer not to need—a gift God might have preferred not to have to give us—but under the circumstances, it serves us well.

As human beings it's our job to align ourselves with God's *economia*, disposing ourselves to receive the good things He offers. But drugs can participate in this *economia*, too. Sometimes the normal intensity of labor oversteps its boundary from pain into anguish. It ceases to edify us and only grinds us down. This may happen when a woman lacks anyone to encourage her, or is restricted to a position where she cannot move her body freely—when her baby is in a bone-crunching back-to-back position, or she starts to lose hope that her baby will ever come—when she is plagued by flashbacks to previous trauma, or hasn't slept in days—or in any of a number of circumstances. When a woman says her experience is no longer for her good, it's time for the compassionate use of medicine. No one else can say she should be content to endure it: only she and God know where the line should be drawn.

As Christians, we seek neither pain nor comfort for their own sakes, but "all things good and profitable for our souls." The martyrs are a good example: we venerate them as saints not because of their suffering but because of their acceptance of suffering for the cause of love. If there is value in the pain of martyrdom, or birth, or any pain for that matter, it's not as an end in itself, but only as a means to work out our salvation.

Bodies

"The body is deified at the same time as the soul."
—ST. MAXIMOS THE CONFESSOR

We'd be fooling ourselves to pretend that childbearing doesn't implicate our most intimate body parts, or that our fears about birth don't relate to those parts. The trepidation so many of us feel about how labor might change us physically cannot be addressed without being a bit explicit and brave. Though none of us really wants to say it, many of us wonder: Will the earthquake of birth split me open along the deepest of fault lines? Will my body ever be the same? Will the physical life I share with my husband be diminished? After birth, will I still be lovable? Will I be me?

The fact is, obstetric tearing isn't inevitable. Many women give birth over an intact perineum. Neither is it simply the luck of the draw: there are things we and our caregivers can do actively, both before and during labor, to prevent a tear. But my purpose this week (the last in our series on fears surrounding birth) is not to talk anyone out of her concerns about tears. That would be foolish, given the huge impact pelvic health has on our well-being throughout our lives. I'll not dismiss this fear but embrace it in a spirit of curiosity, using it as a springboard into bigger issues about our physical lives. Why is the idea of a perineal tear so frightening to us? As mothers, what's the significance of our bodies, top to bottom, inside and out? Do they have any bearing on our inner world? Do they have a purpose to fulfill?

Our society gives a confusing response to these questions. One message that comes through loud and clear is that our bodies and their attractiveness are everything. In the pursuit of loveliness we tweeze, squeeze, starve, cut, and implant ourselves with plastic. With makeup, as T. S. Eliot says in "The Love Song of J. Alfred Prufrock," we "prepare a face to meet the faces that [we] meet." Social media feeds overflow with images of human skin, and a whole generation of girls has learned to pay for the attention of boys with pictures of their bodies. A magic recipe of mouths, legs, and cleavage is used to sell almost every product. The cross-pollination of celebrity with pornography makes every role model a centerfold and every centerfold a role model. The body itself is treated as not much more than one big erogenous zone, a work of performance art.

At the same time, it's implied that our bodies are nothing and the way we conduct ourselves with them is of no account. Anything we do with anyone is considered acceptable if we have their consent. Our sexuality is framed as a journey of self-discovery rather than a call to self-giving love. Physicians purport to remove people's reproductive organs without anything being lost. We speak of our physical selves as a set of parts belonging to us—"my" head, "my" pelvis—forgetting that we are not our own (1 Cor. 6:19). We then assess these parts on the quality of their function, from "a bad back" to an "incompetent cervix," as if they were cogs in a broken machine.

Bodies-as-everything and bodies-as-nothing seem to be two contradictory philosophies. Actually, they are the two sides of the gnostic coin. A gnostic view of the world is dualistic: it holds that our souls are the true realities temporarily imprisoned in our illusory and fleeting bodies. The goal of the spiritual life is to free ourselves from this slavery. A prisoner often has a love-hate relationship with her cell. She wants to break free. She counts the days until her release. But she is also shaped by the walls that confine her. Over time, she becomes so accustomed to incarceration that she develops a perverse love for it, so institutionalized that she fears living another way. These are the same complicated feelings we have for our bodies when we regard them as confining.

Such a way of thinking, though, is nothing new. Gnosticism was the beast St. Paul was wrestling with as he reminded the church at Corinth, "Glorify God in your body and in your spirit" (1 Cor. 6:20). The Corinthian Christians had forgotten that physical actions have a spiritual reality. Twenty centuries more and this pervasive heresy is still at the heart of our culture. If we're not careful, it can sneak into our hospital bags and right into the birthing room.

Gnostic dualism would disdain birth as a mechanical event rather than part of a delicate and mysterious dance of bodies and souls. It would shoehorn our labors into convenient office hours. It would have labor triggered by an obstetrician's vacation schedule instead of by an exchange of hormones and love between a mother and her child. A gnostic view would expect our labor progress to be perfectly linear. When our bodies do not perform according to a predetermined timeline, it would have us use medications to speed things up, even if there is no pressing need. It would see the landscape of birth as a jagged mountain range of heartbeats plotted on a graph and make our birth companions more attentive to ever-scrolling machines than to us, their loved ones. It would have the nurses caring for us refer to us not by name but by number: the number of centimeters our cervix is dilated, or the number of the room we're occupying.

This mechanistic view of birth is summarized in the oft-heard phrase, "All that matters is a healthy mother and a healthy baby." These words seem innocuous enough—in fact, unquestionable. After all, who *wouldn't* want new families to be well? The "healthy mother, healthy baby" mantra gets something important right: in birth, the physical health of the mother and the baby are vitally important. Yet they are not the *only* things that matter. To define *healthy* as merely *alive* sets the bar unnecessarily low. As Christians we understand health differently—as encompassing our whole being, body and soul. Christ comes to bring us not just life in the sense of physical survival, but abundant life (John 10:10). Babies need parents who are not simply undead, but well in every way. So when we hear the "healthy" catchphrase, let's be careful we're not being sold a gnostic bill of goods.

We've seen what childbearing looks like when we view the body as a meaningless machine, but how does the flip side of gnosticism play out in the birthing room? When the body is idolized, women feel pressured to appear attractive even while they are pushing a baby out. Some wear makeup and lace for labor. Where women of our mothers' generation once protested as inhumane the hospital policies that called for their pubic hair to be shaved, many women today remove their own hair to comply with a protocol popularized by pornography. Some elect to have their babies by Cesarean section because they fear a vaginal birth will diminish their sexual value. These mothers are tragically misguided, both factually and spiritually. It seems they do not know that pregnancy itself challenges the pelvic floor, regardless of the baby's exit route, and it's Cesarean, not vaginal, birth that has the far greater overall impact on the body. Nor do they recognize that a woman's worth is far greater than can be measured in terms of a single body part.

The idolization of the body hounds mothers in the postpartum period, too. Our culture's hypersexualization of breasts can impede the breastfeeding relationship. Because functional breasts are considered vulgar, lactating mothers are under pressure to observe a standard of modesty not required of other women. When their babies need to be fed, they face an unfortunate choice between draping themselves with an awkward cover, retreating to a bathroom stall, bracing to deal with comments from strangers, or just staying home. Sometimes pressure comes from closer quarters. Many a mother has related a most intimate dilemma: her husband's or partner's possessive reluctance to "share" her breasts with their baby. Often in the struggle, the child is weaned before he is ready. This is a far cry from the divine call to mutual belonging in the spirit of self-sacrificial love that we see in Scripture (1 Cor. 7:4). It's the siren call of porn, in which a male asserts ownership of the female body for his own pleasure.

We've seen that, in both its forms, gnostic thought takes a toll on us mothers. Whether dismissed as soulless machines or idolized as shiny trinkets, our bodies are viewed as mere objects. But a childbearing woman is not just a victim of heresy; she is also a living corrective to it. And herein lies the hope, for a birthing body refuses to lie back and submit to objectification. The observer's gaze cannot rest on it, because it points beyond itself to the child who is coming into the world by its agency. In a woman giving birth, we see a body in the act of facilitating relationship, in this case an unfolding love between mother and child. In this relationship, her body can no longer be an object; it becomes a subject of love. It has a purpose, a meaning in the world. It is not a confining prison but a door opening out onto new life.

In this way the birthing body reveals a truth about each of us, because every human body—man, woman, and child—is created for relationship. Our physicality exists to make us known to one another. God also was made known through a physical body in the Incarnation. Our Lord was at first a baby who needed to be wrapped and held and (as we see from that delightful corner of the Nativity icon that shows the midwives bathing Him) cleaned after soiling Himself. After His Resurrection He continued to reveal Himself through the tangible details of everyday life: the breaking of bread, the wound in His side, a campfire breakfast, a walk on the road.

And so it is for us. All our relationships—with the world, with other humans, and ultimately with God—have their locus in our bodies, as well as our souls. This is why our worship is so physical. Bodies fold in prostration, incense billows, bells jangle, candles flicker, wine sweetens lips, melodies rise, and chests are enfolded in the sign of the cross. Each of my senses draws me into the beauty of God's presence. In my worship I ask Him to save me, and that *me* is an inextricable bundle of body and soul. As Florovsky wrote, "A body without a soul is but a corpse. A soul without a body is a ghost."[68]

So birth gives us eyes to see the human body afresh. When we turn these eyes back on birth itself, a new vision emerges. In labor, we no longer need to hold our physicality at arm's length, as it were. We can embrace the power of this most carnal, or should I say incarnational, experience. Birth and sexuality, so closely linked in nature but compartmentalized by institutional protocols, can take their proper place in relation to one another.

As God ordained it, pregnancy begins with intercourse and

marks our bodies as having had sex. Sexual intimacy and child-bearing implicate the same body parts. The same abandonment with which we pursue marital love sweeps over us in labor. We lose all sense of shame, becoming like fearless fools for Christ, naked not as we wander the streets but as we pace the birthing room. Our babies too are born naked, nestling skin-to-skin. The same bonding hormones flow. And all this voluptuous fruitfulness is not an offense, for God has made it so. Saint John Chrysostom does not shy away from this: "As if she were gold receiving the purest of gold, the woman receives the man's seed with rich pleasure, and within her it is nourished, cherished and refined. It is mingled with her own substance and she returns it as a child!"[69]

But no matter how sensual birth can be, it is never pornographic. Its laughter, joy, beauty, intensity, and sacredness are in fact an affront to the voyeur. Labor is so personal, so private, so unglamorous, that the objectifying eye finds little material to work with. Such is the power at work that the viewer can no longer fancy himself the dominant one whom all things must serve; rather he can only stand in awe. As the gateway to human existence, the female body commands respect—we might even say veneration. Of course we do not worship the physical form any more than we worship the wood and paint of an icon when we bow before it and kiss it. Rather we worship the creative power of God revealed there. Our bodies exist not to create an image, cropped and filtered and ready to post; instead, they are created *in* an image: the image of God.

If, as our pregnant bodies change—swelling here, loosening there—we forget that they are "very good" (Gen. 1:31), we need only look up. Above our church altar, soaring high over the iconostasis, we see the one "More Spacious than the Heavens." How her icon speaks to those of us expecting a child! Her arms reach out in prayer surrounding the womb-like medallion in which the infant Christ nestles. Her uterus is like a halo around the Son of God, the little space in which the Uncontainable One chose to dwell. There we see a deep mystery taking place: the Creator contained in a creature. As St. Ephrem the Syrian puts it, "While the fetus of the Son was being formed in the womb, He Himself was forming babes in the womb."[70]

From the dome of the church, the Theotokos watches over the community, bringing the curvaceousness of pregnancy right into the heart of our worship. Lest we think our condition is unaddressed, irrelevant, or taboo in the Christian life, she is there reminding us otherwise. As St. Gregory the Theologian emphasizes, "Christ Himself was conceived in a pure but human belly, and slipped out from a woman's womb, thus mixing half of human marriage with divinity."[71] We cannot consider shameful those body parts—a uterus, a cervix, a birth canal, a perineum— through which God chose to travel on His journey into the world. On the contrary, every time we call Christ's mother the Theotokos, the Church implicitly celebrates them. *Theotokos* means "God-birther," much as our word *tokophobia* means "fear of giving birth." By affirming this title in the face of dissent at the Third Ecumenical Council, the Church stressed that Mary was not only the Mother of God (*Meter tou Theou*) or the Bearer of God (*Theophoros*, a title shared by many saints) but the one through whose pelvis God deigned to pass.

This is the shock of Christianity. Christ's Incarnation truly marries human flesh with God's Spirit. After assigning every body part its function and tenderly recreating His design within each new person, He comes to inhabit the work of His hands. If He does not spurn our physicality, neither should we. By altering our bodies sometimes beyond our comfort or recognition, pregnancy offers a chance to start a new relationship with them. We seek not to become free of them but free *in* them. We know them not as empty wells for others to fill with shallow affections, but as vessels of holiness. Whether they should tear or sag or stretch or scar, we can love and accept them in a new way.

FIVE

Braving Labor

Companions

*Two are better than one because they have
a good reward for their labor. For if they fall,
one will lift up his companion.*
—ECCLESIASTES 4:9–10

ver the past weeks we've examined three of the most
common fears about childbirth through the lens of our
faith: concerns about losing control, about pain, and
about damage to our bodies. Though of course the fear we feel
approaching labor is *fearful*, we've seen that it can also be a help.
Fear prompts us to seek support for the journey ahead, reminds
us to use our pregnancy fruitfully, and invites us to deepen our
relationships. It's like the voice of a prophet—not a grumbly
soothsayer foretelling a dark future but a seer calling us out on
our habits and inviting us into a richer life: "The voice of one
crying in the wilderness: 'Prepare the way of the Lord; make
straight the paths of our God. . . . The glory of the Lord shall be
revealed, and all flesh shall see the salvation of God'" (Is. 40:3,
5). The coming four weeks seek to move on from avoiding fear
to building active courage. I'll share four practical coping mea-
sures for labor: this week companionship, then prayer, rhythm,
and the role of our thoughts.

A TWENTY-FIRST–CENTURY WOMAN who happened to stum-
ble into a time machine just as her labor begins, if she traveled into the past, would emerge to find herself surrounded by

a curious cast of characters. Any era she landed in would look roughly the same, as long as she went back more than about a hundred years. Neighbor women and concerned relatives would be gathered around, chatting, working handicrafts, and feeding nurslings. A bigger child would be off fetching the village midwife. Water would be boiling on the stove or fire, bread rising on the table. Men would be nowhere evident, except when they shuffled in every so often to restock the firewood. Only in extremis would a physician be summoned, and even then, in this domestic domain his views might or might not prevail.

One such scene is shown in the icon of the Nativity of the Theotokos. The newly postpartum St. Anna reclines, warmly wrapped in flowing robes, often of blood-red. Saint Joachim, her husband, is absent altogether, or he may be shown overlooking from a distant turret of the house. But her bed is a hub of activity as a bevy of young women attend to her bodily needs. One fans her, another prepares food; one brings oil, another one rubs her shoulders; one is keeping her hydrated, another rocks the infant Mary in a cradle. Unlike in "the other" birth icon, depicting the Nativity of Christ, where the Theotokos has no one but her child with her, it's clear that this mother is recovering from the physical rigors of a very ordinary birth.

Saint Anna's attendants are ordinary too: they are not named but are taken to be those young "daughters of the Hebrews" she summoned as mother's helpers, mentioned in the *Protoevangelion of James* (the apocryphal gospel which is the source for our knowledge of this event).[72] They haven't a halo among them, but their very practical work is part of the holiness that makes "a sanctuary [of Anna's] bedroom." And their sheer number shows how vital the good companionship of other women is assumed to be for the physical safety and spiritual integrity of birth.

Anthropologist Wenda Trevathan argues that this human need for birth companions arises from our very physiology. As creatures who walk on two legs, we have a maternal pelvis shaped so that our babies must make a series of rotations on their way into the world and (for the most part) emerge facing away from us. We cannot easily reach down at birth to clear our own baby's airway or unwrap his cord, but need help from someone who can see more than the back of his head. We cannot guide our own child out of the birth canal without pulling him against the natural angle of his body's flexion—only someone else can do that. [73] The very design of our bodies makes birth a social enterprise.

And even if our birth attendants were originally recruited for logistical reasons surrounding the moment of birth, we also thrive on their emotional support in the lead up to it. They can see and show us other things we lose sight of, too—like how well we are managing, or the fact that, despite how it feels, no one ever labored forever. In the end, though it may have sprung from the biological need for assistance, the psychological support birth companions offer proves equally or even more indispensable.

But our current model for labor support, where we expect men to be our primary companions, arises from a cultural rather than a biological imperative. Over the course of the twentieth century, men's quick evolution from background figures to cigar-smoking hall-pacers to pivotal players totally reversed the historic norm. As geographical mobility increased, people no longer lived near family members and close friends who could help a growing family. Childbirth moved out of the village and into the hospital, seemingly a cleaner and safer setting in which to have a baby.

Unfortunately, by mid-century women found that there was a tradeoff to institutionalized birth. It offered them ready antibiotics and surgical expertise, but it separated them from their loved ones and usual surroundings, often making birth lonely and impersonal. At the same time, emotional closeness was increasingly seen as part of marriage. Women began to advocate for, and finally came to expect, the support of their husbands in the birthing room. It's now a father who is absent for his child's birth, rather than one who attends it, who's the exception.

And we have high expectations of our menfolk. Their labor to-do list is often long:

- Drive wife/partner to birth facility without getting pulled over
- Rub her back, feed her ice chips and hold her hand—preferably simultaneously
- Be in command of the hospital bag and the exact location of all contents
- Remain awake for as long as it takes (several days if necessary)
- Never leave the room, not even for a bathroom break (see timeframe above)
- Don't make inappropriate jokes out of nervousness
- Intuit, say, and do the right thing at all times
- Handle all conversations with medical personnel and curious relatives with professionalism
- Remember and implement everything from the birth classes
- If a Cesarean is necessary, rock a head-to-toe blue disposable suit
- Cut the umbilical cord, and
- Whatever happens, don't pass out.

We are asking each of them to do the tasks once filled by a whole team of experienced village women: hard shoes to fill. But our men have the heavier burden, because unlike the "daughters of the Hebrews" they have probably not been attending births since they themselves were babies. They witness our womanly journey to the brink without knowing what a wild and breathtaking new land awaits on the other side. And we are not just their neighbors or sisters-in-law, but their helpmates, their life. Witnessing our voyage, they must undertake a powerful journey of their own, at various times feeling protective, useless, exhausted, joyful, pained, confused, and awestruck. Nevertheless, they are expected to keep these feelings in check and fulfill all their obligations without a thought for themselves.

As a doula I am constantly astonished by how well many men rise to the occasion. It's remarkable given the brevity of the apprenticeship human history has given their sex. The vast majority of expectant fathers I work with tend their partners with touching attentiveness. They are responsive, resolute, and practical. They tenderly tie back their lovers' hair, hold the bucket while they vomit, and submit to being squeezed to the point of bruising without complaint. They speak sweet nothings, kiss sweaty foreheads, and blink away their own tears.

This can be a true help. Most women supported by their menfolk say they made a vital difference.[74] And fathers bond better with their babies when they've seen them come into the world— which makes sense in view of studies suggesting that oxytocin, the hormone implicated in both labor and bonding, can be communicated through the sense of smell.[75] It seems the love with which labor primes a mother to greet her child is rather contagious, and fathers in the birthing room also come under its spell.

But labor support skills are a gift, and not all men (or women) possess them. A man can be a perfectly good husband and father without being a great birth companion. And while not every husband will shine in the birthing room, not every wife will want him there. The beauty of bringing a baby into the world in our society today is that we can be accompanied by the companions of our choice. When we choose to have our men join us, we do well to recognize that they are no more superhuman than we are. They'll require space to see to their own emotional and bodily needs, and their own sources of support in order to support us.

This is the gap into which many families choose to bring a doula, or professional birth companion. This Greek term meaning "slave" appears many times in Scripture in its masculine and feminine forms (*doulos* and *doula*), often interchangeably with the term for "servant"—*diakonos,* which is the root of our word *deacon.* As a deacon does for a priest and parish, a doula puts herself at the service of the expectant woman and her whole family. She is not a medical caregiver but practices alongside whatever other attendants are present, providing information, comfort, and physical support.

It's a calling as old as humanity that has only recently been the subject of scientific study. A 2017 review of twenty-six clinical trials found that where a doula is present, there is a 34% reduction in dissatisfaction with the birth experience, 31% less Pitocin used to begin or speed up labor, a 28% reduction in Cesareans, 14% fewer babies admitted to special care nursery, and 9% less need for pain medication. Labor is an average of 41 minutes shorter. No ill effects have been noted.[76] Compelling statistics like these have led some to conclude that "if a doula were a drug, it would be unethical not to use it."[77]

Of course, when we remember that for most of history it's been absolutely standard for women to support one another in labor, we see that the intervention consists not in providing some women with a doula, but in depriving most women of access to such support. It's the ethical merit of the current anomalous setup that needs examining.

As carefully as we mull over who will take the role of the village women, we'll also want to consider how they will complement the other characters on the team. Unlike in most countries, the majority of US births are attended by obstetricians, that is, physicians specializing in childbirth—or, to be more precise, surgeons specializing in the complications of childbirth. Their expertise is put to best use in the operating room rather than the birthing room. Many of them have never had the chance to observe the sweep of a straightforward labor from start to finish: they typically leave obstetrical nurses to attend the women in their care and only return when the baby is about to be born. This more distant approach to the management of birth is reflected in the name of their profession. The word *obstetrician* comes from the Latin meaning "to stand in front of," and indeed they place themselves at the "business end," not *beside* but *over* the women in their care.

A midwife, on the other hand, is someone who stands *alongside* a woman as she labors. *Midwife* means *with woman*. These practitioners are experts in the normal course of labor: recognizing, protecting, and promoting it. They attend the majority of births around the world, particularly in the countries where maternity care is safest. Like obstetricians, their primary concern is for the physical well-being of mother and baby, so they monitor vital statistics too. But because their model of care regards physical and emotional care as vitally linked, they're often seen helping women in more personal ways an obstetrician rarely would: mopping brows, breathing together, making snacks, whispering words of encouragement. More often than obstetricians, midwives practice on a caseload rather than an on-call model, so the same person who cares for a woman during pregnancy will also attend her labor from start to finish.

Partners, obstetricians (and the nurses who work under them), midwives, doulas: this is the roll from which our culture suggests we choose our birth attendants. But for Orthodox Christians, the list does not end there. Actually, there are more natural candidates still. For in birth, as in life, the Church is our primary source of companionship. *Companion* is a compound of the Latin words meaning "with" and "bread," so a companion is a person with whom I break bread. Thus my greatest companions are those with whom I share the defining act of spiritual community: the breaking of the eucharistic bread.

My friends in the faith can support me as I labor, either in person or by praying from afar. Perhaps this may be an elderly grandmother from my parish; my godmother or the expected godmother of my baby; a Christian friend who is pregnant at the same time I am; or a spiritual mother. I can also rely on those who worship with us but on another shore: saints with a special care for childbirth;[78] my patron or guardian angel; and especially the Theotokos. With such a cloud of witnesses, I know I need never be alone, but can "run with endurance the race that is set before [me]" (Heb. 12:1). In difficult moments, I can turn to them, asking for their intercession as I would ask a physically present friend for help. Indeed, I may find I look to them more often than I press the bedside call button to summon the nurse.

There are also companions who don't just witness our labor but labor with us. We are joined in a common work with hundreds of thousands of women globally whose babies will share a birth-day with ours.[79] Most of these babies will be born under circumstances less fortunate than our own. Every day there are women birthing amid war, in captivity, after rape, homeless, or without running water. During labor the veil thins between life and death, earth and heaven, here and eternity, and we have a serendipitous chance to stand with these people before God with particular immediacy. As their suffering becomes our own in prayer, let's make their courage ours as well. Indeed, labor unites us with the toil of the entire world. "For we know," the Holy Apostle Paul writes, "that the whole creation groans and labors with birth pangs together until now" (Rom. 8:22–23). As we navigate each contraction, the world also works to bring forth the new life of the Resurrection.

But all birth companions pale in comparison to the comfort offered by God Himself, who is already present at every birth before He's summoned. By becoming a human in the person of Christ, He has made Himself present to our pain, not just seeing it but knowing it from the inside. Even in the valley of the shadow of death we will not fear, for God with Us is here (Ps. 22/23:4). Though His incarnate body was a male one, Emmanuel is familiar with every struggle a human can face. He's familiar enough with childbirth specifically to make labor a metaphor for His own work in the world. "I will not always be silent and restrain myself," God says. "Now I will be steadfast, like a woman in labor. I shall amaze" (Is. 42:14).

Prayer

*There is no need at all to make long discourses, it is enough
to stretch out one's hands and say, "Lord, as You will, and
as You know, have mercy." And if the conflict grows fiercer
say, "Lord, help!" He knows very well what we need.*
—ST. MACARIUS THE GREAT[80]

With my mother's milk, I was fed on tales of the power
of prayer during childbirth. Choking on grateful tears,
my mama would recount the story of my hair-raising
birth: about my slowing heart, the efforts to save me, and the
obstetrician who, as my newborn cries were finally going up,
silenced the whole operating theater to offer a relieved prayer
of thanksgiving for my preservation. My existence is predicated,
somehow, on the faithfulness of these strangers.

Although I'm fully credentialed as an enthusiastic advocate
and beneficiary of prayer, I'm hardly an expert. After practicing
for forty years, I am still very much a beginner, learning from
the example of others. And my work as a doula has given me the
chance literally to sit at other women's feet as they pray their
way through labor. One Catholic mother-to-be took great comfort in repeating a hymn to the Theotokos as she labored in a
busy hospital one winter's night. While big snowflakes drifted
past the high-rise window as if through space, the woman's
mother, nurse, and I prayed and swayed together, supporting her
on all sides with womanly love.

Another home birth I attended was punctuated by the regular

trips of the Orthodox midwife to the family's icon corner to chant the prayer of the hours. Though she was sometimes there alone, the whole team benefited from overhearing her quiet devotion. Over more than a day, the milestones of prayer helped us mark the progress of labor and the passing of time. Another woman, relieved as the epidural she'd chosen took effect, invoked God's blessing on the anesthesiologist, his children, and his children's children!

My own most prayerful labor was my fourth, a planned home birth under the care of an experienced midwife. It began with the blessing we asked over our family dinner one Saturday night when I was forty-two weeks pregnant. My belly stood momentarily to attention, rising up firm and tight under the kitchen table. A few minutes later, it happened again. The contractions were surprisingly strong from the start, and with each one I put down my fork and scooted my chair back, hunching over the counter until my body allowed me to sit back down.

After the meal, my family convened in the icon corner for nighttime prayers. My son helped his father light the incense; my daughter held the cross. When the Trisagion prayers were complete, my children prayed in their own words for me and the baby who was coming. As is our custom, we venerated the icons and made the sign of the cross on one another's foreheads, and I made sure to ask each of my family members for their forgiveness for any way in which I had offended them.

The children tripped excitedly up to bed, knowing that they'd likely be waking up to a new sibling, but I remained behind in the light of the candles. As I had most nights of my pregnancy, I intoned the Prayers of a Woman with Child. "O All-Merciful Christ our God," I prayed, no longer needing to read the words which had taken root in my heart, "look down and protect me,

FERTILE GROUND

Your handmaiden, from fear and from evil spirits that seek to destroy the work of Your hands. And when my hour and time is come," I chanted, wondering what hour of this night that would be, "deliver me by Your grace. Look with compassionate eye and deliver me, Your handmaiden, from pain. Lighten my infirmity in the time of my travail and grant me fortitude and strength for birth-giving, and hasten it by Your almighty help. For this is Your glorious work, the power of Your omnipotence, the work of Your grace and tender-heartedness. Amen."

I heard my husband come down and start to fill the inflatable birth pool standing ready next to the hearth. He anointed the surface of the water with a few drops of holy oil and lit candles in a corner next to a small icon. It was the icon of the Mother of God, Helper in Childbirth, which had accompanied me to scores of doula births, and it reminded me that in the hours ahead, she would be with me as she had for each of the women I'd attended. We called the friend who had sponsored me at my chrismation, who had agreed to be present at the birth, as well as our midwife, asking them both to set off for our house. We hit *send* on an email we'd prepared earlier, informing loved ones around the world that labor had begun and begging their prayers. I began to feel the spiritual support of my community gathering around me like a blanket.

By the time our two helpers arrived, it was the middle of the night. Labor had strengthened, and I was swishing through each contraction in the warm soothing water of the tub. In the dim light of our home, each woman went to work setting up the tools of her respective trade. The midwife arranged supplies on a tray; my friend got ready to pray the Akathist "Glory to God for All Things." From the next room, its words began to filter through. Penetrating the haze of my intensity, I heard her dear voice say:

Glory to Thee for calling me into being . . .
Glory to Thee through every sigh of my sorrow . . .
Glory to Thee for every step of my life's journey . . .
Glory to Thee, ceaselessly watching over me
Glory to Thee for the encounters Thou dost arrange for me
Glory to Thee for the love of parents, for the faithfulness of
friends . . .
Glory to Thee for the unforgettable moments of life . . .
Glory to Thee for the joy of living . . .
Glory to Thee, O God, from age to age!

The voice faded in and out, then quieted altogether. I drank
in the abundance of blessings to which the Akathist had given
words. The midwife reached the wand of the Doppler machine
into the water, and as soon as it was against my belly, the rushing of our baby's heartbeat filled the air. In the great enormity
and tenuousness of life, I knew how utterly fortunate my baby
and I were to be alive. From around the house, my other children assembled. As if they'd been woken by angels, they crept
reverently in to see who was about to be born. I was filled with
gratitude and love for this wonderful team, all silent together,
waiting with me for the next wave to roll in.

As contractions came stronger than ever, I asked my husband
to whisper the Jesus Prayer next to my ear. My sponsor-friend
had told me what a lifeline this ancient prayer of the Church had
been to her during her labors. For hours she'd prayed it aloud
during contractions. When she was given a medication that rendered her incapable of speaking, her husband had taken up the
mantle of her prayer until she could resume it herself after the
drug wore off. Make it part of your birth plan, she'd advised.

Now able to utter only the most basic of words, I too needed my husband to give me voice. "Lord Jesus Christ, Son of God," he prayed, "have mercy on me, a sinner." Like the contractions continually returning, he repeated the prayer. "Lord Jesus Christ . . ." Each recitation, it turned out, was the length of one of my carefully focused exhalations. Every low breath represented a prayer as if it were a knot in a prayer rope. Round and round we went on this imaginary *chotki*, my husband's arms encircling my massive belly. When even his quietest words in my ear were too much, and I had to ask him to stop, my breath continued to speak the prayer for itself. In that moment, I experienced why this is called the prayer of the heart. Once set in motion, it has the capacity to continue pulsing in our bodies without us.

As labor culminated, I began to feel the descent of my baby through my body, the swinging of the primal gates on their bony hinges. Though I had done this three times before, the shock of the feeling was new. There was no way to proceed, it seemed, yet no turning back. My whole self would have to open utterly. "OGodhelpme, OGodhelpme," I gasped, clinging onto the midwife's arm. It was not a vain request, but the most visceral and basic of prayers. It was the unutterable groaning of the Holy Spirit in us when we do not know what to pray (Rom. 8:26). It was the vesperal supplication of King David: "O Lord, I have cried to you; hear me" (Ps. 140/141:1)—the kind even a newborn baby knows how to make.

Indeed, just a few minutes later, my new daughter was let loose on the world with a cry of her own. Scooped up out of the water by her father's careful hands, she met the air with a loud prayer of surprise and need and hunger—the first of many such supplications she would make on her human journey.

Of all my experiences of prayer in childbirth, I've chosen to tell the tale of this labor because it quite naturally encompassed so many different forms of prayer: silence, thanksgiving, the Jesus Prayer, supplication, the Prayers for a Woman with Child, use of holy oil, prayer with icons, repentance, arrow prayers, and begging the petitions of others. I hold this story up as a taste of these several forms rather than a perfect model of any.

But perfect models aren't really needed, as each of us who prays through labor finds her own way to do so. And this is true even of people you'd not normally expect to hear praying. Some committed atheists I have worked with have turned to prayer as their babies were born, using their own words to call on One in whom they didn't know they trusted. They may not have identified as "religious" either before or after the fact, but in their moment of need they instinctively cried out for the kind of aid that no earthly birth attendant can give.

For these people, as for all of us, giving birth strips away the rational considerations by which we normally define ourselves to expose the more basic foundation of our being, the level on which every heart knows and longs for God. No matter what creed we profess, being confronted with our own poverty draws us to seek the riches found in the comforting presence of God. On the threshold of motherhood, the door opens to a richer life of prayer.

This truth is the currency in which many childbirth educators trade. Though it would be an unusual birth class that would provide instruction in prayer, the secular rituals that are taught often share a form with Christian spiritual practice. These teachings contain what St. Justin Martyr might call "the seed of the Logos":[81] that is, though they are still in germinal form, they are beginning to reach toward their fulfilment in the faith of the ancient Church. Mantras and breathing awareness exercises seem to point toward the Jesus Prayer. Birth altars, with their sculptures of fertility goddesses, mimic the fullness of our home icon corners. Mood lighting imitates the flickering of prayer candles. Guided relaxations grasp at the stillness of hesychasm.

Yet such is the power of prayer that even devoid of devotional content, its mere form proves a creature comfort. What desert monastics learned centuries ago, scientific evidence now agrees: the habit of putting aside everyday thoughts to focus on a repeated phrase, sound, or movement moderates our bodies and minds. Studies have shown that expectant mothers who practice techniques like deep focused breathing, visualization, and progressive muscle relaxation experience fewer pregnancy complications, have fewer Cesareans, and give birth to calmer, healthier babies.[82] If these practices are such a help in seed form, how much greater is their benefit when they have been perfected, established and blooming in the Church for two millennia! And if our labor coping skills are so beneficial when they merely take us deep into relaxation, how much more so when they take us deep into the heart of God!

But, from spiritual fathers and mothers to hypnobirthing instructors, anyone who teaches the form of prayer will say it requires frequent practice. Simply taking a few deep breaths while I labor won't make me instantly calm. So I needn't wait for the spontaneous urgency of labor to open the door to a fuller life of prayer: I can take advantage of the shifting sands of pregnancy to begin now.

In her book on the Jesus Prayer, Frederica Mathewes-Green tells how she did just that.[83] When Khouria Frederica was pregnant with her first child, she read somewhere about the fruitfulness of spending prayer time alone in quiet darkness. Figuring she'd soon be waking up with her baby anyway, she decided to acquire the habit of rising in the middle of the night to pray.

That baby came, and two more followed, then grandbabies, and decades later she's still at it. Each night she'll "swim up to consciousness" around 2:30 AM and rise to visit an icon corner in her hallway. After warming up with other prayers and psalms, she'll turn to the Jesus Prayer. Before returning to bed, she says a hundred recitations using a prayer rope, backing up to redo a few knots whenever her thoughts wander. Since those days as a young mother, this nightly practice of the prayer has become so much a part of her, she says, that she needs it "like I need food and light."

As Khouria Frederica found, one of the beauties of the Jesus Prayer is how expansive and flexible it is for every situation of life, despite the fixed structure of the words. If it took her from youth to grandmotherhood, it can take me from pregnancy into labor. As I ask for mercy, I can direct my petition not just to the current moment, but ahead to my birthgiving, knowing that all moments are present to the eternal God. With this prayer I can encompass all those who will be there to support me, whether known or unknown: the lab techs, nurses, security officers, or parking attendants who will become part of my labor story: "Have mercy on *us*." I can pray still further into the future, for all who will accompany my child through life: godparents, relatives, future siblings, school friends, and perhaps eventually a spouse.

Most of all, I can use the words "Lord, have mercy" to infuse my child himself with prayer, both as one who is prayed for and one who (because he is one body with me) prays, so that with the Psalmist he can say, "from my mother's womb You are my God" (Ps. 21/22:11).

Rhythm

Human beings, vegetables, or cosmic dust, we all dance to a
mysterious tune intoned in the distance by an invisible player.
—ALBERT EINSTEIN[84]

Imagine watching a time-lapse video of a familiar busy road. Two times every twenty-four hours there'd be a pulse in the volume of traffic when for a moment cars might lurch to a stop, hood to trunk. Then, just like that, the artery would unclog and flow would resume. This strange phenomenon is commonplace enough to have a name: rush hour. Traffic patterns are based on the standard working day; business hours, in turn, are established around our natural human periods of sleep and wakefulness, arising from the rhythm of night and day. This diurnal pattern comes from the orbiting of Earth around our sun, which takes part in the spiraling movement of the galaxy.

My, didn't *that* escalate quickly! Who knew highway traffic was a secret portal into a mystical vision of the rhythmic dance of the universe? But life's just like this, isn't it? Objects from disparate corners of our experience turn out to share a common pattern: departure and return, inhaling and exhaling, waxing and waning, rising and falling. Like rush hour returning anew each day, things cycle back around on themselves without ever returning to exactly the same spot. They both repeat and move onward, outward.

It is a spiral form: a shape combining a circle and a line,

embracing and directive, feminine and masculine. Spirals have apparently fascinated humans since we began painting them on the walls of caves 26,000 years ago. Everywhere we look, the world provides examples of the beauty and utility of spirals, from a spider's web to a nautilus shell, from the simple functionality of a corkscrew to a propeller thrusting forward in space. It's no wonder that St. Dionysius the Areopagite considered the spiral "the highest type of movement, the form most befitting the angelic powers."[85]

Childbearing also shares this form. The formation of a baby's body is like the revelation of a thousand spirals. He is conceived during a single hundred-hour fertile window of his mother's ever-repeating menstrual cycle. He curls up on himself in the womb like a little Fibonacci diagram. He grows to the rhythmic beating of two drums: the faster one, his heartbeat, rocks him from the inside; the slower one, his mama's heartbeat, throbs loudly all around him and in the ringlets of his umbilical cord. He is knitted together along the lines of several spirals that mark him as unique: the double helix of his DNA, the concentric swirls of his fingerprints, and the spiraling folds of his developing cerebral cortex.

When he is ready, labor begins—itself a hypnotic circling dance. Its timing appears to be affected by daylight and darkness, summer and winter, or (one might put it) the orbiting of planets.[86] As labor is established, it too gains a fractal shape with many nested spirals, something like a fern whose tiny curling fronds make up bigger curling fronds, which compose the biggest curling frond: the plant itself. In this same way, the shape of labor appears the same when viewed on different levels. Each contraction grows from nothing to a powerful summit, slowly easing off until it comes to a resting place on the other side about a minute later. Likewise, over the course of many hours labor builds to an intense climax, with each contraction coming on stronger than the last until the baby comes. Even the path the baby takes as he is born traces a spiral shape while he pivots to navigate the landmarks of his mother's accommodating pelvis.

These same embodied rhythms pulse through the life of mothering, too. Within an hour or so of birth, a newborn has navigated instinctively to his mother's nipple, latched himself on, and drunk himself to sleep, but very soon, he's awake again, smacking his lips and bobbing his head. He needs to return to the breast often, because breastmilk is easily digested and his stomach is tiny, the size of a little marble on the first day. For the next couple of months at least, he'll be asking for milk every few hours around the clock. "Again and again in peace," we almost hear his mama say, echoing the words of the prayer. She has moved seamlessly from the liturgy of labor to the liturgy of breastfeeding.

There are the womb rhythms we seek to recreate for our babies as they learn to live in the world: the sweet endlessness of rocking, pacing and bouncing with a crying baby, the shushing that sounds like the pumping of blood in a placenta. There are the lilting nursery rhymes from which they learn their mother tongue. The other practical work of parenting tends to be highly repetitive, too. There are the liturgies of diapers and dishes— those tasks that need to be repeated as soon as they are complete.

Why should God choose to place these patterns at the heart of our family experience—indeed, of our human experience? He is drawing us in toward His love. Rhythm has the power to bring us closer. Think of the campfire ceremony of dancing and drumming that unites a village tribe, or a concert venue packed with thousands of people all jumping in synchrony. How about an army marching to war to the sound of bugles and drums, or a lullaby passed down the generations?

Scientists investigating the bonding effects of rhythm looked at the brain activity of people doing a task while listening to a strong beat, and found that the group members' brainwaves harmonized nearly instantaneously.[87] Likewise, amid the repetitive beat of the postpartum period, mothers and babies become highly attuned to one another, entering into each other's biological rhythms as both a cause and an effect of their bond. A mother cuddling her newborn can unconsciously monitor and stabilize his body temperature. She raises or lowers it as necessary by adjusting her own temperature, in a way even the most sophisticated incubator cannot. Throughout his early months, if they sleep next to one another, the sleep cycles of mother and child will also converge, making it easier for the mother to wake to meet her baby's nighttime needs.

The same cyclical experiences that harmonize us with one another can also bring us into step with our Maker. The rhythm of the Church gives us a taste of this delicious synchronicity. Again, its shape looks the same zoomed right in as it does panned out. The overall shape of salvation history is an arc that bends away, then comes back to its proper place: a return to the Garden, so to speak. On a personal level, we also follow a cycle of repentance that takes the pattern *fall down—get up—fall down—get up*.

The Church's liturgical life is composed of a series of concentric cycles, too. There's the church year, with each feast, fast, season, and color appearing in its appointed time; inside it, the routine of each week is established around a Paschal celebration on the Sabbath; and within the week, every day is ordered by a personal rule of prayer, often some variation on the monastic services of the hours. On a micro level, our prayer itself often takes a rhythmic form. "In the name of the Father, and of the Son, and of the Holy Spirit," we begin, crossing ourselves with our habitual movement. "Lord, have mercy," we chant so many times that it becomes as constant as our breath.

These rhythms are the Church's way of passing the time, and not just passing, but *redeeming* it (Eph. 5:16)—of reaching into the *chronos* of tick-tock time and pulling out the *kairos* of eternity. The daily grind becomes a smoothing of the rough places in our souls. Repetition fosters in us a humility that reminds us that we are a small part of something much bigger than ourselves. Our hearts become softer, more porous, more receptive to God and our fellow humans. With every repetition, love seeps a little deeper into us.

But if entering into the rhythms of life is heavenly, being out of step with them can feel hellish. What could be "the never-ending dance of love"—a spiral reaching toward the infinite—instead becomes "a descending vortex, sucking us down into annihilation."[88] This can happen in two ways, when we stress one aspect of the spiral to the detriment of the other. If we overplay the directional aspect of the line, we get obsessed by progress and control, and lose the sense of being in the current moment; if we overplay the recurrent aspect of the circle, we feel trapped in a feedback loop and lose hope.

Let's address these two imbalances one at a time. When we make an idol of progress, we can be tempted to squeeze life into a shape of our own making, blasting a tunnel through rock rather than working with the contours of the land in which we find ourselves. Quickly we get out of sync with the natural order of the universe, and this can have unintended consequences. For instance, those who travel frequently or work on rotating shifts may be successful at satisfying their employer but go on to develop sleep, mood, or digestive disorders. In the arena of birth, we use medications to force labor to begin, sometimes simply because our patience has worn thin or our doctor is going out of town, and risk endangering our babies in the process. As mothers, we may expect our newborns to sleep and feed according to our preferred schedule right from the womb, and we get consternated when they continue to dance to their own inner rhythms.

When we're inclined to overemphasize the line at the expense of the circle, rhythm can offer a corrective. For instance, mothers who cope beautifully with labor all seem to have in common that they manage to sync with its tempo. Rather than dancing to the beat of their own will, they simply come into step with the instinctive rhythms coursing through their bodies. Some will stand during contractions, rocking their pelvis like a belly dancer. Some find rituals to greet a new contraction. Some repeat aloud a certain phrase over and over in order to hold on to an encouraging thought. Some use the power of sound waves, raising their voices to moan, moo, roar, or even sing through the intensity. Still others thrive on repetitive massage strokes from a support person on their backs or hips.

With these cycles, we are gradually drawn into a sort of hypnotic trance. We close our eyes. Our head lolls. We withdraw and speak a minimum of words. To someone on the outside, it may look as if we have vacated our bodies, we are off on another planet, we have absconded from the present. In fact, the opposite is true. In these moments we are so utterly focused on what is happening inside us that there is no bandwidth to spend on anything else.

That can work as an antidote to the one side of the problem, but what if we take things too far the other way? When we make an idol of repetition, we can come to regard life as a vicious cycle, with no way out of the monotony. We're like a child in the back seat of a car, starting to think we're always circling, never progressing, and asking again and again, "Are we there yet?" We become like the monk St. John Cassian describes, who "looks about anxiously this way and that . . . and frequently gazes up at the sun, as if it was too slow in its setting"[89]—the desert version of constantly glancing at our watch or our phone. The discontented voice inside us always wonders what's next, rather than embracing the moment at hand.

In the life of motherhood, this can be a particular pitfall. Amid messes that are made even as others are cleaned up, we lose our sense of purpose. We think of ourselves as Sisyphus, that unfortunate king from Greek mythology who was condemned to push a stone up a hill. Every time he neared the top, the stone would roll back down, undoing his great efforts in the blink of an eye. After a morning folding laundry, even as the hamper refills, we too may think, *I'm right back where I started.* We fantasize about how much easier things will be when our work is finally done. *Once my baby sleeps through the night,* we might think, *life will be much easier.* When that moment comes and we are still discontented, we simply move the goalpost. *No, actually: once my baby weans,* that's *when I'll have it made.* Then *once he's weaned* becomes *once he's potty trained; once he's potty trained* becomes *once he's at school.* But that elusive point always remains just beyond our fingertips.

In labor too, we can be tempted to think nothing's progressing. Ten hours in and wanting to know how far we have to go, we may submit to an uncomfortable internal examination. Sometimes, of course, these checks are proposed for medical reasons, for instance when a midwife needs to check the baby's position, suspecting labor might flow better if the mother changed her own position to encourage him to move. Mostly, though, they are suggested simply because time has passed since the last check and people are getting curious. But a dilating cervix is not a crystal ball: its current measurement cannot forecast how soon the baby will be born. A woman might spend days with her cervix open to four centimeters, then suddenly have it yawn to ten centimeters and birth her baby half an hour later. Yet we continue to measure progress using these numbers, as if our bodies were machines on a production line.

Certainly, it's normal to crave information in an uncertain situation, but as with the skygazing monastic, unfortunately every glance at the sun can make us feel worse. In my experience, a woman who is told how dilated her cervix is may often be disappointed by the news. Before the midwife has finished speaking, her mind has created a mathematical model of the situation forecasting the number of hours of labor still ahead. She forgets that "He made everything beautiful in its time" (Eccl. 3:11). She may become disillusioned with the body that is actually serving everyone so well. She struggles to keep sight of the coping mechanisms that hitherto have been working so beautifully. The pain of labor, which previously seemed like a healthy challenge to rise to, now becomes an overwhelming ocean of subjectivity from which she will never be released. She would not have faced this had she simply declined to be examined in the first place.

There are other, healthier ways to mark time in labor, honoring the linear dimension of the spiral so that we don't get stuck in the circular aspect. We need to be told by a doula or nurse, a husband or partner that there is movement, that everything is progressing just as it should, that this will not go on forever, because in the intensity of the moment we may be unable to remember this by ourselves. In addition, dividing labor into a series of manageable tasks helps us mark our progress.

Our breath is a wonderful tool to help with this. Respiration has its own rhythm, which continues whether we are aware of it or not. Some women follow a prescribed breathing pattern they have been taught; many cope by simply bringing their awareness to their own instinctive breathing patterns. When one laboring client started to panic and hyperventilate, I began counting breaths with her. Exhaling slowly together, we noticed that each contraction only lasted five or six respirations. By getting through five breaths, she could get through a contraction, and by getting through one contraction at a time she got through labor.

In labor—as in motherhood and life—we thrive best by embracing both the directional and the cyclical aspects of the spiral. Let us strive always to enter into the returning pulse of the present, without losing sight of the goal toward which we are pressing.

Thoughts

*There is an interaction and mutual influence of the soul
toward the body and vice versa. . . . The attributes of each
communicate with each other because of the ineffable and
natural bond which unites the soul and the body, even though
the exact reason for this remains essentially unknown.*
—ST. NICODEMOS OF THE HOLY MOUNTAIN[90]

n his book entitled *Our Thoughts Determine Our Lives,*
twenty-first–century Elder Thaddeus of Vitovnica
teaches:

*Our life depends on the kind of thoughts we nurture. If our
thoughts are peaceful, calm, meek, and kind, then that is what our
life is like. . . . We also influence ourselves and radiate peace all
around us—in our family, in the whole country, everywhere. This
is true not only here on earth, but in the cosmos as well. . . . However, when we breed negative thoughts, that is a great evil. When
there is evil in us, we radiate it among our family members and
wherever we go. So you see, we can be very good or very evil.[91]*

The elder explains why our thoughts have such efficacy:

*In our minds we conceive everything we do, say, and plan. With-
out this, we cannot do or say anything. Everything first receives
its shape and form in the mind: all of our energy is first made*

manifest in our thoughts. Thoughts are the power that conceives
everything in the center of our being (our heart).[92]

This mystery lies at the heart of our Christian experience. Miracles of matter and mind are our daily currency, our bread and butter. We worship a Creator by whose Logos the universe came into being. "In the beginning was the Logos, and the Logos was with God, and the Logos was God. He was in the beginning with God. All things were made through Him, and without Him nothing was made that was made" (John 1:1–3). Though *Logos* is usually translated "Word," it means more than just a verbal expression. It's more like an organizing principle—in this case, where it appears with a capital letter L, it means *the* organizing principle of the cosmos. It is the glue holding everything together, giving all things their form, their ground for being. In this, Logos is *like* a word, since our words are also an organizing principle, giving form and structure to our thoughts.

And so God uses His words to draw things out of nothingness into being: the phrase "Let there be" was all it took (Gen. 1:3). As the Psalmist notes, "He spoke, and they were made; / He commanded, and they were created" (Ps. 148:5). As beings made according to the image of the Logos, we humans share in this creative energy. We are not mere lumps of clay—we are lumps of clay filled and transformed by divine breath, capable of bringing shape to the world around us. We can make a choice and carry it out. We can pray in our hearts and see God work an answer to our prayer in the world. We can speak, and it becomes so. We can purify ourselves, and others see the skin of our faces shine. We can eat wine-soaked bread from a spoon and find our souls healed.

But it's not only Christian theology that makes the interaction between spiritual and material evident: such miracles are part of the fundamental experience of being human in the world. I see a baby lick a lemon for the first time, and my own mouth fills with saliva. I think of an intense experience from the past, and my cheeks flush and my heart pounds as if I were there all over again. I speak a soothing word, and my child relaxes. An athlete visualizes herself soaring over a hurdle and completes her race with a better finish time. A person's amputated limb itches just as badly as the one still attached to his body.

But there could be no better anecdotal evidence than that which birth provides. One midwife relates the story of a remarkable experience with a client having her second baby. At some point in labor, the midwife gave her client an internal exam to see how far her cervix had dilated. As she was doing so, the birthing woman sighed, "I just want to open up and let this baby out." To the midwife's astonishment, with these words, her client's cervix "yawned open another two centimeters beneath my fingers. . . . Pretty fancy, I thought, to be able to tell your body exactly what you want to happen and have it comply."[93] It wasn't long before that child was in its mama's arms.

Another birth worker, this time an obstetrician, tells of being with a mother who was frantic and hyperventilating at the height of labor. She advised her, "When a contraction comes, see if you can't go somewhere else in your mind." And this is exactly what she did. The woman became completely still. At first the helpers wondered if her labor had stopped, but the monitor indicated contractions were still coming every three minutes. After a time, the woman suddenly opened her eyes and pushed her baby out. At a follow-up visit later, the OB asked the woman where she had been all that time she was so quiet. "I went to a white room," she said. "My favorite uncle, who died recently, was there chatting with me. It was a beautiful spiritual experience." (The doctor confided she'd never worked with a departed uncle-doula before and never suspected they could be so effective.)[94]

How can it be: one woman opens her womb by the power of her mind, and another gets physical endurance to birth her child from communing spiritually with the dead? Leafing through a modern obstetrics textbook, we won't find much in the way of recognition, let alone explanation. Whether our thoughts can really effect changes in the physical world is considered a question for pop psychology, not gynecology. But to birth attendants in other ages, the answer would have been straightforwardly obvious. Old medical texts contain tales from nineteenth-century physicians of established labors that were suddenly suspended upon their arrival and sometimes didn't resume until weeks later.[95] The surprise of having an unfamiliar man enter her bedroom, it was observed, was enough to put a woman's body on hold until she felt safe to proceed.

Such effects aren't just a quaint vestige of older times. Experience shows that labor is still inhibited by stimulation of the neocortex through excess talking, questions, and eye contact from birth companions. The difference is, in earlier times the influence of the mind on the body was treated as an asset rather than a flaw. What in a modern hospital would be diagnosed "failure to progress" and treated with a C-section was regarded as the *success* of the woman in protecting her baby against a perceived threat to their safety or modesty, calling for greater sensitivity from the attendants.

If sometimes our thoughts have a positive function in labor, though, they can also be disruptive in a negative sense, making our job harder. The Church Fathers speak of the dangers of giving in to our *logismoi*—the intrusive thoughts or images that plague even the holiest saints. They come to us unbidden, always flowing past on the tide of our minds, imploring us to adopt them and make them our own. The danger comes when we stop to engage them in conversation, then eventually invite them to stay. Once they have penetrated our heart, they take us hostage, drowning us in a disorienting deluge. While the Logos provides the true reference point for all of reality, its etymological cousins the logismoi become a false lens through which we perceive the world—little counterfeit versions of the Logos, so to speak, clouding rather than clarifying our vision of the truth. While the Logos organizes things into a coherent whole, logismoi divide our minds into a million dissipated pieces.

The logismoi that come to us in labor usually converge around our pain. The thought *ouch* appears, beckoning us to follow it down a dark path. It's no sin to have such an impression; it's how we respond to it that is the issue. If we let the thought be, it passes. If we latch onto it, it leads us to the next one, a little further down the road: *This is really bad.* Next we come to *Poor me!* Before we know it we've reached a state of mind where our pain is all that exists: *I'm dying! This is never going to end! Somebody just kill me now.* We have lost all sense of control over our fate; we have become nothing more than slaves to our impressions.

Looking at the situation through the lens of Logos rather than logismoi, we see that this trap is an illusion. No matter how intense the sensation or how few the alternatives, even in the most desperate of circumstances, we retain a measure of creative control. In labor, as in many of life's hard situations, we cannot always choose a way out of the experience, but we can always choose a way in.

Viktor Frankl, an Auschwitz survivor, wrote, "Everything

can be taken from a man but one thing: the last of the human freedoms—to choose one's attitude in any given set of circumstances."[96] We need not assent to every tempting thought that comes by; we can decide how to respond, from self-pity and cursing to resolve and thanksgiving. This is the radical freedom of the young mothers Ss. Perpetua and Felicity exchanging the kiss of peace among hungry beasts in the amphitheater, of the Three Holy Youths praising God in the midst of the flames (Dan. 3:51)—and it can be ours as well.

If we are not captive to the destructive thoughts of labor, how will we use our freedom to tackle them? The Church Fathers recommend a spirit of *nepsis*, or attentive watchfulness, so that we can see these thoughts coming and be on guard. Nepsis is a sentinel who looks out for intrusive thoughts trying to scale the wall of our hearts under cover of darkness. The *Philokalia* defines it as "the opposite to a state of drunken stupor; hence spiritual sobriety, alertness, vigilance."[97] In labor, a spirit of nepsis might mean simply stopping to be mindful of my thoughts and feelings as contractions come and go. They may be very intense, but instead of being entirely sucked in by them, I can stand aside a little and regard them as "interesting sensations that require all of [my] attention."[98] Observing without engaging with my logismoi in this way allows me simply to let them drift past. There is no need to do battle with them rationally. Like flies zipping around a room, Mother Gavrilia says, logismoi will leave when they find no food.[99]

What constructive thoughts will take the place of the logismoi? Having avoided the destructive power of our thoughts, how can we harness the creativity Elder Thaddeus speaks of? Our goal, as the Fathers of the *Philokalia* remind us, is to put the mind into the heart (also known as the *nous*): that is, to bring our busy thoughts to rest in the quiet center of our being where we are at one with God.

Some mamas use "birthing affirmations." They may repeat their chosen words as part of a guided relaxation, visualizing mental images to go with them. Or they may write their selected phrases onto cards and display them around their home, or string them into a banner to decorate the birthing room. Often, birth companions pick up on the phrases, encouraging a woman by using the words she herself chose. As with all our words, we are wise to use discretion in choosing birth affirmations. Some phrases we read in childbirth preparation books sound like prayers to the universe, the female body, or birth itself, rather than to God. Other affirmations use terms drawn from faiths contrary to Christianity: *om*, for example, isn't just a meaning-less syllable but evokes a theological concept that sits uncom-fortably with Christian faith. I needn't use a phrase just because I found it in a book. Instead, I can choose the words that speak most to me as a Christian and as an individual:

I was made for this work. I birth my baby with ease. I surrender. My mothers did this, and so can I. Breathe, open, release. Or simply, *Relax.* I might pick verses from Scripture, such as: *See, I have set before you an open door, and no one can shut it* (Rev. 3:8). *Do not be afraid* (Luke 1:30). *The joy of the Lord is your strength* (Neh. 8:10). *He will comfort those with young* (Is. 40:11). *I shall not die, but live, and tell of the Lord's works* (Ps. 117/118:17). *You possess my heart, O Lord; You took hold of me from my mother's womb* (Ps. 138/139:13). *As the eyes of the maidservant look to the hands of her mistress, / So our eyes look to the Lord our God* (Ps. 122/123:2). And above all, *I can do all things through Christ* (Phil. 4:13).

SIX

Becoming a Parent

Expertise

Do not trust in rulers and in the sons of men,
In whom there is no salvation.
—PSALM 145(146):3

Trust in God with all your heart,
And do not exalt in your own wisdom.
—PROVERBS 3:5

Today begins a new leg of our pilgrimage through pregnancy. Having spent much of the journey so far pondering gestation and birth, over the next six weeks we'll cast our eyes a little further down the road to the initial weeks of life with a baby. We live in an age when most people enter parenthood feeling completely unprepared, but when we attend to the deep purpose of our journey, every moment of pregnancy becomes a chance to gather the wisdom we will need in our new roles.

I'LL NEVER FORGET HOW IT FELT, my first day as a mother. After a sleepless night of labor I'd given birth when the sun was high in the sky, but by the time the midwife left us in the later afternoon, the washing machine was humming with receiving blankets and the living room was so tidy no one would have guessed it had just been the scene of a major event. The door clicked shut behind our last visitor, leaving just my husband, our squishy pink perfect child, and me—our family. It was the moment of contentment we had longed for.

My reverie was broken by a sudden flood of urine against my shoulder. Our son's first diaper had burst its banks. Apparently the theoretical knowledge that as parents we'd be changing diapers hadn't yet translated into the practical realization that we'd actually need to do it, many times a day. And we'd never actually changed a diaper before, except for one we'd managed to put on a friend's baby backwards.

This diaper change too was only a mild success, so I went to give our son a bath. Though his body was so slippery and his head so floppy it was terrifying, between the two of us we managed not to drop him in the water. My husband proudly chose a little outfit from the waiting stash, but getting each sleeve over every single one of the relevant fingers at the same time without breaking any proved tricky. Now our little one was crying, so I settled into the best chair and carefully latched him on. He seemed to know what he was doing—I, less so. I wanted several more arms than I had and was concerned my baby wouldn't get any air with his nose right up against me. I needn't have worried whether all was functioning as it should: my efforts were rewarded with both spit-up (all over the selected outfit) and a very sticky meconium poop. So the evening went on.

As night rolled around, I was surpassing frontiers of exhaustion I'd never known existed. The sheer responsibility of keeping someone else alive, combined with loss of sleep during labor, was a powerful cocktail. How I looked forward to bedtime, when I could put this baby down and go to sleep! My bed looked softer and sweeter than ever. Finally the stars aligned and our baby was in his basket, clean and fed and sleeping. But as my head hit my own pillow, a strange sound stirred in the quiet darkness: a bone-chilling chirpy wheeze from the baby's corner of the room. He couldn't breathe! Like a shot, I was out of bed with the light on. My baby grimaced awake, wondering what the fuss was about, and gave a reassuring little sneeze.

But throughout that first night my husband and I slept for only minutes at a time, every sound from our child's mucusy newborn lungs rousing us to acute but helpless vigilance. With the new day's light, it began to dawn on us: our son's needs were a continuous cycle of dependence that continued around the clock with utter disregard for our inexperience. We wondered: *Isn't there someone better qualified for this tremendous job? How could everybody up and leave him with us when we have no . . . idea? Wait, what about tomorrow night? Is this what it's going to be like* forever? I felt like placing an emergency call to the midwife: *You mean, we're in charge now?*

I've heard a variation on this story from most every client I've served. Getting ready to leave the hospital, new parents tell me, they signed discharge papers, shouldered their bags, took their baby, and walked right through the revolving glass door. Passing security, they felt like imposters, somehow, thieves—utterly unfit to be transporting such precious cargo. *How could they let us get away with this?* Even experienced parents say they forgot how tiny and reliant a newborn really is. It seems to be a rite of passage for every freshly minted parent: the terrifying and exhilarating moment when we first realize, the buck stops here.

In such a moment of self-doubt, my natural inclination is to look for an "expert": someone who seems to know better than I do. For me that first night, it was the midwife. But equally it may be a fellow mother whose baby is a stage ahead of my own. I dash quickly out to buy whatever piece of equipment she recommends in hopes of ever having a life one-tenth as put-together as hers appears. Or maybe I turn to a parenting expert whose bestselling book outlines the latest baby-care method. For the price of a paperback, it promises an easy life if I follow its prescriptions to a tee. With millions of copies sold, I figure there must be something to this advice.

It's only reasonable that I should feel small before the task of acquainting an entirely new human with the ways of the world. On such shifting sands, who wouldn't want self-assurance that could be purchased for $12.99? If I could, why wouldn't I retain a little control, a little predictability, a little order? Who would fault me for turning to those with greater experience? And that is what an "expert" is: from the Latin word meaning "to try," an expert is someone who is tried and tested, who has learned from experimentation and experience.

Yet the paths that look like shortcuts to expertise sometimes lead me astray. Heaven forbid I should forgo all advice from those more experienced than myself. And doubtless each of the various parenting paradigms and products of our time has its own merits. But following *any* particular prescriptions too slavishly turns my attention away from the real baby with whom I am forming a relationship. Instead, my focus becomes directed inward onto myself (*Am I doing this right?*) or projected away onto the details of the method itself (*How long till I'm supposed to feed him next?*). I assess myself and my baby according to the standards of the system, and if we deviate from the textbook, I presume the flaw is not in the method but in us. Family life becomes less about curious observation, mutual response, and creative experimentation, and more about effective performance, efficient management, and iron imperative.

The fact is, no one can be a *general* expert in parenting. If anyone has knowledge, it has been gained through highly specific relationships with particular people. There are many experts in the world—mothers of ten, developmental psychologists, PhDs in lactation support—but none of them has experienced *this* child: the one whom God has given *me*.

And this baby is different. He is entirely new in the world. He is a unique package of particular gifts, needs, traits, tendencies, and quirks—an enigma too intricate to be encapsulated in one theory or "solved" with any trick. The method that works a charm for every baby on the block may not even touch him. I won't know until I try that it's something totally different that he needs. He offers me the chance to learn not just to be *a* mother, but *his* mother, responding to his distinctive character as it is presented to me. His pedagogical methods are unique: no other child, and certainly no adult, could impart these precise lessons. And there are no shortcuts to this knowledge. It cannot can be transfused but only gained slowly, through trial and error with the actual person whom God gives into my care.

The challenge we face, then, is to give our own motherly knowledge its proper value alongside others' advice. The experience clock does not start ticking at birth. After carrying my baby as near as my own heart for many months, I am as close to an authority as anyone comes. Maybe I've noticed some patterns to my baby's movements, different times of day that are busier than others, which like the movements of a new neighbor acquaint me with the habits of a person I've not officially met. I may know physiological "facts" such as whether my baby is male or female, and whether or not development looks to be proceeding typically. Perhaps I even have a deep inner sense of who this person is: a familiarity with him based on an intuitive kind of knowing that does not need facts.

Or maybe it all remains clouded in mystery. But no matter how profoundly aware I am of the limitations of my maternal knowledge, it runs deeper than I might remember. Well before our babies are born, our very bodies contain a great wordless wisdom, and perhaps recognizing that can show us the way toward trusting our inner sources of knowledge, too.

One example is the cravings for which pregnancy is so notorious. The specific foods we desire are thought to reflect the nutritional needs of our growing child. Sometimes it's quite clear these urges don't arise from our own preferences, such as when we crave substances not normally considered food—for instance, dirt when we are deficient in iron. With little conscious knowledge of our child's needs, our bodies are able to pinpoint and provide for them in the most specific ways.

This is evident in labor, too: though I may be unaware of my baby's position, I move my body into postures that ease his way. If his hand is up next to his face so that his descending head needs a little more room on one side, I will instinctively raise a leg on that side. No one needs to tell me which foot to put up on the stool: I know. After birth, my instincts continue to inform my parenting. On a whim I may walk in on my child at just the right moment, or reach out an arm to catch him not a second too soon. Such motherly hunches must have averted countless mishaps over the course of human history, and the world would likely be very different without them. It's this profound intuitive, embodied, relational knowledge of our babies that we bring to parenting from before our first day on the job. No magic formula, product, or method can replace it.

And our babies have their own expertise to contribute, too. We see this with the newborn "breast crawl." If he's healthy and alert after birth, a child only minutes old will work his way up from his mother's stomach to her chest and latch himself on. With the help of his stepping reflex, he digs his heels in and inches toward his mama's nipple. Her areola, which has darkened throughout pregnancy, provides him a clear target. Without full head control, he nevertheless bobs around until the nipple meets the roof of his mouth, triggering the sucking reflex which has been developing since his thirty-second week in the womb. After half an hour of wriggling, he reaches his goal. His mother need not prompt or position him: if anything, it's he who shows her how this works.

Spiritually, too, our babies may be able to teach us lessons we may have forgotten. Though we adults regard ourselves as the ones who need to be wise in order to show children how to live, in some ways we are called to become more like them—to put away our grownup reserve and be reliant and joyful and trusting in a childlike way, as Christ teaches. He says, "Unless you are converted and become as little children, you will by no means enter the kingdom of heaven" (Matt. 18:3).

It's a mutual learning, then, that takes place in a family. We teach our children how to live as people in the world, and they teach us how to be parents. They begin with the lessons appropriate to their own stage, like how to hold up their head, or how to get someone's attention from across the room, and only very gradually move on to the more complex questions like how to cook an egg, or what it means to be a good friend. We too begin with the lessons appropriate to our stage, such as how our baby prefers to be held, or how to live deeper into the love that lays down one's life night in and night out. Over the course of many years we move on to questions like how much screen time is too much, or when to say yes if a teenager asks to use the car. Neither of us need know it all before we get started: little by little, we can grow alongside one another into our respective roles. If we gain any expertise along the way, it is the expertise of love.

The Latin word for love, *amare*, is the root of our English word *amateur*. An amateur does what she does not for reward or recognition, but for the love of it. In the eyes of the world, amateurish knowledge is considered lowlier than expertise. After all, what new parent would seek to become an amateur? But Christianity totally flips the precedence of experts over amateurs. In our faith, love wins over competence, humility trumps wisdom, and the servant is king. In fact, as St. Paul points out, "It is written: 'I will destroy the wisdom of the wise, / and I will set aside the understanding of the experts.' . . . Instead, God has chosen what is foolish in the world to shame the wise" (1 Cor. 1:19, 27 HCSB).

As amateur parents, like Paul we may feel as if we're "what is foolish in the world," especially compared to those who seem to know what they are doing. But it's exactly we foolish ones who are "chosen." Parenting creates new, humbler people of us, and these new selves bring low our old selves who thought they knew everything, or at least *should* know everything, in order that we can become more willing to learn. This opens us wider to our babies—not the babies the textbooks say they should be, nor the babies other women have, nor the babies their siblings may have been, but the people they actually are. It unfastens the gates of our hearts before God, from whom true wisdom flows.

Village

It is not good for man to be alone.
—GENESIS 2:18

It takes a village to raise a child. So this week, I'm asking, who's my village?

These days most of us don't live in an actual village—a quaint clutch of countryside cottages with smoke-streaming chimneys—so this isn't a question of geography. Instead, it's an issue of community: who are the people who celebrate and mourn with me? In which relationships do I find my belonging and purpose? Who are the ones I sustain, and am sustained by, in times of need? Or, in the words of the lawyer who questioned Jesus, "Who is my neighbor?" (Luke 10:29).

For new and expectant mothers, this is a vital question. At a stage when the very person we thought we were is being picked apart and stitched back together along raw new seams, we long for security among a welcoming tribe of mothers, grandmothers, aunts, sisters, cousins, and neighbors. We want the expectations of others to provide a structure in which we can find our own distinctive way. We yearn for living proof that the growth that threatens to stretch us to the point of bursting can be safely completed—that, like others before us, we'll live to tell this tale. We need to know that we will have their practical guidance as an anchor on the high seas of life with a tiny infant. Their wounds from this struggle, vulnerably shared, provide a sign that we are not alone. Their dignity gives us courage to follow them into a role which, be its tasks ever so humble, holds unquestionable value for the future of humanity.

Until very recently, daily living provided us with these bonds. The work of human existence was undertaken *together* inside a fairly small, cohesive community. Before engines were invented, our daily circles were only as wide as the terrain over which our legs could carry us. On the daily trudge to the village well, women could meet to exchange news and advice. Scrubbing clothes in the stream, they might confide, argue, cry, or sing with each other, albeit with one eye open for a straying infant or disoriented senior. As squads of young ones roamed from house to house, women would feed, shepherd, and co-mother their friends' children, just as their own mothers' friends had done for them. Visiting one another to help with bigger chores that were not to be done alone, they could hear from cherished elders about the old ways. When someone was sick, bereaved, menstruating, or postpartum, her ailments could be tended and her work covered by others who could serve, knowing their own moment of need would surely come in time. Life was hard and dirty and tiring, but it provided ample opportunity for rich, authentic, interdependent relationship.

Though a life of connection is our natural human habitat, the setting in which we are designed to thrive best, it's not the one in which we find ourselves. The villager is a vanishing species as even the world's most traditional societies become urbanized and industrialized. Now, most of us mother within four sound-proofed walls and have highly choreographed meetings with friends. Our convenient cars and washing machines keep us from meeting at the crossroads or riverbank. Relatives often live in faraway lands to which work has taken them, and we are lucky to see them a few times a year. Our peers are glimpsed through the rose-tinted lens of social media, giving us the impression we are the only ones with messy, loss-spattered lives. Our marriages are pressurized to the point of implosion as we attempt to fill all the village roles within a nuclear family. The priority with which we could be vesting our relationships is instead given to possessions: acquiring, cleaning, maintaining, organizing, and disposing of them.

Though we are freer and more leisurely than previous generations, we hobble around wounded, neutralized, and impoverished. Without adequate support, we feel adrift, lonely, exhausted, depressed, anxious, guilty, inadequate, judged, and ashamed of our dependence on others. Through no fault of those who love us, our gaping need to see and be seen, know and be known by other human beings remains unmet. Pregnancy brings this truth out of the shadows and to the forefront of our attention. How aware it makes us of our own limitations! Some of us are able to turn to our own mother—the lynchpin of our village, the umbilical cord that ties each of us into our community. But many of us, for whatever reason, must become mothers without the support of a mother of our own. And few of us are so fortunate as to have experienced confidants we can come to with our darkest doubts and silliest questions. Cut off from the ones to whom we "should" be most closely moored, we float adrift.

Sometimes, like the distant memory of a familiar childhood smell, we'll catch the passing whiff of the metaphorical village, with its holy scent of bread rising, cook fires sparking, and incense seeping from under the church door. At women's retreats or a music festival, we'll fall back into rhythm with other human beings. On a trip to an agrarian country, or amid the din of a big family, we'll taste the pure joy of life shared. If we're fortunate we'll even get a bit of this from our maternity care. At birth classes, new parents' meetups, or even just in the clinic waiting room, women will exchange a meaningful glance or word that says, *I see you there. I'm here, too.*

Other times, we try to reconstruct the village from scratch. We'll join internet groups connecting us to "our tribe." These online spaces, with their own specialist acronyms, language, culture, and concerns, litter our feeds like virtual villages across the technological landscape. Whether we baby-wear, have a child born through embryo adoption, oppose vaccinations, or produce an oversupply of milk, there's a group for that. With a click, we jump from community to community, sampling a number to see where we feel most at home. The constraints of geography and time melt away, and at any hour we might care to visit the well, someone is there offering a continuous stream of advice and anecdotes from halfway around the world.

Among those crowded into our safe little niche, it seems we'd find some solace, and at times we do. But too often our online encounters prove to be a mirage, only contributing to the alienation we want to escape. Awash in a stream of constant content, we find little depth. Unlike in a true village, where for better or worse we are defined in conversation with other people, on the internet we define ourselves. Our self-selected affiliations serve only to confirm us in the suspicions we had all along. When we find things uncomfortable, we unfollow, unfriend, or block. The camps grow entrenched. The divisions between mothers are driven deeper. We sit alone, scrolling and clinging ever tighter to our personal philosophies.

Like the social media village, the baby shower represents another valiant attempt to resurrect the village under unfavorable historical circumstances. Throwing a shower has become *the* way to show love and support for a pregnant friend. In many an Orthodox parish, it almost seems to be one of the liturgies we serve. One woman from a southern US state confided that baby showers happened so frequently in her busy church that she had started to consider them a line in her weekly budget.

For women to gather as one of their own embarks on her maiden voyage into motherhood is far from unique to our culture. There are precedents in societies around the world, sharing certain universal elements: conversation and laughter, food and stories. But if we imagine describing our formula to a time-traveler recently arrived from another era, we realize how oddly prescriptive it is: a shower is a baby-themed party at which the honoree's friends present her with specific gifts she has chosen for her child in advance. The party's sub-theme may vary—forest creatures or childhood books, pink and navy decorations or green and blue; the guest list may be tweaked to include men and/or children. Still, the basic recipe remains unquestioned.

They're ubiquitous, they're often fun, but in my experience the average baby shower doesn't usually offer the kind of support that arises from deep knowing and being known. The women I work with often speak of the showers thrown for them with humble gratitude for their loved ones' generosity; they also express overwhelm at the task of organizing and storing all their bounty, and the flicker of a sense, somehow, of a missed opportunity.

Though experienced women at baby showers may tell stories from their births or early parenting in passing, the emphasis tends to be mostly on preparing the expectant mother as a consumer, not a person undergoing a profound spiritual and physical metamorphosis. Sage maternal advice centers around recommendations for recently released products. Brand names ricochet through the air like pinballs. It's as if these women's friends simply bought the baby a T-shirt: "300 cumulative years of mothering experience gathered in one room, and all I got was this lousy onesie." Though it's a disappointment, perhaps it should be no surprise that today's baby shower—a brainchild of the postwar consumer era born at the advent of the advertising industry itself—is better for corporations than for expectant mothers.

To many of us the materialism of such a rite of passage seems perfectly normal, but to people of other cultures, it can be foreign or even shocking. I recall the baby shower organized for me by a fellow expat while I was pregnant with my first baby in the Balkans. Throughout, one of the women who came—a local friend whose face bore the creases of her signature giggle— sat stiffly at one corner of the sofa. She later confided that she wanted to support me but struggled to figure out how to participate. She knew that gift-giving was a vital part of this ritual, but in all her fifty years, she had never bought a present for an *unborn* baby. To her mind, helping me assemble necessities for my child before his birth was tempting the devil, more akin to a curse than to a blessing.

And speaking of blessings, some communities have adopted the Blessingway ceremony as an attempt to reach the itch that the usual baby shower formula doesn't quite scratch. Like a shower, it's a gathering of the village, but with an emphasis on furnishing a woman's spirit rather than just her home. Sometimes those gathered read poems, tell stories, make music, or create art. They may wash the mother's feet, massage her, make jewelry for her to wear at the birth, or share intentions and prayers. At such events, I notice, true connection between people can shine through more readily. For Orthodox faithful, however, the trick with Blessingways is their heady cocktail of heterodox spirituality. Native American, Hindu, and Buddhist imagery is employed almost interchangeably to invoke the inner life. Such events express faith, but not a faith we share.

Perhaps the rise of the Blessingway is a sign that it is time for Christian women to develop new cultural ways of helping one another prepare for birth. Say my sister offered to throw me a shower: we could choose the parish hall as a venue, rather than a trendy brunch place, and begin festivities with a specially arranged Akathist open to the whole church community. When offered gifts, I might request home-cooked postpartum meals and charitable contributions for local foster babies in place of crib sheets and diaper pails. Rather than baby food tastings or playful quizzes, I could ask each attendee to decorate a card with a favorite quotation from Scripture or the Church Fathers, and string the cards together as a mobile for my baby. After the party, I might hand out prayer ropes and put my guest list to work as a prayer team supporting my family.

To center my budding parenthood within the faith in this way is to affirm that my village is the Church. Our Lord Jesus Christ, too, "looked around in a circle at those who sat about him, and said, 'Here are My mother and My brothers! For whoever does the will of God is My brother and My sister and mother'" (Mark 3:34–35). Likewise from the time of the apostles, the Church has served as the primary community for Christians: "Now all who believed were together, and had all things in common" (Acts 2:44–45).

But for some of us, this truth is a little abstract. What does church-as-village mean when parish life isn't particularly encouraging? What if work or transport arrangements stop me from getting to church often enough to develop meaningful relationships? How about when the only motherly advice I get comes from people who parented in another culture or era? In such situations I may grieve the death of the village all the more profoundly because deep connection is lacking precisely where I would most expect to find it.

There is yet solid hope, for the community of faith is not confined to its members still walking on the earth. Even when I feel isolated, I am in fact surrounded by the nurturing love of "so great a cloud of witnesses" (Heb. 12:1). These witnesses are the angels, saints, prophets, apostles, ascetics, and queens of old; but literally speaking, a witness is a *martyr*. Some martyrs, whose names we know and icons we venerate, shed their blood unto death on the sandy floor of Roman arenas; others shed their blood unto life on the crisp sheets of the birthing bed or the straw floor of the stable.

In "the God of Abraham, Isaac, and Jacob, the God of our fathers" (Acts 3:13), we are united to every generation of humanity upon the earth. Our true village is in fact the heavenly city on the hill, populated by throngs of our spiritual and physical forebears interceding for us—the God-bearing mothers, grandmothers, and foremothers through whose bodies the divine breath came into us. Above all is the Mother of God: by giving birth to Life, she gave us the fullness of life. In the words of St. John of Kronstadt, she is "truly our mother by grace in accordance with the words uttered by Christ on the cross to the beloved disciple: Behold thy mother! and to her: Behold thy son!"[100] Her prayers guide, strengthen, and support us, even when the earthly village fails.

Our communion with fellow heavenly villagers, our ancestors throughout all ages, may sound like a theory, but in fact we experience it in deep and concrete ways. I served once as doula for a woman who had been a young teenager when her mother died. Years later, her preparations for the birth of her first child brought a new cycle of grief. She could not share with her beloved mother the developments of her pregnancy. She grieved for the child she was expecting, who would never know his maternal grandmother in this world. She mourned the many pertinent questions she'd not thought to ask when her mother was alive. She couldn't glean from her experiences, get her advice, or ask her to attend the birth.

My client's time came, and as she labored, her mother was both conspicuously absent and curiously present. We spoke of her often, and every little mention wore a bit thinner the veil of death separating us, so that I felt I was getting to know this woman I'd never met. Midnight passed with the birth drawing near, ushering in this baby's birthday, which also happened to be my client's older brother's birthday. With a sudden smile, my client realized what this meant: she and her mother were each bringing their firstborn son into the world on the same date. They were going through their birthpangs together, decades apart. All along, her mother had been with her not only as a companion but as a co-laborer, *beside* her in this experience but also somehow *within* it. A long while after it seemed the time for growth in their relationship had passed, the shared experience of giving birth brought my client closer to her mother than ever, and perhaps closer than if she had been physically present.

With this way of looking at things, the border between earth and heaven, between the living and the dead, starts to blur. The village to which we belong starts to look less like a provincial settlement with dung-covered cobbled streets and more like a glorious eternal city in which we live with the mothers of this age, of every age, and of the age to come. When the human community falters, we do not need to reinvent the village, because a true and perfect village already exists. Here we are offered a deep encounter not only with those we meet at the village well, but with all those we meet at the wellspring of Living Water. When we need guidance, let us ask their prayers, wrapping ourselves more cozily in the communion of heaven like a blanket.

Nightwatch

"Let not your foot be moved;
Neither let him who keeps you slumber.
Behold, He who keeps Israel shall neither slumber nor sleep.
The Lord shall keep you;
The Lord is your shelter at your right hand."
—PSALM 120(121):3—5

It was 3:15 AM. My husband was snoring. I was not. I'd just fed my baby for the third time since retiring to bed for the night and was swooning with the effort of keeping my eyelids apart. The little person in my arms started to squirm, her two weeks of life on the outside insufficient to acquaint her with the novel sensations of digestion. I gave her squishy palm-sized tummy a little rub, but it didn't seem to help. Neither did she want more milk. Her conversational complaints slowly became a loud monologue of discontent.

My husband scooted deeper into his pillow. Briefly, I considered rousing him to go change our little one's diaper and see if that would help. Usually he did the honors at nighttime, offsetting the job that I, as the one with the milk, could not delegate. But he had been up late with a work deadline and would be getting up in a few hours to take our other children to Saturday morning violin lessons. Waking him to help might prove as much effort as changing the silly thing myself. Sighing unbecomingly, I swung myself out of bed and flicked on the light.

Through bleary eyes I noted the greeting card I'd pinned up

above the changing table. Sent by my sympathetic mother-in-law two babies previously, it was a prized possession. "We shall not all sleep," the cartoon baby was saying, "but we shall all be changed." *Little did St. Paul suspect*, I thought wryly, reaching for the wipes.

The fresh diaper did nothing for my baby's crying. It was now an all-out ululation, and I still had no idea what was wrong. The tension built in my jaw. Picking up my baby, I held her stiffly to my shoulder, swaying as comfortingly as the frustration swirling inside me would allow. My shushing was ineffectual and my coos, to the extent I could hear them over the screaming, sounded forced. Why could this baby not be quiet and sleep? How could my lucky husband sleep through this torturous sound? At this point I didn't care if her cries woke him. *I* hadn't had more than two consecutive hours' rest for a fortnight and I deserved sleep *now*!

Pacing over to the window, I looked out over a slushy winter night and the sleeping suburbs all around, my self-centeredness simmering just under a boil. Out of the corner of my eye, I saw a light flash dimly on. It came from the upstairs window of a neighbor's house. Lucky people, I thought, who can stay up till all hours of the night, safe in the knowledge that they can sleep in as long as they like on a Saturday morning! Here I have a human alarm clock, set to go off again in a couple of hours, without so much as an off switch.

But hang on: whose window was that? The light seemed to be coming at my friend's window, the one with a nine-month-old. Likely she was also up with her baby. Maybe I wasn't the only one. I felt a little anger drain from my shoulders. I thought of another friend with a newborn who lived on the other side of town and wondered if she was up, too. If I were a bird, I mused—a night bird soaring high above this sleeping city—at how many homes would I see a light burning? How long would it be until another window was illuminated, the warm light of attentive parental love spilling out into the Midwestern darkness? How often would a light go out, signaling all was once again well in that place?

Slowly it dawned on me that, far from being alone in my plight, I was part of a huge secret army of caregivers keeping vigil through this night. Right now, other mothers and fathers were feeding, rocking, soothing, changing, holding, and tending their babies. There were those up with an older child who had been sick or had a bad dream. There were parents in hospital, propped up next to incubators, or pacing linoleum floors as they labored to give birth. There were people caring for others not their children—beloved parents dying, or friends in crisis. There were those whose hearts, or whose monastery bell, had awakened them to pray for those in need. Like night watchmen, each of us took our turn to watch and to sleep, but at no time did the world have to keep turning without the collective witness of our love.

Looking out, I noticed myself quietly humming the tune of a nineteenth-century Anglican hymn. From deep inside me, its verses rose to the surface of my consciousness and up to God:

We thank thee that thy Church unsleeping,
While earth rolls onward into light,
Through all the world her watch is keeping,
And rests not now by day or night.

As o'er each continent and island
The dawn leads on another day,

The voice of prayer is never silent,
Nor dies the strain of praise away.

The sun that bids us rest is waking
Our brethren 'neath the western sky,
And hour by hour fresh lips are making
Thy wondrous doings heard on high.

As my voice died down, the baby in my arms grew a little heavier. Her protestations were interrupted now by little breaths of calm as sleep encroached. Her sweet smell rose to my nostrils like a cake starting to bake gently in the oven. Finally her warm body melded into mine, and I could feel the precise moment when sleep took her over. Still I stood at the window, the quietness ringing in my ears.

THIS WEEK, THE THIRD in our six-part series on life in the early days with a baby, we consider the challenge of "nighttime parenting." I find this a useful phrase, because it conveys the startling truth that we don't get to stop being parents for half the day just because our side of the earth is facing away from the sun. Before parenthood, we understand—in the abstract— that newborns don't sleep through the night. Having never encountered the brightness of the sunlight by which our bodies and societies are regulated, they are born without a circadian rhythm. To them as to God, the darkness is not dark; the night is as bright as the day (Ps. 138/139:12).

We know, too, that human offspring are born prematurely, relative to other mammals. While little horses, giraffes, wildebeest, and deer stand up just minutes after birth, for example, it takes our babies a good year to learn to walk. Initially, this makes them highly dependent. They cannot so much as throw off a blanket or turn over in the night without our help. It is not normal for them to sleep through, or to let us do so. We know all this.

Experiencing the reality of it, however, is a different matter. It's hard to convey how all-consuming sleep deprivation is— or even to recall it when one has not been there for a couple of years. New parents often speak of being *bone*-tired, *deathly* tired, and it does feel like a kind of death. Lack of good rest depletes us each day more and more, and yet we must find a way to carry on through the emptiness. The image of the burning bush, constantly spent but never used up, speaks deeply to our weary souls. (Fittingly, within Orthodoxy the burning bush is understood to prefigure the Theotokos, who must have seen her fair share of disrupted nights.) Far beyond a feeling, tiredness becomes a way of life—the foggy lens through which, however temporarily, we see the world. Slowly we realize there is no way back to normal. Normality itself has moved.

We dream of sleep-training our babies, to get them to rest through the night so that we can, too. Parenting authors have developed some elaborate methods to achieve this, some of which specify the timing, the duration, and even the amount of eye contact or touch for each nighttime interaction between parent and child. These schemes may "work" for some babies. (Lord knows, we sometimes just need something that works.) But they also come at a price. It takes a lot of effort to follow a rigid schedule rather than our babies' cues, which are so finely engineered to get a physical response from us. And even a scheme that works does not put us back in control of our sleep schedule—it simply puts the parenting author rather than the baby in the driver's seat!

But whether or not I sleep-train my baby, I will nevertheless need to sleep-retrain *myself*. Like a monastic novice, I take on a new rule of life that shakes up my former routines. My family is my little community; the bedroom where I tend my baby at night is my humble cell. Nighttime ministry is part of my vocation, and I wake from sleep regularly to do my service. Amid the hardships of this rule there is holiness; in its routines, liturgical shape; amid its isolation, solidarity and companionship. In order to master this training, I need to develop two skills: resting in peace and rising with thanksgiving. And, with the disturbed sleep of the third trimester, I have the chance to begin practicing now.

Of the two, restfulness seems to come more naturally; wakefulness doesn't always lend itself readily to thanksgiving. We spend many billions of dollars on prescriptions, apps, pillows, herbs, sleep studies, and therapeutic mattresses to counteract it. We fret over how long we slept, how deeply we slept, and the dreams we had—all in pursuit of the perfect eight uninterrupted and consecutive hours of sleep. (*As if!*, cries the chorus of new parents.) We speak of our night wakings as causing a sleep *deficit*, as though rest were justly owed to us and not a loving gift of God (Ps. 126/127:2).

However, historians have found that the division of the day into two distinct blocks—roughly, two-thirds devoted to wakefulness and a third for sleep—is a modern innovation. Before electric lighting was available in homes, there is evidence that people followed a different pattern. Sleep was segmented; night was considered a play of two acts separated by an interval. We'd go to bed when darkness fell, wake naturally for an hour or two during the middle of the night, then lie down for the "second sleep" until daybreak. The time in between was used for prayer, lovemaking, reading, writing, or even visiting. It's probably no coincidence that the monastic practice of waking for midnight prayer divides the night along exactly these lines.

We live in the era of the electric bulb and the LCD screen. When we're disturbed at 2 AM, it's most likely by a social media notification, not by happy friends on the doorstep. It isn't easy to revert to other ways. But it's helpful to know that our expectations for sleep, which seem so fundamental, are in fact socially mediated. When our adult rhythms clash with our newborns', arguably it is we, not they, who are out of step with nature.

Rather than feeling sorry for ourselves when we must wake with our babies, we can take a leaf out of our ancestors' book and use the chance to pray. Rather than cursing under our breath, we can practice thanking our babies for helping us to cultivate the night with prayer. Awakened in the dead of night, we can open our eyes, determinedly saying, "At midnight I [arise] to give thanks to You" (Ps. 118/119:62). Dragging ourselves from bed, we can feel Christ taking us by the hand, tenderly whispering, *Talitha, cumi*: "Little girl, arise" (Mark 5:41). As darkness weighs heavily on our eyelids and we have to blink ourselves awake, we can goad ourselves with the words we hope to hear from Christ at the resurrection of the dead: "Wake up, sleepyhead!" (see Eph. 5:14). As dawn light falls on our feeding babies we can cry, "From the morning watch until night, / Let Israel hope in the Lord" (Ps. 129/130:6). As we call it a day and get up for good, we can recall the night past as one well-used: "I remembered you on my bed, / I meditated on you at daybreak" (Ps. 62/63:7).

Our sleep retraining also requires that we practice a second skill: restfulness. We'd imagine that this would kick in naturally when we get the slightest chance. But for new parents, resting often requires some intention. The familiar advice is to "sleep when the baby sleeps," cobbling together a sufficient daily ration of rest from the naps a newborn takes around the clock. This sounds simple enough, and studies indicate it's the best way to get a good rest, as breastfeeding mothers synchronize their sleep cycles with their babies sleeping nearby and often wake spontaneously at the same time.

But doing this requires a mother entirely to reprioritize her life around the survival of her newborn and herself. Most newborns doze until they are hungry, dropping off again when their tummies are full, so a mother who literally sleeps whenever her baby sleeps spends every waking moment feeding her child. She has no time to buy, prepare, eat, or clean up after her own food; no time to bathe or wash her clothes; no time to call a friend or sit quietly just being herself; and certainly no time to devote to any older children. It may be possible for her to live this way for a time, but only if a team of helpers is committed to meeting her basic needs so that she can meet her baby's, and only if everyone is reconciled to a lower standard of tidiness and personal hygiene than they may be accustomed to.

Aside from practicality, another unexpected obstacle to sleeping when the baby sleeps is the vigilant instinct that many of us find suddenly switches on with great force once our baby is born. With the action of the Spirit brooding over the waters at the beginning of time (Gen. 1:2), we hover over their beds, just checking to see they're still breathing. In the morning, we rouse before they do, startled that they have not woken us. Occasionally this vigilance oversteps its bounds and becomes a troublesome hypervigilance. Even when we *can* sleep, we *can't*: our attentive brains refuse to switch off and insomnia strikes, or we rest without entering into deep sleep. "I sleep," as the Song of Songs puts it, "but my heart keeps watch" (5:2).

When we have trouble resting, the words of Psalm 126(127):1–3 remind us,

> *Unless the Lord guard the city,*
> *Those who guard it stay awake in vain.*
> *It is in vain for you to rise early,*
> *To awaken from your rest,*
> *You who eat the bread of grief,*
> *When He gives His beloved ones sleep.*

And the very next verse goes right on to say, "Behold, children are the Lord's inheritance; / The fruit of the womb His reward." By juxtaposing the topics of vigilance and parenthood, the Psalmist speaks directly to our strung-out souls. We are reminded that, as our children's maker, it is the Lord who is their keeper, and not we ourselves. While we're sleeping, He watches over them on our behalf. "I will both sleep and rest in peace," we can declare as we tuck ourselves in, "for You alone, O Lord, cause [my family] to dwell in [safety]" (Ps. 4:9).

Interruptions

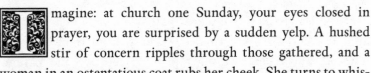

In unforeseen events let me not forget
that all are sent by Thee.
—MORNING PRAYER OF MET. PHILARET OF MOSCOW

Imagine: at church one Sunday, your eyes closed in prayer, you are surprised by a sudden yelp. A hushed stir of concern ripples through those gathered, and a woman in an ostentatious coat rubs her cheek. She turns to whisper to the person next to her, who leans to pick up something small, round, and brown from the ground. You feel something pelt you smartly in the back. Chaos is descending all around. Some people cry out; others come to their aid. The singing stops as your priest peers worriedly around the iconostasis.

Dashing up from the back of the church comes the figure of that old fool Symeon, your hometown Emesa's most notorious madman.[101] Behind his gruffness and a forelock of greying hair, his eyes are strangely bright, and today you see them glint mischievously as he flashes by. Quickly, he mounts the ambo, reaching into the pocket of his threadbare cloak and cackling as he bombards the most respectable members of your community with . . . what? "Nuts!" someone exclaims. An astonished deacon shoos him down, and several elders mount a pursuit. As delighted as a child winning a game of tag, Symeon dodges them all. A golden stand packed with lit candles wobbles and crashes to the ground, and a table replete with coffee-hour pastries is overturned before Symeon slips nimbly through the heavy doors, elaborately signing himself with the cross. While his spritely footfall fades away, the good people of sixth-century Emesa look at one another in bafflement, then quietly begin gathering nuts from the floor.

BEING PELTED WITH NUTS when I am *trying* to pray: that's how it often feels to be a mother. I can be in the middle of any-thing—a task, a thought, a mouthful, or a moment of rest—and, *bop*, an interruption from one of my children will intrude like a well-aimed nut. The most mundane needs (hiccups! poop! water! blankets!) barge to the front of the queue, demanding to be seen to *now*. If I delay, the urgency of the request only increases; if I try to teach my children to wait, that's another interruption.

My life lurches from one interval to another, apparently with-out moments of intention in between. I crave the chance to do something, *anything*, even use the toilet in peace. Yet I've grown so accustomed to these punctuations that I don't know how to live without them. So if for a moment no one interrupts me, I start interrupting *myself*. I break up my sentences into a chain of clauses and leave a trail of half-done projects around the house. Sometimes I reach the end of a day unable to identify a single thing I saw through from start to finish.

It starts in the postnatal period. The baby's hungry, so the beans on the stove burn; the baby fusses, so you hustle out the narthex door; the baby wakes, and in the bedroom a nascent moment of marital intimacy is snuffed out. But your children don't interrupt you any less when they get older—their inter-ruptions simply take other forms. While you're dressing, a young child begs for help tying her shoes. An older one heckles your conversation with comments of her own. You take a sick day off work when it's your schoolchild, not you, who's ill. A tween needs rides to umpteen activities, breaking up your day. You spend a long night waiting up for a teenager to come home after her first evening out. Even an adult child can command her mother's attention whatever hour of the day she might call.

If interruptibility is one of the arts of motherhood, pregnancy gives us plenty of opportunity to practice. Pregnancy is an interruption all its own, an interlude in the course of normal life, starting with the suspension of our menstrual cycle. Then comes the intrusion of nausea and vomiting. Next there's the phase punctuated by sharp kicks in various body parts we'd been unaware of until they were poked from the inside. By the time we've reached term, our day is broken into a multitude of little chunks, shards of time delineated by trips to the toilet, medical appointments, and exhaustion-fueled catnaps.

Childbirth, too, is a time set aside, an interruption to normal living and behavior. A birthing mother instinctively withdraws to an environment of privacy and darkness in which the hormones of birth most readily flow: in traditional societies, a hut or tent reserved for birthing and menstruation, and in ours a dim bedroom corner or a hospital shower. There, the flow of labor takes the form of contractions interspersed with restorative breaks. The respite is as much a productive part of labor as the work itself, and in terms of duration more so. In the end, it's hard to tell what's the interruption and what's the process being interrupted.

Sometimes the flow of interruptions itself gets interrupted; contractions don't merely get interspersed with rests, but stop altogether for a time. This can happen during the middle of labor if a woman feels disrupted or exposed. It's quite common, for example, for someone who was experiencing regular contractions every three minutes before she left home for hospital to find herself explaining half an hour later to a nurse, "Well, I *was* in labor . . ."

Other times, there can be an interruption toward the end of labor in the phase known among midwives as "rest-and-be-thankful." Once a woman's cervix is fully open, contractions may cease for minutes or even hours, allowing her and her attendants the chance to nap, eat a meal, or take a walk, gathering their energy before the final stretch. But practitioners who attend births in highly medicalized settings and aren't familiar with what happens when labor proceeds undisturbed can mistake these healthy biological mechanisms for a problem. They may diagnose a case of "stalled labor" and advise the woman she needs drugs to fire her body up again.

I too tend to see the normal interruptions of motherhood in a bad light. In my darker moments, I catch myself thinking of my children as Interrupters-in-Chief—an inconvenience, an annoyance, the enemies of my productivity. When an elderly lady in the park says tenderly to me, "Such beautiful days. They go so quickly. Enjoy every moment!" I wonder what on earth she is talking about. I might enjoy a moment if I *had* a moment. But what moments are there to enjoy amid all the interruptions? Our profit-motivated society feeds this temptation. Maternal selflessness is not regarded as heroic; a mother's children are seen as disrupting not just her time but also her economic productivity, which is the capitalist measure of human worth. The childbearing years are defined mainly in the negative, as a glitch on a woman's résumé, a time when she isn't making money or advancing her career.

Interruptions can even appear troublesome viewed from within our life of faith. For many followers of Christ, the disruption of the prayer life is one of the hardest aspects of new parenthood. I may wish I could devote unbroken time to standing in the icon corner or in church, concentrating my attention on God. By contrast, the real-life prayer time I am able to snatch at the steering wheel, the changing table, or the kitchen sink looks inferior. I yearn for some imagined future when I will have the leisure and the inclination to pray with concentration for whole swathes of time. If I don't guard my heart in the Liturgy, the Cherubic Hymn, "let us now lay aside all earthly cares that we may receive the King of all," just rubs in any subsequent squawks from my baby.

The world offers us plenty of suggestions for increasing focus and productivity in our disjointed lives. We use bullet journals and switch off our phones at bedtime. We make monthly meal plans and limit our social media use. But what if there were a deeper solution? What if I stopped viewing the interruptions embedded in the path to parenthood as maddening? Could they be cobbles that pave the way for a smoother journey? Might an interrupted life be good training for the Kingdom? What if, instead of regarding my baby's interruptions as devilish, I recognized them as Christlike?

Much like St. Symeon of Emesa, the nut-throwing fool-for-Christ, our Lord was a big interrupter. When people spoke, Jesus listened attentively, so He didn't interrupt in that sense; nevertheless He continues to cut in on people's lives, overturning their worldly presuppositions in the most unexpected ways, as in the case of the money-changers' tables. His topsy-turvy, inside-out, upside-down gospel dethrones the mighty and lifts up the humble and meek. It transforms prostitutes into saints and exposes scriptural experts as hypocrites. Even the laws of nature are disrupted. A perilous storm is interrupted by His voice, a dead man strolls from his tomb, a basket of food feeds a whole crowd with leftovers to spare, and water becomes the most flavorful wine.

Christ was comfortable with interruptions from others as well. When children came to climb on His lap while He preached, He didn't shush them and tell them to wait quietly for their turn, but pointed out that His uptight adult followers might take a page from their book. When some men desperate to help their paralyzed friend ripped a hole in His host family's roof, our Lord did not tell them to *get down right now*, but turned His attention to the man in need and healed him on the spot. A blind beggar shouted at Him on His way into town, but He didn't hurry on to His next appointment; He stopped, heard the man out, and declared that his faith had made him well.

Perhaps most poignant of all illustrations of Christ's gracious dealing with intrusions is the miraculous raising of Jairus's daughter, inside which like a matryoshka doll is nested a smaller story, that of the healing of the hemorrhaging woman (Matt. 9:18–26; Mark 5:21–43; Luke 8:40–56). Unexpectedly, Jesus is approached by a temple ruler, a desperate daddy on a last-ditch mission. "My little daughter lies at the point of death. Come and lay Your hands on her, that she may be healed, and she will live," he begs.

The crowd surges around Jesus, pressing Him on to His destination of Jairus's house. But along the way He is stopped in His tracks. He has felt power drain from Him and turns to ask who touched Him. Trembling, a middle-aged woman emerges from the throng. She is suffering with a menstrual disorder, and though according to law she should have shut herself at home so as not to spread the impurity of her blood through physical contact with other people, she has ventured out of the house in hopes of catching a glimpse of Jesus. Seeing Him pass so closely, she was unable to resist reaching out for Him. But rather than conferring on Him the ritual taint of her condition, He conferred on her the wholeness of His. Far from being angered, Christ tells her, "Be of good cheer; your faith has made you well. Go in peace." And for the first time in more than a decade, she feels the flow dry up.

But no sooner has this encounter concluded than a messenger arrives from Jairus's house with terrible news. It is too late. "Your daughter is dead," the messenger tells the leader. "Why trouble the teacher any further?" The interruption of the hemorrhaging woman seems to have cost Jairus's dearest one her life. Yet Jesus proceeds to the house, which has now become a scene of loud mourning. Those gathered mock Him for His assurances that all will be well. He barges into her bedroom, where her budding body, poised on the prime of life, lies empty and limp. He reaches toward the twelve-year-old, born around the same time the hemorrhaging woman had first begun to bleed. Grasping her hand as He grasps Eve's in the Resurrection icon, He raises her up, saying, *"Talitha, cumi"*—an Aramaic phrase which might be translated, "Up you get, lambkin." Just like that, her eyes flutter and life flows back into her.

Far from thwarting a miracle of God, the woman's audacious interruption enabled a far greater glory to become manifest than Jairus had even conceived. Christ did not just heal the girl's sickness, as a regular physician might do: He conquered her death. He interrupted the Great Interruption. Jesus' willingness to be diverted from the charted course multiplied the miracle, restoring two women at opposite ends of their fertile years, strangers twinned by the miraculous mercy of God, back to the lives in which they belonged.

It seems Christ is quite at home amid the randomness and

disruption of our lives as well. Hiding out among inconvenience and surprise, circumstance and coincidence, He reminds us again and again that many gifts come to us posing as interruptions.

For me, it's my work as a doula that has schooled me in readiness to be interrupted at every moment. When the call comes that a labor has begun, it inevitably signals a change to the day's arrangements. I must abandon a party mid-conversation, reschedule a big appointment, leave a task half-finished, forfeit sleep. My long-suffering husband suddenly becomes responsible for things I had planned to do myself. Our children wake to find me missing from my bed. It has not always been easy, to say the least.

Nevertheless, out of the ashes of my best-laid plans, blessings have emerged. I remember one client who contacted me unexpectedly at thirty-six weeks to say she'd lost her mucus plug and started in with contractions. Before heading to bed that night I scanned my planner, noting, then (as cheerfully as I could) writing off, a parent-teacher conference scheduled for the next day. My client would surely be calling me in the night. But next morning I woke, pleasantly surprised to be greeting the light from my own bed. I made it to the school meeting, but now tomorrow's birthday celebration started to look compromised, so I hurried to make my daughter's cake. Her birthday rolled around, and I got to watch her blow out her candles with my client still pregnant.

Over the next two weeks, my client phoned me daily to share her symptoms, sure each time that today was the day things would really kick in. During that borrowed time, by God's grace I baptized a new godson, taught Sunday school, attended a conference, closed on a new house, redeemed some expensive tickets, attended a different birth, and finally entered a strangely empty new phase in the calendar. I was able to participate in every last commitment and count it all as gain, even as my poor client continued to have the sporadic contractions presaging labor. Gradually, it started to come as a happy surprise each time I got to carry out a plan I'd made. If the day happened to bring any achievements, I gave thanks. Life turned itself inside out so that the wins, not the losses, became the interruption to the pattern.

It made me wonder: why should I be surprised when my plans are occasionally stymied, but take it for granted that they so often succeed? Amid the world's complex web of interconnected events, how could I have come to expect that God should routinely grant the desires of my heart? Slowly I came to see that everything I experience requires a near-miraculous alignment of circumstances. Only by virtue of God's providence do I live to take another breath. It is by His grace, not my own determination, that I proceed: "A man's heart plans his way, / But the LORD directs his steps" (Prov. 16:9, NKJV).

As Dietrich Bonhoeffer wrote, "We must be ready to allow ourselves to be interrupted by God. God will be constantly crossing our paths and cancelling our plans by sending us people with claims and petitions. . . . It is part of the discipline of humility that . . . we do not assume that our schedule is our own to manage, but allow it to be arranged by God."[102]

By helping us treat everything that comes to us as sent by the Lord, this theology of holy interruption transforms the water of our lives to wine, the nuts thrown at us into manna, and our interrupting children into harbingers of unexpected blessings. By allowing the sacred to be continually punctured by the mundane, we witness the sacred and the mundane intermingle. The barrier separating the two becomes thinned and permeable so that we can more readily see into heaven. The diaper that fills just as we are leaving the house becomes a chance to refocus on the person in front of us. The bus we miss because we forgot the changing bag at home becomes a chance for travel encounters we would not otherwise have had. The cry in the night becomes a chance to grow by setting aside our own comfort for the sake of the Other. There are no more intrusions into "my time," for we understand that God owns time. Every plan confounded is a gift, a sacrament, an invitation to see God all around us.

Milk

Indeed your breasts shall be like clusters of the vine.
—SONG OF SONGS 7:9

or many newbie mamas, the idea of breastfeeding in a public place is intimidating. Latching a squirmy baby in comfort and privacy is challenging enough, but when we're away from home, the need to find an appropriate place, deal modestly with ridiculous amounts of clothing, and handle others' reactions makes this an advanced skill.

Now imagine breastfeeding not merely in public but in church—not sneaking in a quick feed on a back bench, but right at the front while a community of monks looks perpetually on. This is the predicament of that quintessential first-time mother, the Most Holy Theotokos—or at least of her sixth-century icon, the Mother of God Milk-Giver, found in the iconostasis of Hilandar Monastery on Mount Athos. This icon represents breastfeeding at its most public. It shows Mary with the infant Christ seated on her lap, her head inclined to Him. She is veiled, but poking out of the pleats of her robe is a conspicuous breast, nipple and all, and nary a nursing cover in sight. Christ grasps it eagerly, not sparing a hand to bless us as He often does in iconography. Where we might expect to see Him look into His mother's face or ours, He has eyes only for her bosom.

If we are ever scandalized by the Incarnation of Christ and tempted to run for the hills in shock, the Milk-Giver icon returns us firmly to our doctrinal place. It faces us with some implications of our belief in the two natures of Christ as fully human and fully divine: after inhabiting His mother's uterus for forty weeks or so, linked to her pumping blood by an umbilical cord and placenta, the eternal God passed out through her parted flesh, then spent His babyhood in utter dependence on her breasts for His physical survival. The Scriptures do not shy away from this juicy reality. "'Blessed is the womb that bore you, and the breasts that you sucked!'" cries a prophetess from the crowd in St. Luke's Gospel (11:27 RSV). Neither is our Orthodox worship coy. One of the hymns of Christmas declares, "Today is born of a Virgin He who holds creation in the hollow of His hand. . . . He is nourished with milk from the breast, He who rained manna on the people in the desert."

We who are made female in the image of a God-man who sucks the breasts of a human mother also learn something about ourselves from the Milk-Giver icon. As startling as the Incarnation may be, the voluptuousness of our own bodies may come as an equal surprise. Our experience of lactation is very visceral and tactile—sometimes uncomfortably so. The mammary glands we previously classed only as secondary sexual characteristics come roaring into action; we leak milk from one end and blood from another; an unused breast sprays while our child is feeding on the other side; we soak through our shirts when a stranger's child cries in the grocery store; we awake drenched in our own sticky sweetness. We are touched out, spent, "always eaten but never consumed" (as the Liturgy of St. Basil says of the eucharistic Body of Christ). At times we feel like a milk machine, or a cow, or the Trevi fountain. Our lives are submerged in bodily fluids. Milk becomes life.

Alongside physical rigors, the requisitioning of our breasts for our babies' benefit brings internal perplexity. In a hypersexualized world, nipples dripping with jeweled tassels for men's amusement are plastered on billboards, but nipples flowing with milk for babies' nourishment are illicit—blocked on social media pages, tutted at by strangers, and relegated to public restrooms. As milk fills our own breasts, it stirs up new questions regarding the "ownership" of our bodies. We scramble to reconfigure both our self-concept and our intimate relationships. In this environment, the Milk-Giver helps us redeem the scandal of our own incarnation as people made in the image of Christ, both in body and spirit.

Even when it is inconvenient or undesired, lactation is such a fundamental aspect of motherhood that it persists unbidden. Mothers who've weaned their nurslings may still be lactating weeks or even years later. Those who feed their babies formula from the start find their milk comes in regardless of their plans. Bereaved mothers make milk for the babies they've lost. Until it eases off, an unneeded supply can cause discomfort and sometimes infection.

An exception illustrating this rule is St. Perpetua, a noblewoman martyred in the third century at age twenty-two, leaving behind a nursling son. During her time behind bars, she kept a diary that can still be read today. Perpetua recounts the period when her baby came to live with her in prison after a time of separation. Being able to breastfeed him again gave her the physical and spiritual comfort she needed to stick to the path to which she was called: "Forthwith I grew strong and was relieved from distress and anxiety about my infant; and the dungeon became to me as it were a palace, so that I preferred being there to being elsewhere." As her date with the arena drew near, her son was removed from her, but her milk miraculously dried up and her son was weaned happily, so that she could put her concern for their mutual comfort aside as she prepared for death. "As God willed it, the child no long desired the breast, nor did my breast cause me uneasiness, lest I should be tormented by care for my babe and by the pain of my breasts at once."[103]

It does take a miracle (or drugs) to suppress the lactation of a new mother, and that's because, for mammals, breastfeeding forms part of a biological continuum spanning human pregnancy, birth, and infancy. Milk, we could say, begins at conception. From the first missed period, our bodies prepare to feed the one who will be born. For many women, one of the first signs of pregnancy is the darkening areolas which will act as bullseye targets, helping the baby navigate to his food supply. Throughout pregnancy, increased prolactin enlarges our breasts, and toward the end we may be able to express a drop or two of colostrum, the honey-colored first milk known as "liquid gold" for its amazing protective properties.

After our baby is born, pulses of oxytocin—the bonding hormone that primes us to fall in love with our babies—continue with a new function. During labor they caused uterine contractions that birthed the baby and placenta, and clamped off the open blood vessels at the placental site; now they also cause cells in our breasts to contract, squeezing out milk. Within an hour of birth, a baby instinctively starts rooting around, turning with gaping mouth toward anything that brushes his cheek until he finds the breast. He knows it by the smell of the oils its glands secrete, which matches the scent of his amniotic fluid, and he finds it conveniently located right within his mother's arm's reach, the exact distance from her face that his nearsighted newborn eyes can see. Throughout their breastfeeding relationship, day and night, her breasts never cease making milk, even while she is doing other things.

Because lactation is the biological default, breastfeeding is often described as "natural," but I don't find this a helpful way of thinking of it. The word *natural* makes us think of something that comes effortlessly, whereas breastfeeding is a skill each mother-baby dyad needs time to learn. This entails, at best, a huge sacrificial offering from the mother of energy, faithfulness, and stamina; at worst, tears, pain, blood, and illness. This offering, made out of great love, merits recognition and honor. Neither does calling breastfeeding "natural" do justice to the women who feed their babies in other ways. It implies that they are somehow doing something unnatural, when in fact we're all just trying to do our best. In a society so notoriously poor at supporting mothers to breastfeed, where most women give up earlier than they want to, it's more remarkable that women do persist.

Why? Why *do* most women breastfeed, even in the face of such tough physical and emotional challenges? Why is it worth it to us? What is the deeper significance that gets us through unforeseen difficulty? Or, to ask the question another way, what are we doing, in theological terms, when we breastfeed?

The basic reason we breastfeed is that our babies get hungry and ask us. If we are observant, we see them asking for it when they quietly smack their lips, head-butt our chest or flicker their tongue. If we miss those signs, babies escalate their complaint, with full-body squirming, grimacing, and wailing. Their desperation for the breast is so classic that the Holy Apostle Peter uses it as an example of how Christians are to thirst for God: "[A]s newborn babes, desire the pure milk of the word, that you may grow thereby, if indeed you have tasted that the Lord *is* gracious" (1 Pet. 2:2–3). Astonishingly, our milk can satisfy this powerful desire, both staving off hunger and quenching thirst.

Attending to our nurslings' physical cravings in this way is a kind of ministry to the "least of these," and through the mercy of Christ, we mothers hope to hear Him tell us, "'I was hungry and you gave Me food; I was thirsty and you gave Me drink'" (Matt. 25:35).

Second, we breastfeed our babies because it soothes them. They may approach the nipple with furrowed brow and balled fists—stressed, rigid, and crying—but within minutes our magical milk transforms them into punch-drunk ragdolls, eyes rolling as they slip sleepily off the breast with a drop of milk running from the corner of their smile. The abundant sweetness of milk, which in Scripture is often paired with honey (Deut. 31:20; Song 4:11; Is. 7:22), gives our little ones a taste of Paradise. We become the promised land flowing with milk and honey, symbols of joy to come, and with every gulp they "taste and see that the Lord is good" (Ps. 33/34:9).

The motherly ability to quieten a baby at the breast has proved not just socially handy but vital for human survival at certain times in history, from Israelite slaves in Egypt at the time of Moses concealing their firstborn boys, to Jewish families trying to escape detection in Europe during the Holocaust. The secret ingredient here is the amino acid tryptophan, which promotes sleep and feelings of well-being.

Though they won't have known the mechanism behind it, the inspired writers of the Old Testament knew this phenomenon well and used the comfort of the breast as a metaphor for the comfort of God: "I have calmed and quieted my soul, like a child quieted at its mother's breast; like a child that is quieted is my soul," writes the Psalmist (131:2 RSV). The prophet Isaiah spells it out further: "'Rejoice with Jerusalem, / And be glad with her, all you who love her . . . That you may feed and be satisfied / With the consolation of her bosom, / That you may drink deeply and be delighted / With the abundance of her glory.' For thus says the LORD: . . . 'As one whom his mother comforts, / So I will comfort you'" (66:10–13 NKJV).

Third, we breastfeed to enhance intimacy with our wee ones. A magnet on my fridge reads *Love people. Cook them tasty food*, and it's true: the sharing of nourishment seems to be a universal love language. But human milk is a uniquely effective idiom for expressing mutuality and oneness: liquid love, we might call it. It's deeply personal and responsive, varying from mother to mother, from baby to baby of each mother, and from feed to feed with each baby—a sensitive medium to communicate with someone who does not yet speak another tongue.

Researchers observing the sleep of bedsharing mothers and babies, for instance, note that breastfeeding pairs are highly attuned to one another even as they snooze.[104] They instinctively turn toward one another belly-to-belly in the "cuddle curl" familiar to families throughout history, creating a protected space for a baby at the level of his mother's breast, between her bent knees and folded elbow. While it facilitates feeding, this position also helps sync the pair's sleep cycles, temperature, heartbeats, and breathing, with each adapting toward the other to harmonize their shared life. Even without knowing, the sleeping mother also rouses briefly throughout the night to check her baby for temperature, breathing, and hunger cues umpteen times—much more frequently than co-sleeping mothers who feed their babies formula, the study found.

Fourth, breastfeeding is a teaching method. In the Greco-Roman world, human milk was considered a tool for educating children, essential to their formation as good citizens.[105] The instruction our babies receive from our milk can be looked at from a modern scientific viewpoint, too. Research demonstrates that the foods we eat affect the composition of our milk.[106] Every drop is full of information about the outside world, giving our baby a literal taste of the surroundings into which he's growing. How beautiful it is, then, to see a breastfeeding mother approaching the chalice at Divine Liturgy, knowing that she shares with her nursling every crumb that passes her lips—that the Mysteries nurture not just her but also the one she nurtures. Through her milk, she teaches him the faith, and he can receive spiritual food even before he is received by baptism into the Church.

One Orthodox mother of three, blessed with an abundant flow, expressed and donated around 14,000 ounces (105 gallons!) of her milk as an act of charity to families struggling on their breastfeeding journeys: mothers with autoimmune illness, mothers of twins, and mothers receiving essential medical care that prevented them breastfeeding. Sitting pumping under the icon of the Mother of God Milk-Giver that her family had commissioned when she was expecting her first baby, she would think about how sharing her milk was sharing her faith. She told me, "It is a beautiful experience, to be able to freely give of that which I have been freely given. I always love considering how my donor babies will receive a bit of the Holy Mysteries on days I have Communion. I wonder how that will play out in their lives. Perhaps it will lead them Home someday."

Finally, we breastfeed our babies because it's good for them. "To your good health," we toast wordlessly as we latch them on. As the writer of the Epistle to the Hebrews knew, breastmilk is easy on the stomach and a perfect first food (5:14). This one substance provides all the nutrition and fluid infants need for the first half-year after birth, so that they grow from the tiniest speck into a crawling child sustained entirely by our bodies' nourishment.

But a lactating mama doesn't keep just one organism alive and well: she sustains whole colonies of living cells, because in addition to being easy to digest, milk is filled with the good bacteria that aid its own digestion, much like yogurt or pickles. White blood cells also attack destructive bacteria, which is why milk that has been in the fridge a couple of days actually has a lower bacterial count than when it first went in, while oligosaccharides line the digestive tract to prevent any surviving bacteria from invading the cells. Whey proteins, meanwhile, kill off viruses and fungi. Through his saliva, a baby can convey a message about any threats his immune system is facing; his mother responds with milk containing antibodies customized to treat his illness. Thus our milk is medicinal without being sterile. In fact, it's very much alive: nature's closest thing to the "living water" Christ promised to Photini, the woman at the well of John 4:4–26.

Miraculous as it is, earthly milk is not the nourishment of which Christ says that whoever drinks of it "will never thirst. . . . [It] will become in him a fountain of water springing up into everlasting life." As new mothers are quite aware, the richest breastmilk cannot keep our babies from ever thirsting or hungering again. Our own milk is but a shadow of the milk with which the Creator nourishes the Universe. He is the true sustainer of our babies, not we, for God sustains us all: "For *You* latched me onto my mother's breasts," writes the Psalmist. "You were the midwife who caught me when I was born. From my mother's womb You are my God" (Ps. 21/22:10-11, my translation).

Our milk points us beyond our earthly sustenance to the

heavenly bread of life. It directs us to the Eucharist, the living food from His own flesh with which God feeds His children, as we mamas do in our own humbler way. The Liturgy understands the Holy Mysteries as the Body and *Blood* of Christ, and it sounds odd at first to speak of it as His milk, since the second Person of the Holy Trinity became incarnate as a male human being. But to the ancients, this wouldn't have sounded so odd. Blood and milk were considered closely related, as milk was thought to be made of menstrual blood not shed during pregnancy. We now know this is not the case, but for a newly postpartum mother, both bleeding lochia and oozing milk, whose nipples may be cracking as she and her baby figure things out, the association rings quite true on an instinctual level.

Neither would this have been an unfamiliar idea to the mothers and fathers of the Church. The second-century St. Clement of Alexandria says, "the Father's breasts of love supply milk."[107] In the fourth century, St. Ephrem the Syrian calls God "the Living Breast."[108] The English female mystic Julian of Norwich, who died in the early fifteenth century, is more explicit still. In her *Revelations of Divine Love* she writes, "The mother can give her child her milk to suck, but our dear mother Jesus can feed us with himself, and he does so most generously and most tenderly with the holy sacrament which is the precious food of life itself. And with all the sweet sacraments he sustains us most mercifully and most graciously."[109]

After all these considerations we can return to the Mother of God Milk-Giver with fresh eyes. As we sit in front of her icon, feeding our babies, she draws us into a dynamic movement of love circulating at the heart of the nourishing relationship between God and His people. We see her sustaining her son, yes indeed—but we also see it is He, the Source of Life, who continually sustains her. A hymn of St. Ephrem the Syrian says, "She gave Him milk from Himself that prepared it, she gave Him food from Himself that made it! He gave milk unto Mary as God: again He sucked it from her, as the Son of Man."[110]

Likewise He feeds us continually with His eucharistic Body, and we bear this food within us in our bodies when we go out, so that we mothers become the nourishment not only of our little ones but also of the whole world. The meaning of the icon, and our participation in it, spins outward like a Milky Way, expanding throughout the human story and reaching out to its fulfilment in paradise, where we and our babies will drink the sweet and life-giving milk of God and never thirst again.

Forty Days

God blessed the seventh day and sanctified it, because in it
He rested from all His works God began to make.
—GENESIS 2:3

BOUNCE BACK: postpartum secrets from the super-
models." "Bye-bye baby bulge, hello skinny jeans."
"Operating room to boardroom: this supermom CEO
was back at work two days after birth!"

With such words, the world bustles us new mothers out
the hospital doors and straight back into our customary lives.
Our grandmothers often stayed a week in the maternity ward,
resting and getting to know their babies free of daily responsibilities, but here in the twenty-first century we are routinely
hurried along after thirty-six hours. (Admittedly, under the circumstances we might not want to stay longer. It's hard to rest
when we're billed by the day and woken by beeping machines
throughout the night.) A third of freshly minted mothers in the
United States take *no* time off work.[111]

Like an afterpain, the pressure to move on kicks in right after
the baby's born. It's a rare family that gets to spend the irreplaceable Golden Hour following birth completely undisturbed,
despite scientific evidence demonstrating its lifelong benefits. As
a doula, I've often been asked to act the birthing-room bouncer,
playing for time with impatient friends and relations so that a
mother and child can spend their sacred first moments looking
into one another's eyes rather than mugging for pictures. Many

times, I've had to repeat the family's wishes for space to a health-care professional eager to get the cord cut so she can clock off for the day. Yet when we protect their endangered natural habitat, a unique electricity surrounds a mother and baby meeting one another for the first time. Face to face and skin to skin, their love charges the air with a radiant energy that does not fade for many months.

Elsewhere in the world, the days and weeks following child-birth are honored and set apart with ancient customs. Through-out Latin America, the first forty days of an infant's life are a time of *cuarantina* (quarantine) when a new mother devotes all her energy to feeding and bonding with him inside the home. She is not expected—she is expected *not*—to cook, bathe, keep house, or have sex. In Mexico a mother will have her hips wrapped tightly in cloth to "close the bones" of her vulnerable, open body. When a Chinese woman "sits the month," female relatives see that she follows a detailed wellness protocol focused on restoring warmth to the postpartum body.

In India, the period is called the "sacred window," and women return to their mothers' homes to be nurtured and nourished for the sake of their long-term vitality: "forty-two days for forty-two years," the saying goes. In Vietnam—despite what we hear about women squatting to birth their babies in the rice fields, then carrying on as if nothing had happened—moth-ers also observe a time known as "lying in a nest." The precise rituals, teas, herbs, soups, foods, and massages prescribed differ from place to place, but most traditional societies find some way to set apart the month or so after birth as a sanctioned time of retreat, quiet, recuperation, privilege—a Sabbath rest after the work of pregnancy.

Some societies also have practices to mark the completion of the forty days and the woman's return to the community after her time away in the shadowlands. A tale often told in the Beriba language of Benin "depicts the ancestors in the act of digging the woman's grave throughout the pregnancy. If she survives the days after the delivery, they begin to shovel the sand back; forty days after the delivery, the grave will finally be closed without her."[112] As for us, the closest we get to such a ritual is the six-week medical checkup, at which healthcare professionals may inspect our reproductive organs and presume to grant us "permission" to resume our sex lives.

From a practical standpoint, these other cultures are more realistic about the timescale for postpartum recovery. Most women find it takes much longer than they expected. Vaginal bleeding continues for an average of twenty-four to thirty-six days, even for women who have had a Cesarean, and though lochia isn't painful, its heaviness can be inconvenient and startling. (Only clots larger than a fist are considered abnormal.)

For several months more, little energy is left after baby care for doing anything more than just the basics. A year is how long one study, based on interviews with new mothers, concluded it takes to recover physically and emotionally from birth;[113] ten years is the estimate of one birth worker.[114] Conditions like *diastasis recti* (where the abdominal muscles remain separated) and incontinence can take years to heal, or may even remain for life. Perhaps it's most honest to admit that, in both enriching ways and challenging ones, after having a baby we are forever postpartum. Acknowledging and embracing this can help take off some of the pressure we feel to bounce back.

For babies, too, it takes time to adjust to life after birth. A human infant is born prematurely relative to other mammalian species. Unlike theirs, his mother's pelvis is shaped for walking upright as well as for giving birth, and he must be born while he is still small enough to navigate it. During the first few months, his diurnal rhythms, behavior, and comforts are still those of the womb, but the sensations he experiences—hunger, heat, cold, space, brightness, and din—belong to the outside world. So he is a fish out of water, a living, breathing culture clash, inhabiting a world in which he does not fully belong. He is still growing into his surroundings. For this reason these months are often called the fourth trimester.

Our culture wasn't always blind to such realities. As recently as a hundred years ago, Western mothers too observed a formalized period of "lying in." But our modern consumer economies now have little tolerance for women who want retreat from the world. In the US, time to rest and heal is framed as a luxury for the moneyed few rather than a necessity for all. Society supports our freedom to work, combining motherhood with a career, but it does not support our freedom *not* to work by guaranteeing paid maternity leave; so a postpartum Sabbath becomes the privilege of those who can afford to take the financial hit. Our own mothers and aunties, too, need to be at work and cannot take the time to nurture us back to full strength, so paid postpartum doulas and pizza delivery take the place of loving hands and homemade bone broth. At the same time, the idea of a "confinement" period strikes us as old-fashioned and counter to our aspirations. Why would any self-respecting woman want to be *confined?*

In such a baffling cultural climate, many of us scurry through the postpartum days, asking ourselves, *how long till I'm back to normal? What's wrong with me that this is taking so long? Am I the only one who is completely immobilized by this weighty new love?* These surely are not new questions; our great-great-grandmothers must have asked them too. What's new is that our wider society no longer provides the welcome answers: *There is nothing wrong with you! You are just what your baby, and our community, needs. As a mother, you now have no* normal *to go back to. You have been inducted into the extraordinary. It's disorienting and exhausting, but it's here to stay, so put up and rest up while you can. Here, have a sip of this.* Instead, what is returned to us is the lonely echo of our own voice, asking.

But if we listen carefully, we can still hear a still, small response to our concerns. The Orthodox Church, alone in the Western world, has quietly retained the first forty days after birth as a precious and sacred time, guarding this ancient practice even when all the surrounding culture has abandoned it and other churches have cast it aside. Though it is not universally observed, the enduring existence of this practice within the tradition is a testimony to the world of the irreplaceable importance of this time. During this time, we are officially excused from our usual disciplines like attending Liturgy, just as it's assumed we will be needing time off *all* responsibilities other than holding, feeding, and loving our newborn.

Right when we're most tempted to keep ourselves to unrealistic expectations, the Church affirms that we need not try to carry on as usual. By entering into this practice, we accept the Lord's invitation to withdraw for a period of quiet transformation as we ready ourselves for a radically new stage of life. By the fortieth day after birth, we are more ready to emerge from our spiritual chrysalis in a fuller new form, and the Church honors our metamorphosis with a service known as churching. She welcomes and reintegrates us back into the body of the faithful, but as mothers—changed people with a new beauty and even more to be thankful for.

Why forty days? It's the approximate timespan many cultures follow, but in the Christian tradition, the number forty also has important symbolic significance. A bit as we might say "umpteen," it stands for a large imprecise number, so that if forty days or years elapse from one event to another, the gulf is so wide it divides time into two epochs. (We experience this for ourselves with the forty interminable weeks of pregnancy!) Forty days of mourning, forty days of fasting, forty days of Pascha: in the Christian life, forty is a numerical signal that an old era has been fulfilled and a new one is beginning.

A forty-day retreat also has an illustrious biblical precedent. Like Noah and his family, who weathered forty days and nights of rain in the ark, we are freed to take this time to tend only to the inhabitants of our cozy little vessel as it navigates choppy seas. Like Moses, who spent a forty-day stint up on Mount Sinai and returned with the Divine Commandments, we disappear from the world (in a haze of sleepless nights, rather than celestial cloud) to try to ascertain our way forward into this life, though frankly it's a bit hard to see for all the dazzling glory. Like the Israelites, whose forty *years* wandering in the desert eating manna for their daily bread prepared them to enter the Promised Land, we depend on others to provide physically for us while we are consumed with the work of figuring out our new role—and any meal we're given tastes like heaven. Like Christ in His forty-day wilderness sojourn, we benefit from a spell of ascesis and prayer, clinging to God as we fortify ourselves for the life-altering ministry that now begins.

Historical evidence suggests that women once looked forward to their churching as a social occasion. Many still do, but sadly for others the tradition has become a source of confusion and hurt. They see it not as an opportunity extended out of a desire to honor our holy task and protect our well-being, but as a misogynistic attempt to keep us away from church while we're still unacceptably messy. We know the practice is not aimed solely at excluding us, because we are not forbidden to return to church earlier than forty days if it's truly helpful—for example, when a new mother becomes ill and needs to receive Communion.

But some of the language of the churching prayers remains a stumbling block. There are many references to the "uncleanness" and "impurity" of our state, and a resulting need for "purification." If these words were simply referring to the physical griminess that early motherhood entails, many of us would agree. I know I've been there—covered with spit-up and longing all day to be "purified" in a hot shower! But those of us with the Trisagion prayer "cleanse us from all impurity" tucked inside our hearts understand reflexively that it's sin, not just dirt, that the prayers impute to us. This hurts. We're very far from perfect, we know, but any implication that our birth-giving is a sin feels gravely unjust. In fact, we sense it's more like a brush with divinity.

Knowing the damage the language of these prayers can cause, some priests adapt them on the fly, skipping over the offending verbiage as they go through the service. Such an instinct turns out to be well-founded historically as well as pastorally. Only in the late Byzantine era was the innovative purity language introduced into the churching prayers. Before that, it was completely absent, and thanksgiving, not purification, was the focus of the rite; the couple's marriage prayer that they would receive "the enjoyment of the blessing of children" had been answered, and it was time to thank God that everyone was alive and well. A carefully researched version of the prayers that returns to this original emphasis has now been released and blessed for use by the Antiochian Church of North America,[115] but until something similar is used across all jurisdictions, our dilemma remains.

What are we to make of the talk of impurity in the otherwise life-giving practice of churching, which is there even if we choose to skip over it? We know that God gives us "the law as a help" (as the Liturgy of St. Basil puts it, echoing the words of Is. 8:20), and that the Church does not intend the tradition as a spiritual hindrance—but how can we accept a gift wrapped in such prickly packaging?

Here we can look to the churching of Christ, in the light of which all churchings happen. At forty days old, He was brought by the Theotokos and Joseph to the temple in Jerusalem, where He was received by the elderly Simeon and the prophetess Anna. As a Jewish family, they understood that ever since the first Passover, every firstborn son belonged to God, and so to fulfill the law they came to exchange an offering for the loan of their child. Since they were poor, the custom allowed the Theotokos to present two turtledoves rather than the lamb required of prosperous families; in fact, though, she obeyed the law by presenting the very One who fulfilled it: *the* Lamb Himself.

This is an event we commemorate in a feast called the Meeting of the Lord, whose hymns are also sung at our own churchings. "'O pure Lady, you are carrying fire!'" says Simeon in the ode. "'I am afraid to take God in my arms as a babe [. . .]! Isaiah was cleansed by receiving the coal from the Seraphim!' cried the old man to the mother of God. 'You fill me with light, entrusting to me with your hands as with tongs, the One you hold.'"

Here is a key to a healthier understanding of the purity language. As Simeon experienced, the divine energy, such as that radiated by a mother and her baby embracing each other in the moments after birth, is sometimes too hot to handle. The intimacy of their love shines with such holiness that those outside it must shield their eyes from the sight. For everyone's sake, it must be guarded, protected, held sacred. A word I learned when I lived in the South Pacific comes in handy to illustrate this: it's the word *tabu*, meaning "holy," which at the same time is the source of our word *taboo*, meaning "set apart, forbidden." It's the most sacred things that must be most preciously guarded.

But as well as inspiring awestruck adoration, an encounter with the holy also causes us to question our own worthiness. "Woe is me," cries Isaiah in the passage to which Simeon alludes, "because I am pierced to the heart, for being a man and having unclean lips, I dwell in the midst of a people with unclean lips; for I saw the King, the Lord of hosts, with my eyes!" (Is. 6:5). Perhaps the humility of Isaiah can help us understand the uncleanness the prayers impute to our postpartum state. If like him we allow ourselves to be particularly humbled by a particularly close encounter with the Almighty, the impurity language ceases to threaten us and can instead be the vehicle for a deeply personal confession of our own poverty before God.

I wonder what treasures we would garner if we treated our postpartum selves with the tenderness and reverence our Church traditions accord us. Rather than approaching these weeks as a time to hurry through, if we set them aside as a unique window during which to look within, then what would happen? What if we sought not to get *back* to our usual self, but to lean *forward* into a richer new reality?

SEVEN

Preparing for Birth

Nesting

Firm is your dwelling place, and your nest is set in the rock.
—NUMBERS 24:21, NKJV

This week we embark on the final stage of our pilgrimage through pregnancy. As we prepare, body and heart, for what is to come, we enter a strange liminal zone. We're readying for huge things—for the birth of our babies, and for our own rebirth as mothers—and it's easy for us to focus only on what is to come. Over the next few weeks we will seek to lay claim to the deep inherent value of this period, not just for what it leads to, but for what it presently is.

A CURIOUSLY PLACED ART INSTALLATION? Detritus from an oddball pagan ritual? Or evidence for the existence of leprechauns? Well might a person wonder what on earth she was looking at if she stumbled across the creation of the Australian bowerbird.

Hidden in the undergrowth, this bird's masterpiece looks like a miniature thatched cottage, ingeniously engineered to stand with support from a nearby sapling. The roof is woven from thin black orchid stems. Decorating his doorway are gloopy baubles made of orange caterpillar droppings. He has carpeted his threshold with fine moss sourced from the riverbank miles away, flying back and forth to transport each piece. Outside in his cottage garden are the collections he has built over the years: avant garde piles of objects grouped by color—a stack of purple berries here, a heap of hot pink buds there, a motley mound of creamy bones, lichen, pebbles, and plastic bottle caps on that side. In the center he's placed his most prized possession: a single neon seed-pod. For hours each day he meticulously rearranges his trove; if the wind or a rival should vandalize it, he quickly replaces each treasure in its correct spot.

This bower is not the nest into which his young will be born, but it serves an important role in his reproductive life. When a female bowerbird comes along, she'll inspect the bowers of the area to see which one pleases her most and will choose its architect as her mate.

Many animals attend carefully to the beauty and order of the physical surroundings in which their heredity is forged, so in this respect the bowerbird isn't unique. In the last days of pregnancy, a rabbit will dig a hole, fetch straw to fill it, and pluck out her own fur to line the nest. A pregnant wild sow may travel a great distance from her herd to find just the right stump; next to it she'll use her snout to hollow out an indentation in the ground where her newborn piglets can keep warm. A dog paces around, searching out soft items from around the house—blankets, cushions, even stuffed animals—to make her puppies a landing spot. But, of all the creatures on earth, human nesting behavior is most extravagant of all.

In the weeks before birth, many women notice the instinct kick in. A realization is dawning: our gravid days are numbered. We are not just pregnant but expecting a *baby,* who will be here before we know it. Under the deep loam of third-trimester exhaustion, a new energy stirs like the springtime shoots of motherhood. We begin to create space in our home for our baby. We want to prepare as cozy, warm, clean, and orderly a landing spot as we can. We fold and sort baby clothes into piles. We sort the Tupperware cabinet, excavate the junk drawer, declutter the linen cupboard. We rearrange furniture. We surprise our families with spontaneously repainted walls. We feather our nest with the piles of internet purchases and gifts that wait on our doorstep. We potter, tinker, and tweak.

Sometimes we get tired and discouraged. The to-do list seems so long, we wonder if we'll get everything done in time for the new arrival. The projects we begin create mess before they yield order. The people we rely on to help us take longer than we thought. We start to wonder, will we ever be ready? Actually, it's a fair question. Can we ever be perfectly ready for the unknown? Could we ever be *all set* for a role as big as parenthood? Will the humble nest we are feathering ever be fit to receive a new child of God?

There's an exercise I sometimes invite the families I work with to complete. Parents sit down with a pile of catalogs and start cutting out pictures of the products they figure a baby needs. When they're finished, a large collection of scraps is spread out on the ground. They talk through the merits of their selections: cool-looking stroller accessories, diaper pails they've seen advertised, and pacifiers friends recommend.

When they're done, I ask them to remove half their chosen items, so that only the most essential ones remain. Sometimes this proves hard, but in the end the wipe warmers and scratch mitts are set aside. Next I invite them to pare their selections down even further, leaving just their top three picks. When they're done, each mother or couple has thoughtfully assembled a mini-layette for their baby based on their own family's priorities. For some it might be a sidecar crib, a swaddling blanket, and a wrap carrier; for others, a changing mat, a rocking chair, and a car seat. Along the way, there is often a fruitful conversation about how the things most needful are fewer than we suppose.

For a worthy welcome does not require an elaborately feathered nest. Let's consider the innkeeper of Bethlehem, receiving the pregnant Theotokos and her betrothed on the eve of Christ's birth. He didn't turn them away on the grounds that his stable wasn't kitted out properly for guests. It may not have been up to the standard of his regular accommodation, but he offered what he had. There was no room; nevertheless he "carved out" a space, a literal cave in the rock, which gave the Savior a safe landing place. He made room in his life that night to get up and see to another family knocking at the door, even after all the rooms were filled. Perhaps he scooted the manger back against the stable wall, shooed the animals aside, quickly shoveled a bit of muck, and scattered fresh straw to pad the floor. By doing so, he was blessed to have the Christ-child born under his roof.

Now, it's understandable if I want my baby to land in a nest a little more luxurious than the newborn Christ's. But for me, too, a simple nest can be a fitting one. My baby cares not a whit about color-coordinated nursery accessories. What makes a difference is the space I create to accommodate him. Can I hollow out a place of safety, belonging, and comfort for him in this world? Will I make of my own life the nest in which he can grow?

This room-making takes many forms. While I am busy rearranging my home to make space for a crib or a bedroom, my very body is also being rearranged. My ribcage pushes outward to fit my growing child, my bladder is tucked away into an improbably tiny space, my blood volume has increased dramatically, and the connective tissue in my pelvis is softening to ease my baby through my bones at birth. Even my feet broaden to help me keep my balance and strength under extra weight. Heartburn, carpal tunnel, swollen ankles—these are all symptoms of making space.

My daily schedule is also in the midst of a great reshuffle. There are appointments and classes, essential naps and additional nighttime bathroom trips to squeeze into my already busy days. I may spend hours preparing food for the good of my baby— learning about nutrition, planning meals, sourcing ingredients, preparing dishes, and eating them to benefit the one who shares every mouthful I consume. Much of my time in pregnancy is carved out for baby-related activities. Pregnancy itself, it might be said, is one big phase carved out for "baby-related activities"!

And the same could be said of the decades of parenting that follow. Our whole life as mothers takes a new concave shape, formed to fit our little nestlings. This spiritual truth is manifested quite clearly on the physical plane, in the space created for my baby by my encircling arms, right next to my heart. At first, I spend many hours each day, perhaps a total of six or eight out of every twenty-four, simply sitting and holding him while he drinks milk. I pass untold additional time toting him around while I do other things because he fusses when I put him down, or strapping him to my chest for a walk, or (as a reported eighty percent of parents do at some point[116]) co-sleeping with him in my arms.

We are designed to thrive in this mutual embrace, for— unlike some animals who scurry off to a life of independence as soon as they are born, and others who stay quietly in the nest while their parents go off foraging for food—human beings are carrying creatures. In that sense we're a bit like great ape mothers, who carry their young continually, keeping them close in order to transport, nurse, and protect them. After a few months, when the babies are strong enough to grip their mother safely, she transfers them from her front to her back, but still she carries them.[117] The family returns regularly to their nest, but it's she, not the nest itself, that offers protection.

And so it is with us. Beyond any space we might create in our homes, *we* are the true nest our babies need. The motherly act of *holding*, simple and primal as it may be, is deceptively powerful.[118] Scientific studies show that holding her baby eases a mother's pain, promotes better sleep, and protects her mental health. Meanwhile, his mother's cuddles regulate a baby's heart rate and temperature and help him grow—so much so that premature babies are often prescribed "kangaroo care" (where they are carried skin-to-skin in wrap carriers, rather than stowed in incubators) as a medical intervention.

Why should the feeling of being touched, held, and nested firmly in our arms be so soothing to babies? Perhaps because it's familiar from life inside their mother's body, where strong uterine muscles cradle them. But to say "cradle" gets it backwards. It is, after all, the enveloping comforts of the outside world—cradles, swaddling blankets, warm arms—that attempt to recreate the original environment of the womb, rather than the other way around. We would better say not that we "cradle" our babies in our arms, but that we "womb" them there.

And why, in turn, is the womb such a comforting place to nest? Might it embody for us the "protective enclosing of the world in the care of God"?[119] Could it be that the muscular hold of the uterus reminds us of something yet deeper in our human past—returning us to the paradise of God's womb in which we have our origin? St. Ephrem the Syrian writes strikingly of God as "the Majesty in Whose womb the universe is placed as if [in] the palm of the hand."[120] And again: "As He dwelt in His mother's womb, in His womb dwells all creation."[121] It is from this divine womb, Ephrem says, that the Son comes forth, and inside which we can be united to Him: "If anyone seeks [Christ's] hidden nature behold it is in heaven in the great womb of Divinity."[122]

This notion is more comfortably at home in the tradition than it may at first sound. Saint Ephrem's language reflects the words of St. John the Evangelist when he calls Christ "the only begotten Son, who is in the *kolpos* of the Father" (John 1:18). The Greek term used here, usually translated "bosom," has many shades of meaning. Likely originating in the Proto-Indo-European word for an arch, it stands for most anything that forms a sheltering enclosure, including *pocket, bay, the folds of clothing, lap*, and (most importantly for our purposes) *womb*. While we don't know which of these connotations he had in mind, St. John clearly means to say that the Son came forth from His Father's deepest and most intimate recesses.

To understand these depths as womb-like is a stretch for us, but to the Jewish recipients of John's Gospel, it would have been quite comfortable. In their Scriptures, God reveals Himself to Moses as *'êl ra-hum*, the Compassionate One (Deut. 4:31). To the ear of a Hebrew speaker, the word *compassion* (*ra-hum*) had an obvious association with the word *womb* (*re-hem*). God is the Merciful, the Womb, the strong protective One who holds His children at gut level, beneath His heart. His love for us is bloody, encompassing, and fierce, and it never lets go. For "can a woman forget her nursing child, / And not have *compassion* on the son of her *womb*?" asks Isaiah. "Surely they may forget, / Yet I will not forget you" (Is. 49:15 NKJV, my emphasis).

Our Lord invites us to nest in the compassion of His womb. But, as the Theotokos shows us, the invitation can be made reciprocal. While Mary accepts a place in the bosom of His love, she too welcomes Him into her innermost being—into her body and heart. The Theotokos takes *ra-hum* on the Son of God by offering him the shelter of her *re-hem*. She has compassion, has "womb," on Him. To the baby for whom no room is found in the inn, she offers the refuge of her body. To the Son who has nowhere to lay His head, she gives a place in her home.

Wherever Christ goes, He takes humanity with Him, whether that be to the heavenly Kingdom or into the shelter of a mother's care. By taking Him in, then, the Theotokos receives us too, offering us a place of sanctuary in a trying world. A beloved hymn the Church sings in her honor—discovered to be at least as old as the Egyptian papyrus fragment from AD 250 on which it appears—expresses the comfort we find there. "Beneath Thy compassion we take refuge, O Birthgiver of God. Despise not our prayers in our necessity, but deliver us from harm, O only pure, only blessed one." Like the Theotokos, we mothers are called to make a nest in the wombs of our hearts where God, our fellow human beings, and especially our children can "take refuge." We are invited to become for them the same unconditional, enfolding mercy that God is for us.

If this week we find ourselves organizing the basement, picking nursery curtains, descaling the teakettle, filing paperwork, or assembling a crib, let's remember: we are more than bowerbirds arranging pretty seedpods. Nesting means creating in our wombs, arms, and hearts a place our babies can call a heavenly home.

Thinning

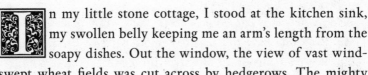

When one turns to the Lord, the veil is taken away. . . .
We all, with unveiled face, beholding as in a mirror
the glory of the Lord, are being transformed
into the same image from glory to glory.
—2 CORINTHIANS 3:16, 18

In my little stone cottage, I stood at the kitchen sink, my swollen belly keeping me an arm's length from the soapy dishes. Out the window, the view of vast windswept wheat fields was cut across by hedgerows. The mighty River Tweed coursed toward the North Sea in the valley below, delineating the permeable border between England and Scotland. Flocks of tiny birds swooped in and out of the traveling mist. This was a land of tolling bells and mysterious standing stones, saints and kings, twisted roots and coal-fired stoves—a gorgeous but strange world into which to be bringing my second child.

Squinting my eyes, I could almost see the crops dividing under the hooves of an ancient Scottish cavalry as they beat a terrifying path up the hill toward my door. With my supersensitive pregnancy nose, I could smell the blood of former centuries that had soaked this earth as the border was pushed back and forth. And for a moment I could sense just how it felt to be the pregnant woman who lived here in those days, a toddler on her hip and a husband away in the fields, breathing "Lord have mercy" as she saw the invaders ride up.

My Northumbrian home was what is known to Celtic spirituality as a "thin place." In such spots, the veil between the earthly and the eternal is a little thinner than usual; the border is effaced, we might say. The *now* and the *not yet* kiss, and we get a glimpse from the everyday world into other worlds: those gone before, or those yet to come. In a thin place, the presence of the divine can be sensed more tangibly, and every person, every event is charged with high-stakes spiritual significance. The transcendent seeps through into the everyday world, filling hearts with awe and wonder. In a thin place, I may feel very small under a vast sky, yet I know that my life, like all others, has deep meaning and purpose.

We've probably all come across these thin places at some point. We don't have to travel to remote parts of Britain to find them. We may encounter one in a library or a cemetery in our hometown. We may discover one in a deep forest, on a windy clifftop, or by a roaring waterfall. We may sense a thin place as our car zips past a roadside shrine marking the location of a traffic accident. Like many seekers through the centuries, we might make a pilgrimage to one, either a holiday-maker's pilgrimage to the radiant beauty of a national park or monument, or an explicitly spiritual pilgrimage to see a monastery, miraculous icon, or sainted land. Maybe we've even created a thin place in our home icon corner, the habit of prayer wearing away at that spot in the veil a little more each day.

But sometimes the thin places are found still nearer by. Sometimes they run like channels right through our hearts. During a Divine Liturgy, for example, a thin place may suddenly open up inside, letting glory shine in, stinging our eyes with holy tears of thanksgiving and humility. In particular phases of life, our hearts can be thin for entire seasons at a time. Great Lent is often like this, as we carry the candlelit spirit of Presanctified Liturgy with us from week to week. Long after the service is over, our hearts seem to make their own prostrations, singing, "Now the powers of heaven with us do minister invisibly. For behold the King of Glory enters . . ."

The days following the death of a loved one can be a twilight time, too. Though the breath of the person has gone, we may feel her presence with great immediacy, as if at any moment she could walk into the room. The grief and vulnerability that we feel at the loss of our beloved seem to open us more to her immortal spirit, removing some of the limitations of our earthly relationship and allowing us to grow closer than we previously could. I experienced this acutely with the loss of my child through miscarriage. I never got to see him alive: he was born into the light of God rather than into the light of the sun. But having a primarily spiritual rather than material relationship with him has allowed me to carry him more closely than I did when he was in my womb. The blessing of his love has worn the veil between earth and eternity in my motherly heart to just a gauzy sheet.

Another period of thinning happens around the time of childbirth. In order to give birth, a woman must become "thin" enough to squeeze through a narrow gate into the new land of motherhood. The intense sensations of labor take her on a solitary inner journey through shadowy border country, each contraction a stepping stone leading her down the path. As the hours pass she is removed further and further from her companions. The faraway look in her eyes intensifies while she goes deeper in. As if distracted by strains of music from the other side, she pays no attention to the trivial things happening in the room. She appears to be hypnotized, or asleep, and confirms this with the occasional snore, yet mysteriously she can also hear if someone a block away is speaking too loudly.

During this time, the birthing woman is having a profound encounter with the next world. Spiritual forces are close by on every side. Death brushes up against her like brambles on the path. In this place, time does not pass, and she sees the faces of those who have gone before, along with those yet to come. She becomes so permeable that she feels herself one with all the mothers in the world who are birthing with her—with all the mothers birthing through the ages—and with every creative force surging in the universe. It's only when the journey reaches its climax and her baby is born that she returns to the "normal" world, emerging victorious from the deeps with the prize in her arms. She has brought to birth not only a baby but also a new self.

This is the point of maximal "thinness" toward which we have been slowly working for the past three trimesters. Here in the final weeks of pregnancy we have arrived at the verge. The barriers of everyday life bulge and stretch under the heavy weight of our bellies. Everything feels very personal. Things that would usually roll off us now strike us to the core. We are raw, ripe, needy, and weepy. We are neither coming nor going, neither here nor there, neither this nor that. Instead we have a foot in each world.

This time has been honored with a name, albeit one we have to source from another language: *Zwischenzeit*. This is the German word for the *meantime*, the *in-between*. It's a very early stage of labor, taking place well before what is recognized as "first stage." And there is a physical aspect to our thinning which is every bit as essential to the process of becoming a mother as the spiritual work we do. Our body, just like our heart, is effacing.

One glaring example is right under our noses: the skin of our bellies stretches taut and itchy over our babies, often leaving stretch marks along whose lines we feel we just might crack open. The distance separating our babies from the outside world is so insignificant that we can sometimes see the contours of their fingers or toes sweep across our skin.

A thinning more hidden, but just as physical, is also taking place. Though we may or may not notice them, contractions start to gather the muscles of the uterus up toward the top of our bellies, which fans them out at the other end. The cervix (the fleshy internal gate between womb and world which opens to release a baby at birth) becomes soft and thin before it can fully dilate. This is quite tangible: if during a medical checkup I consent to an internal exam from my midwife or obstetrician, she can tell me my effacement in percentage terms. If my cervix is zero percent effaced, it's thick and firm like a nose; if it's fifty percent effaced, it feels squishy and pliable like lips; and if it's one hundred percent or fully effaced, it has melted away to a mere membrane. Though a heart's thinning cannot be measured in the same way as a cervix, both spiritual and physical efface-ment are necessary to the birthing process.

But our thinning serves another purpose beyond our family-making and into the world. By becoming a thin place, both in body and in spirit, we pregnant women demonstrate the voca-tion that all humanity shares. For every human person is called to be a thin place in the universe. As human images of God, we are the interface of the sublime and the ridiculous: on the one hand, worms and, on the other, gods (Job 25:6; John 10:34). The fault line between this world and the next is bridged by our bodies and souls. The "thinner" we become, the closer the two worlds are brought. Softening and stretching our lives to transparency, we allow the divine light to shine through us and illumine the world.

This process, like the effacement of late pregnancy, is often uncomfortable. It's often challenging and intimidating to be in— let alone to *be*—a thin place. Our hearts and wombs ache. We get stretch marks on our souls. Sometimes we question whether there is still anything left of ourselves or whether we have faded into nothingness. Our identities, which formerly felt so solid and sure, begin to shift and change. But this is the way of humility. As St. John the Forerunner said, it is so that He can increase that we decrease (John 3:30). We are not melting away and consumed but, in the words of Abba Joseph of Panephysis, have started to "become all flame."[123]

Lest we lose heart, Christ is the prototype for a thin place in the world. He is the One who connects heaven to earth; He *is* Heaven on earth. It's He whose sacrifice cannot leave the temple curtain intact but rips it from top to bottom, spilling the Holy of Holies out into the whole world. In His presence, the barrier of sin we have erected between ourselves and God is lifted, allowing us to look into the brightness of His face.

Christ's full effacement—the thinning of the veil that allowed the glory of His uncreated light to shine through—took place in the thinner mountain air atop the Mount of Transfiguration, identified in the tradition as Mount Tabor. A mountain is the classic meeting point of heaven and earth, and it was also on a mountain—Mount Horeb—that the Holy Prophet Moses met God in the Burning Bush. Indeed, the disciples whom Jesus has brought up this mountain with Him perceive Moses there, along with Elijah. These two figures, brought together, represent the gathering of all things into one: Moses, the law-bringer, died and was buried in the earth before he reached the Promised Land, while Elijah, the quintessential prophet, was taken alive directly to heaven in a fiery chariot. Having experienced the glory of God already, both Moses and Elijah appear comfortable in the presence of the light shining forth from Christ. Not so for the disciples. They fall on their faces, terrified (Matt. 17:6).

But as the Troparion hymn for the Transfiguration says, this wasn't the full extent of it. Christ only revealed His glory "as far as they could bear it"; the Uncreated Light of God "is a light too fierce for human eyes," as St. Gregory the Theologian puts it. And the glory the disciples glimpsed on Tabor was not intended for standing and staring at. After his mountaintop experience, Peter wanted to put up a shelter for Christ, Moses, and Elijah, so that they could all stay awhile (Matt. 17:4); but the three chosen disciples could not remain there. They had to go back down and join the crowds.

Yet though the glory the disciples glimpsed on the mountaintop was novel, the Church Fathers are clear that the true change of the Transfiguration occurred inside the disciples, rather than inside Christ. Saint Maximos the Confessor tells us it was their senses that were transfigured, enabling them to perceive the true glory of Christ, which in fact had been there all along. Saint John of Damascus writes, "He was transfigured, not by assuming what He was not, but by manifesting to His disciples what He was, opening their eyes." And St. Andrew of Crete confirms, "He did not at that moment become more radiant or more exalted—far from it—but He remained as He was before."

And so it is with our experience of late pregnancy. As we are transfigured into mothers, our bodies and hearts are effaced paper-thin, but the radiance that comes shining through is not novel; rather, it is a latent beauty that is revealed. We do not gain new powers to birth babies, endure pain, or cope with sleeplessness; instead, the inherent abilities already inside us are given the chance to shine. If, despite the discomfort of being stretched thin, we take our time, we can learn how to live well in between. Understanding that thin places have their own value and are neither a place to remain nor a place to rush through, we are free to enjoy these final hours of life as we know it as, in imitation of Christ, we become a place where heaven and earth touch as if through a mere membrane.

Waiting

For the vision is yet for an appointed time;
But at the end it will speak, and it will not lie.
Though it tarries, wait for it; because it will surely come.
—HABAKKUK 2:3 (NKJV)

The tools of a doula's trade make an odd collection: a rolling pin, an exercise ball, a shawl, honey sticks, and bendy straws. Deep at the bottom of my bag is the strangest specimen of all: a wad of crumbly grey-brown plant matter that could pass as a dust bunny. Actually, it's a treasure in disguise, a dormant miracle: a resurrection plant, also known as the flower of Maryam (the Theotokos). It's not native to the doula bag; its natural habitat is the desert, where it blows around from place to place like tumbleweed. "He made everything beautiful in its time," says Ecclesiastes 3:11, and this plant sometimes has to wait a long time before becoming anything remotely beautiful. It can survive for months or even years without water, but when it finds moisture, it does what we all must do in labor: it blooms.

The resurrection plant has been long used by birth attendants, especially in the Middle East, not as an herbal remedy but as a visual aid. It illustrates that we too sometimes have to bide our time until our moment of beauty arrives. At a tricky birth, I set my plant out in a dish of water where she who is laboring can watch and wait. Slowly, slowly, each tendril unfurls. "Has the earth travailed in one day," the plant seems to ask, "or has a nation given birth at once?" (Is. 66:8). Over several hours, its foliage releases from a tight ugly ball into a beautiful green flower before our eyes. The woman, too, gradually finds a way—slowly, slowly—to bloom open into new life.

Waiting, the resurrection plant reminds us, is essential to making babies. First I await my period, then when it doesn't come, I wait for the pregnancy test result. I wait at home for morning sickness to stop and in medical practitioners' waiting rooms to be seen. I wait to feel my baby's first kicks and for my bump to start showing. I wait for my due date, then (if I'm average) I wait several days more. Even when my baby is born, the waiting continues. I wait for his next feed, then I wait for him to finish that feed. I wait for him to wake up; I wait for the day he stops waking me up. I wait until he can walk, until he's potty-trained. Even much further down the road I still wait: for the bathroom to be free, or for my teenagers to finish getting ready so we can leave the house. At every stage of motherhood, the moment when I can stop waiting seems to be some way off, perhaps just around the next corner.

Standing on the threshold of full term (a five-week period beginning at Week 37 that outlines the normal range of human gestation), I don't need reminding, but as Mister Rogers sang, "It's very, very, very hard to wait. Especially when you're waiting for something very nice." It's hard enough to wait for a feast day or a vacation, when I can count down to an appointed day. But with only four percent of women giving birth on their baby's "due" date, I can't even be sure how much longer my pregnancy will last. Every twinge in my body puts me on high alert. What is *that?* Could tonight be the night? But every morning I awake, still pregnant, and the sun, heavy under the weight of possibilities, drags laboriously across the sky as another day that proves *not* to be my baby's birthday elapses.

This way of life is seriously countercultural. In a world that wants its burger ready before it even pulls up to the drive-through, waiting for something as important as babies looks like insanity. In a society that can cancel its Uber ride without charge after only five minutes' delay, going weeks "overdue" seems unfair. In a culture that anxiously checks on a friend who is a little late for coffee, letting labor begin in its own good time appears foolhardy. And in an environment where there's an app for every inconvenience, relying on nature to time a baby's arrival looks like a technological oversight.

These pressures make it incredibly tempting to take matters into our own hands. We find ourselves awake at 3 AM, Googling pineapple, curry, castor oil, and a hundred other questionable induction methods in search of a "natural" way to kickstart labor on an unnatural schedule. It's as if we think that if *we* don't do something, *nothing* will happen—as if we've forgotten that nobody ever stayed pregnant forever. Many of us are seduced into signing up for a conveniently scheduled induction, even without a pressing need. Hospital statistics—which show strangely few babies being born at weekends, on public holidays, and during the night shift—suggest that medical necessity is not the only factor in the timing of births. Under the medical-industrial model, convenience for both parents and their care providers also plays a strong role.

Trying to hurry things along may give a reassuring illusion of human control, but forces bigger than ourselves still have the final word. Astonishingly, science cannot yet identify, much less replicate, the precise mechanism that triggers labor to begin on its own. We do know that going into labor seems to require a moment of synergy between mother and baby, when both send the biochemical signal that they're ready. On the mother's part, this readiness is mediated by estrogen, which wires up new connections between uterine cells so that they'll be able to act together during labor. Estrogen production ramps up through the end of pregnancy, so by the time labor begins, her womb is perfectly primed for coordinated contractions. Spurring it into action before this process is complete is likely to result in contractions that don't do anything much except hurt.

A woman's cervix prepares in advance of labor too, becoming thin and stretchy as latex and easing forward so that it opens toward the outside world, rather than the inside of her body as usual—factors that can be measured on the so-called Bishop's Score. There's no medical shortcut for this prerequisite; unless a woman's Bishop's Score indicates her cervix is already favorably inclined to labor, an induction is likely to be unsuccessful, and a Cesarean will be necessary if her baby is to be born right away. Ironically, this means that the only good candidates for induction are women who are ready to give birth on their own!

The baby also makes vital preparations for his birth. In the final days before labor he lays down glycogen stores at an accelerated rate, as if packing a picnic before setting out on the long journey of labor. He'll need all he can carry, because these energy stores are only enough to last ten to twelve hours after birth. Then, just before labor starts, the final building block of his prenatal development falls into place: his lungs are lined with slimy surfactants so that he can take his first breaths without them collapsing. Remarkably, these surfactants also act as his starting signal for labor, releasing certain proteins into his amniotic fluid which create an inflammatory response in his mama, triggering contractions.[124] Her body only begins labor once she is assured that his lungs are fully mature and ready to support his independent life.

Fascinating though they are, these details are more than biological trivia. They tell a lyrical story of God's tender provision for our babies as they venture from the womb. He has put intricate protective mechanisms in place—seeing, for example, that the processes that start to bring a baby into the world are the same ones that ready him to survive in it—to ensure that our babies are not born before all is ready.

But these protections may be subverted if we intervene to bring labor forward even by a little. What if I lost patience a few days before my uterine muscles learned to synchronize or my cervix was prepared to stretch? What if I scheduled an induction just hours before my baby was to have packed his glycogen picnic, or while the insides of his lungs were still sticky? I'd get not just the same result on an expedited schedule, but a departure into an altogether different kind of birth where I lost the control I was aiming to seize. Clearly, I would only deprive my baby of the biological advantages God gave him if I were persuaded there was a compelling reason—and while there *are* sometimes compelling reasons for induction, impatience simply isn't one of them.

Could it be that God knows better than we do how to time a baby's birth? Could it be that by bearing through the final days of pregnancy (trying as they are) I give my child a precious birth-day gift? But if so, how am I to find the strength for it? The epistle writer gives this answer: "Let us run with endurance the race that is set before us, looking unto Jesus, the author and finisher of *our* faith, who for the joy that was set before Him endured the cross, despising the shame, and has sat down at the right hand of the throne of God" (Heb. 12:1–2). He's addressing first-century Jewish Christians, encouraging them to persist in their faith, patiently enduring the hardship they face for the sake of the eternal prize they hope to make their own. But his words also bear great meaning for women on the cusp of motherhood. Let's consider five aspects of his counsel.

First, notice that by waiting, we are not just walking in place; we're running a race (though maybe it's more of a speed-waddling marathon than a hundred-meter dash). There's a reason it's so exhausting: waiting takes a lot of strength, as the disciples learned one night in Gethsemane. It's often harder to do less than more. Among midwives, for example, the ability to *appear* to be doing nothing but knitting silently in a corner while keeping a hawk's eye on what is happening is a highly prized skill developed through years of experience. It takes more internal work, they say, to sit still and let labor take its own course than it does to be "useful" by manipulating, controlling, and interfering.

I too must work hard to wait. Again and again I answer the same tiresome questions: "Still pregnant, huh?" "What are you doing here?" "Haven't you had that baby yet?" I come for extra appointments to monitor my baby's well-being during those days following forty weeks. I shed many frustrated tears as my waiting brings the expected hour to fruition. Like the muscles of my back, my spiritual muscles grow sore as I exercise my patience.

And this is the second detail to draw out of the Hebrews passage. I am to run my race "with persistence," elsewhere translated as "patience," "longsuffering," "endurance." Patience is helpful during the last weeks of pregnancy, but in motherhood it becomes a straight-up survival skill, for it's by staying patient in moments that tempt us to "lose it," Christ tells us, that we possess our souls (Luke 21:19). As St. Paisios says, "A mother asks God to grant her patience. Let's say she's got the table set for dinner and the little child pulls the table cloth spilling everything on the floor. This is as if the child is saying to the mother: 'Mom, be patient!'"[125]

Impatience, on the other hand, according to St. Isaac the Syrian, only doubles our hardships into a suffocating foretaste of hell. "For a man's patience casts off his distress, while faintness of heart is the mother of anguish, . . . from which ten thousand trials gush forth: confusion, wrath, blasphemy, protesting and bewailing one's lot"[126] (sounds familiar). But though the trials of an impatient person are many, he goes on, "the remedy for them all is one: humility of heart." Humility does not take from us the difficulties that require our patience, but it relieves us of the impression that we are the ones who make the world turn, helping us to rest under divine providence. As St. Basil the Great says, a humble heart allows us to "be glad and bear with patience everything the world throws at us, secure in the knowledge that it is then that we are most in the mind of God."[127]

How, in turn, do we acquire the humility that remedies our impatience? This question brings us to the third point of our verse from Hebrews, which calls Jesus "the author and finisher of our faith." Much like labor, humble patience cannot be called up at will. Too often when I *try* to be humble, I only get self-conscious, proud, angry, or despondent. Instead, patience is a fruit of the Holy Spirit (Gal. 5:22) and a gift from God, who Himself is "longsuffering and abundant in mercy" (Ps. 144/145:8). I may not have any patience of my own to summon, but He who humbly endured mocking, spitting, jabbing, and death at the hands of those He was saving has plenty to share with me. And if I can rely on Christ to finish my faith, how much more can I rely on Him to finish my pregnancy! According to Clement of Alexandria, "The flowers of marriage are children, which the Divine Husbandman plucks from the meadows of flesh."[128] God has lovingly tended this flower in me all pregnancy long, and I can trust Him to gather it at the peak of its bloom.

A fourth point about the Hebrews text regards the "joy that was set before Him," on account of which Christ endured the Cross. As a runner in the marathon of pregnancy, I too will find strength to complete the race by visualizing the finishing line, and like Christ's, my goal also is joy. Motherhood is an invitation into a world more rich, vibrant, immediate, and beautiful, where both sorrows and joys feel bigger. It's as if love suddenly makes a new dimension of life accessible to me, and I am able to see the technicolor of what surrounded me all along. As I slow down to my baby's pace, moving to the rhythm of oxytocin pulsing between us, I tune into his almost psychedelic sense of wonder arising in a brain with twice as many synapses per neuron as an adult's, and I too notice and cherish the smallest of things. This is the inexpressible joy that is our goal in these final days.

Ultimately, though, pregnancy points us forward to something even greater than the joy of motherhood. And this is our fifth and final point from the Hebrews passage. After running His race with endurance, Christ "sat down at the right hand of the throne of God." His patience was directed toward the Kingdom—and ours is, too. A pregnant woman, we could say, is an eschatological creature. Even just looking at her, we know she is not a finished work. She makes manifest that "'what-is-not-yet' is already buried in the 'what-is'"[129]—that our present life is not all it can be or will be. Her very body is a symbol pointing ahead to the end times when her pregnancy will be fulfilled in motherhood, just as creation will be fulfilled in heaven. "Thy Kingdom come. *Maranatha*!" her belly prays.

But while it may not always be so visibly apparent, at core *every* human soul is eschatological, for as Scripture says, "He indeed put eternity in their hearts in such a way that man may not find out the work that God made from the beginning to the end" (Eccl. 3:11). And so pregnancy is a moment that teaches all of humanity to cry with the Psalmist, "My soul *waits* for the Lord / More than those who watch for the morning—*yes, more than* those who watch for the morning" (Ps. 129/130:6, NKJV). "Behold . . . as the eyes of the maidservant look to the hands of her mistress, / So our eyes look to the Lord our God / Until He shall have compassion on us" (Ps. 122/123:2).

As we await the hour which "is coming and now is" (John 4:23), let us turn the yearning of our expectant hearts toward God. Let us allow these precious last weeks to do their work in us, drawing us ever deeper into a spirit of patient humility. And may this time of waiting be for us a fruitful training ground for motherhood and for eternity.

Going Forth

The end is where we start from.
—T. S. ELIOT, "LITTLE GIDDING"

We've made it. "The time is fulfilled" (Mark 1:15). At thirty-seven weeks, we've officially arrived at full term, and this pilgrimage through pregnancy is reaching an end.

A bit bedraggled, perhaps, but victorious, we now stand at the walls of the holy city that has been our destination all along. Beyond its gates, we can see the people within—fellow travelers who went ahead on the path and reached the land of parenthood before us—as they bustle around, looking competent and self-assured. In comparison, we may feel unqualified for what we know awaits us on the other side. We're not sure we meet the criteria for entry. No one asks to see our passport or credentials. Yet there are the open gates, beckoning us through.

Parenthood, people often remark, is the only job a person can get without any certification, training, or experience. It may be the most important work we can never become qualified to do. But those who talk like this evidently haven't been paying attention. For, if after all this we are not prepared for parenthood, what have we been up to these many weeks? Why have these three trimesters been such hard spiritual and physical work? What has been the purpose of pregnancy, if not to train us for this moment?

In fact, we only become parents by graduating from a grueling nine-month training expedition—what I've called a pilgrimage.

Each day, we have walked on courageously without a break, our packs growing weightier by the moment. We've camped out in the wilds of the unknown. We've drunk deeply from the clear streams of joy. We've met and wrestled with the beasts of death, pain, and self-doubt. We've followed the path well-trodden by the feet of countless women of immense strength and beauty, in whose company we glimpse a little of these qualities in ourselves.

And the journey has changed us. Every aspect of our lives has been conditioned so thoroughly that we're entirely reshaped. We emerge not sculpted and hard, as we might expect from such a training, but with softer, humbler, messier contours. It might seem an odd, ineffective sort of training which leaves us less trim than we were before setting off. And this would be true if it were a worldly assignment we were preparing for. But mother-hood is a sacred land governed by the strange, upside-down rules of the Beatitudes. It is the meek who inherit the earth. It is the weak who are strong. It is by becoming leaky and porous that we let love in and out. It's by decreasing that we grow. It's our own insufficiency that reveals God's sufficiency in us, empowering us to become mothers.

And so throughout this pilgrimage, the kind of training we have received has proven to be precisely the preparation we needed. God has walked us through the steps that led to this point of readiness. All that has happened has prepared us, our babies, and the world for the moment at which they will enter it. From the kicks in the bladder that wake us like a monastery bell (discussed in Week 30) to the stretch marks on our bellies reminding us to become thin places in the world (Week 35), the rigors of pregnancy have proven not a curse but a chance to grow into the people we are going to need to be. From the instinctive prostrations of a laboring woman (Week 12) to the dark waters through which our babies pass as they are born (Week 19), our bodies point the way for our souls, ushering us along the path of self-giving love by which humanity is saved. From the umbilical links to our foremothers of every generation (Week 14) to the eucharistic form of breastfeeding (Week 32), the symbolic shape of childbearing shows forth God's redeeming action in the world. Reflecting on all that He has wrought in us over these nine months, like Isaiah we cry, "Here am I and the children whom the LORD has given me! / *We* are for signs and wonders in Israel / from the LORD of hosts" (Is. 8:18, NKJV).

Physically and spiritually, pregnancy has done its job. And yet . . . and yet . . . the point at which we've arrived is not a destination but a new starting place. When a pilgrim arrives at the holy city, she quickly discovers that she still isn't "there yet." As a sojourner, she may stay for a short time, but soon she must return home to begin the real work of pilgrimage in her daily life. It's like the Divine Liturgy: at the end of a service, the work of the people is not finished but carries on into the everyday, in what has been called the "liturgy after the Liturgy." Having been fed by the Body of Christ, we become the bread with which the world is fed, and so we are sent out to continue the Eucharist with the words, "Let us go forth." This is how it is for us. We have completed the odyssey of pregnancy, but the path of motherhood stretches ahead. Our lives do not remain settled in the place of readiness but always open out into a new stage.

And so both we and our babies leave this moment behind; we leave our pregnancies, and our babies leave our bodies. Throughout motherhood we will know this experience again and again. Our little ones leave first our wombs, then our arms, then our sphere of commanding influence, and finally our homes. Their job is continually to go forth, and ours is to allow them to do so.

Being a mother, as one scholar puts it, is "a lifelong process of 'being there to be left'."[130]

Under the current circumstances, being left may sound like just the ticket. Our backs are sore, our ankles swollen, and our sleep disturbed from having to share space with another person. We may be desperate to have our "own body" back. On the other hand, there is a great sweetness to the organic unity we share with our babies in pregnancy that is hard to leave behind. I remember that every time my own postpartum tummy grumbled I would think for a second it was my baby kicking—then, with a certain regret, I would recall that he was sleeping in his bassinet rather than inside me. I would not have traded his babyhood for anything, yet I missed the utter oneness we had shared in pregnancy.

In Serbia, where I spent that first pregnancy, it is traditional for a newborn going home for the first time to be greeted outside the hospital by a brass band. Never mind the baby's delicate ears: passersby can hear the horns from several blocks away, blaring out the message that a new human being is coming forth into the world. The music is raw and wild, riotously joyful but hardly beautiful—it's almost painful, in fact. The players are men, always men, often looking disheveled and worn, as if they know for themselves that the life in which this child is joining them is not going to be easy. They certainly don't look like the types to get sentimental about a little bundle of joy. Yet there they are, gathered just for the occasion, making raucous music together, no holds barred.

Like the soundtrack of the Serbian newborn's departure from hospital, our own going forth is one part bitter, one part sweet. But as this pilgrimage through pregnancy together draws to a close, my prayer is that we "shall go out with joy" (Is. 55:12

NKJV). Many challenges wait for us on the path, but looking back over the terrain we've covered during these months, we can take heart. We have not been alone, but guided and tended by One who "gently lead[s] those who are with young" (Is. 40:11 NKJV). As surely as He has brought us to this moment, our Lord will show us the way ahead.

Questions for Reflection and Discussion

PART ONE: WELCOMING A NEW REALITY

Week 6: Fiat

1. The author's obstetrician asked her, "Are you happy about this pregnancy or not?" How would you respond to this question?
2. On a spectrum from initiators to responders, where would you place yourself?
3. What holds you back from saying "yes" to this pregnancy?

Week 7: Co-Creators

1. If you could change one thing about the environment in which your tiny baby is growing to allow him to become his best self, what would it be?
2. What influence do you have on your developing child? What do you not have the power to influence?
3. What is the most freely creative thing you've ever done?
4. What would you like to work on being more thankful for?

Week 8: Recognition

1. Have you ever encountered Christ in an unexpected place?
2. What does it mean that humans are made in the image of God?
3. How would life be different if we saw Christ in every human person, the way Elizabeth and John recognized Jesus in the womb of His mother?

4. Practically speaking, how could you incorporate prayer for your unborn child into your daily life?

Week 9: Hospitality

1. Consider a time you were warmly welcomed into someone else's home. How did you feel? What did your host do or say that made the difference?

2. A host cannot share from an empty store cupboard. What can you do now to stock up the shelves of your heart so that you will be able to give generously to your little guest?

3. Hebrews 3:6 says we are God's home. What does this look like in your life?

PART TWO: EXPERIENCING PREGNANCY

Week 10: Self-Denial

1. To what extent do you consider pregnancy to be a selfish act? To what extent do you consider it an act of selflessness?

2. What things are you giving up during this pregnancy? What are you gaining?

3. What is your attitude toward limitations in your life?

4. "He must increase, but I *must* decrease" (John 3:30). What do you think this statement of St. John the Forerunner means?

5. God loves a *cheerful* giver, and each of us should "give as he purposes in his heart, not grudgingly or of necessity" (2 Cor. 9:7). How much self-giving is too much during pregnancy?

Week 11: Death

1. What is a "little death"? What little deaths are you experiencing at this time?

2. Why do you think maternal death rates vary so greatly from

country to country, when women's bodies are the same the world around?

3. Make a list of questions to ask when choosing a care provider who will safeguard the health of you and your baby. Some ideas to get you started: *What percentage of women in your care undergo Cesareans? Have any mothers died in your care or at your facility? If I choose you, will you will be the one to catch my baby, or is it possible that another practitioner will be covering for you at the time?*

4. What can you do to *fruitfully* bring the monastic practice of the remembrance of death into your daily life during this pregnancy?

Week 12: Weakness

1. What are some signs that weakness is despised in our society?

2. How have you protected yourself with an "impermeable exo-skeleton" in the past?

3. "Blessed is the person who knows his own weakness because awareness of this becomes for him the foundation and the beginning of all that is good and beautiful." What do these words of St. Isaac the Syrian mean?

4. In what areas are you being invited to grow in compassion at the moment?

5. How easy is it for you to accept the help others offer?

6. With whom do you feel safe enough to "open up" as one needs to in order to give birth?

Week 13: Strength

1. When have you felt strongest, like a force of nature?

2. What is *dynamis?* How does it differ from *exousia?*

3. What parallels do you see between battle and motherhood?

4. What does it mean to be "empowered" versus being "overshadowed by God's power"?

5. "The Lord is my strength and my defense; He has become my salvation" (Ex. 15:2 NIV). What does this verse mean to you?

Week 14: Links

1. Why do you think children are so fascinated with belly buttons?

2. What happens to a baby's blood when the cord is clamped and cut before it stops pulsating?

3. What does the author mean when she says that family-making is more like geometry than arithmetic?

4. Who are the "begats" in your family line, without whom you would not be a person? Who are the "begats" in your spiritual life, without whom you would not be a Christian?

Week 15: Trinity

1. "Pregnancy is the icon of human connectedness."
What do you understand by this statement of Frederica Mathewes-Green?

2. What does it mean for the Trinity to be "a mystery to participate in"?

3. When have you experienced the distinctness of yourself and your baby? When have you experienced the unity?

4. For Sarah, whose home appears behind the three figures of the Trinity icon, the encounter with the Holy Trinity was deeply healing, both physically and socially. After living her whole life with the burden of infertility, after their visit she was blessed with a pregnancy and finally became the foremother of many nations. In what areas of your life might this pregnancy become a time of growth, recalibration, and healing?

Week 16: Unknown

1. What is your deepest fear in this moment? How is it related to the fear of the unknown?

2. What are some different ways of knowing a person? Is it possible to know someone without knowing anything *about* them at all?

3. Who knows you best of all? What does it feel like to be deeply known?

4. What gifts is the child in your womb bringing to you and to the world that no one else could give?

Week 17: Naming

1. What is the meaning of your own name? What relationship do you have with your name?

2. "He called My name from My mother's womb" (Is. 49:1). What do these words mean to you at this moment in your life?

3. List the names of possible candidates to be your child's godparents. What might happen if you started to pray for these people and their future role in your child's life?

PART THREE: EXPLORING BIRTH IN SYMBOLS

Week 18: Light

1. How do you imagine the world looks, sounds, feels for your baby just now?

2. Share a time when you experienced "gladsome" light—perhaps the joy of sunrise, candlelight, or a shooting star. What was that like?

3. At a baptism, oil is used to anoint the waters before immersion. Why do you suppose this is?

Week 19: Waters

1. Recount an experience you had of the life-giving power of water, or one of its destructive power.

2. What is the function of amniotic fluid?

3. In what ways could it be said that birth is a baptism into the world?

Week 20: Pascha

1. What do you know, or what can you find out, about the story of your own birth? Can you identify any ways in which the events of your birth, or stories about it, have had an impact on you over the years?

2. Our seed brings forth fruit because it first dies (John 12:24). What have been some instances of this in your life?

3. Check out the context of Colossians 1:24. What do you think St. Paul means when he says "I fill up in my flesh what is lacking in the afflictions of Christ"? Is it folly to think that we too could do such a thing?

4. Can women really be saved through childbearing?

PART FOUR: FEARING LABOR

Week 21: Control

1. The author asserts that the fear of losing control in labor takes many forms. What form, if any, does it take for you?

2. Where in your life do you especially like to feel in control?

3. Are you more naturally drawn to make a specific birth plan or to go with the flow? What might be the pitfalls of your approach?

4. Does God "control" our lives?

Week 22: Pain

1. What do you understand by "the curse of Eve"?

2. Can pain ever be "positive"?

3. John Keats wrote, "Call the world, if you please, 'the vale of Soul-making.' Then you will find out the use of the world."[131] Do you agree?

4. Say someone offered you the chance to live free of any pain for the rest of your life—would you take it? Why?

Week 23: Bodies

1. In what ways has your body changed over the course of your pregnancy so far? What feelings do those changes bring up for you?

2. Do you agree that our age is marked by gnostic heresy? Why or why not?

3. What does it mean that our bodies are created for relationship?

4. How would the world be different if we truly treated our bodies as if they were good?

PART FIVE: BRAVING LABOR

Week 24: Companions

1. Over the past hundred years, men have gone from unwelcome intruders to expected actors in the birthing room. What are the positive aspects of this change? What are the negative aspects?

2. If you expect that your baby's father will be with you during labor, what will his needs for support be, and how will they be met?

3. How will you incorporate the ancient treasury of womanly experience and knowledge into your birthing?

Week 25: Prayer

1. This chapter contained many examples of women's use of prayer in labor. Which one most spoke to you?

2. What are some techniques commonly taught by childbirth educators that find their fulfillment in the practices of the Church?

3. What is your unborn baby's current experience of prayer?

4. How can you use the shifting sands of pregnancy as an opportunity to rebuild your prayer life on a deeper foundation?

Week 26: Rhythm

1. Where do you observe rhythms in the world around you? Where do you observe rhythms inside you?

2. How does rhythm bond humans with one another? How does rhythm bond us with God?

3. "Do not remember the former things, nor reason about the things of old. Behold, I will do new things, which shall now spring forth" (Is. 43:18–19). What relevance does this verse have for a woman in labor? In the postpartum months?

Week 27: Thoughts

1. As Christians, "Miracles of matter and mind are our daily currency, our bread and butter." Do you agree?

2. The author gave several examples from everyday life of the interaction between mind and matter. Can you think of a few of your own?

3. Which of the "arrow" prayers (what we might call spiritual birthing affirmations) from this chapter most spoke to you?

Note down a couple of your own. These can form the beginning of a list you can refer to while you are preparing for labor.

4. How could you further develop this skill of observing your thoughts without assenting to them? How might it benefit you to do so?

PART SIX: BECOMING A PARENT

Week 28: Expertise

1. In what fields do you consider yourself an expert? Do you feel more or less confident in your knowledge than when you first started in this field?

2. Who are the greatest experts on birth and parenting in your life?

3. In what respects are you already an expert on the baby you're carrying?

4. What is an "amateurish" parent?

Week 29: Village

1. Who are the current members of your village?

2. What could you do to deepen your ties to those in the village of your church?

3. What form does your everyday relationship with the village of heaven take? Has there been a time when you have felt its presence especially strongly?

4. Do you agree that baby showers, as they are commonly held, are better at meeting the needs of corporations than of expectant mothers?

Week 30: Nightwatch

1. In the story from this chapter, the author was reminded by the light from her neighbor's window of the work of others keeping the night watch with her. What could you do to remind your future postpartum self of the same?

2. In what ways could the regular night wakings of later pregnancy be considered a gift? How can you "redeem" this gift?

3. "The night shall be light to my delight. For darkness shall not be dark because of You, and the night shall be bright as day" (Ps. 138/139:11–12). How does this text read for a mother?

Week 31: Interruptions

1. What does it mean to say that interruptibility is "an art"?

2. Can you think of a time in your life when, as it did for Jairus's daughter, an interruption revealed the providence of God?

3. How would we react to interruptions if we truly trusted God?

Week 32: Milk

1. "Oh, taste and see that the Lord is good" (Ps. 33/34:9). Where in your life at the moment are you experiencing the milky sweetness of God's goodness?

2. The Milk-Giver icon is so important to the Church that there are not just one but two feast days dedicated to it. Why do you think it is so venerated?

3. Is the Milk-Giver icon immodest? Would it be immodest for a mother to feed as she is shown feeding?

4. Imagine you were a mother struggling or unable to breastfeed. How might you feel about the Milk-Giver icon?

Week 33: Forty Days

1. "Return, O my soul, to your rest, because the Lord showed you kindness" (Ps. 114/115:7). Why have women traditionally rested during the weeks after childbirth? Why do they not usually do so in our own society today?

2. Would you like to live in a society that still practices *la cuarantina*? Why or why not?

3. Are you "good" at resting?

4. What could you do now to start practicing for the still quietness of the postnatal period?

PART SEVEN: PREPARING FOR BIRTH

Week 34: Nesting

1. What is still on your nesting to-do list? What is the worst that could happen if your baby came before it was done?

2. Do you think expectant parents can ever be fully prepared for their baby's arrival?

3. What is the connection between the concepts of nesting, holding, womb, and compassion?

Week 35: Thinning

1. Think of a thin place you've been. What was it like to be there?

2. Who is the "thinnest" person you know (spiritually speaking)? What is it about that person that makes him or her thin?

3. What is uncomfortable about thin places? What is beautiful?

Week 36: Waiting

1. On a calendar, color in a block extending three weeks in front of your due date and two weeks after: five weeks in all. This is the normal range within which your baby might be born. How does looking at a "due month" feel different from looking at a "due date"?

2. Is there such a thing as a natural induction method?

3. What does it mean during this time to keep your prize in sight?

4. To God, "what is has already been, and what is to be has already been" (Eccl. 3:15). Does God ever wait for anything?

5. Why does the author say that humans are eschatological creatures?

Week 37: Going Forth

1. In what ways do you feel ready to become a parent?

2. Do you agree that a mother is "there to be left"?

3. How does this stage of pregnancy help you to understand the "joyful sadness" of which our faith speaks?

4. How has the pilgrimage of pregnancy changed you?

Losing a Baby

A voice was heard in Ramah, lamentation, weeping,
and great mourning, Rachel weeping for her children,
refusing to be comforted, because they are no more.
—MATTHEW 2:18

I pray no one need read these words.

This section is intended for those whose forty-week pilgrimage has come to an untimely end through miscarriage or stillbirth. Such a topic may feel out of place in a book about pregnancy, but very sadly, for many of us, loss and pregnancy will go hand in hand. Any room of more than a handful of women contains someone who has suffered a pregnancy loss, but too often this part of life remains hidden, and we are left to mourn alone. I would not want this book to conspire with that tragedy.

Pregnancy loss is a very varied experience. Some of us do not know anything is wrong until miscarriage is upon us, and others find at a medical appointment that their baby has died in their womb. To some of us this happens only once; for others a miscarriage will be just the latest in a terrible series of losses. We may lose a baby early or late in pregnancy. Medical studies show, however, that no matter how far a woman's pregnancy has progressed, many of her emotions will be the same.[132] It is a depth of sadness that cannot be understood fully unless one has experienced it.

One woman who has experienced it is Rachel, the childless

wife of Jacob from the Old Testament. If we are brave enough to look on it, her icon, the Lament of Rachel, shows that she shares our feelings. Her pain is palpable. Lacking the strength to stand, she sits cross-legged, her arms raised above her head, weeping. Surrounding her on the ground are the souls of many tiny children, tightly swaddled, a lick of hair on each forehead, every eye closed in death. Although each one may look the same to the eyes of the world, clearly she sees that each one is unique and of infinite value. No one baby can replace any other, and no child she might bear in future can make up for the ones she has lost.

I too am someone who has lived through this. I'll tell my story for anyone who fears she is alone. I miscarried a baby in early pregnancy between the births of my second and third living children. It was painful but uncomplicated, and I did not need medical attention. I remained peacefully in my bed for a day and a half while contractions were going on, reading the psalms, crying, and listening to the birds sing outside my window. My husband needed to be at work, but during the worst of it a kind aunt came to care for my children and sit with me, leaving behind an evening meal for my family when she went home.

Once everything had passed, I was able to find the remains of a baby in the biggest clot. It was too poorly formed and little to tell, but we sensed that this was a boy and named him Seraphim. We wrapped his body in a doily that my grandmother had embroidered, cutting off pieces of the doily for our living children to keep and remember him by. I inscribed the verse from Psalm 21(22):29 on the cloth with a Sharpie: "They that are fat upon the earth shall eat and worship; all they that go down to the dust shall bow down before Him, and none can keep alive his own soul."

A bit later we brought Seraphim to church in a little wooden

box, where close members of our community met us for a service that our priest had assembled for the occasion. Then we
took our baby home and buried him, still shrouded in his doily,
in a prayer garden in the yard. Seraphim's siblings helped fill the
soil back into the hole his father had dug. Over the place of his
burial we planted forget-me-nots that return every year.

Even as someone who works with childbearing women, I did
not anticipate the gravity of this loss. Only later was I able to
identify more clearly the source of my trauma. Thankfully I was
protected from any sense of being at fault or deficient because of
what had happened. But I felt my miscarriage had reversed the
order of creation, putting death before birth. I was the mother
of this tiny person, and by dying he had become my senior in
the Kingdom. Everything was backwards. Yet because I had
never known the child of my own womb, there was little room
for complicated feelings. My huge sadness had a kind of sweet
purity to it that left room for a sense of wonder.

Over the weeks that followed my miscarriage, I began to look
for the meaning and value of this event in the life of our family.
I marveled that my children had a sibling who was closer to God
than any of us, whose prayers we could ask. I rejoiced that my
child, whom I had not been able to bring to baptism, had been
baptized directly into the vast sea of God's mercy. I thanked God
through my tears that this experience was mysteriously uniting
me to a community of grieving mothers in all times and places,
and not least to the Most Holy Theotokos.

Ten years on, my Seraphim remains an active part of my
life. He is brought to mind every day by the conspicuous gap
he leaves between his sisters. His patron saint is as close to our
family as any of my living children's patrons. The anniversa-
ries of his miscarriage and due date are emotional fixtures in

our family's annual calendar. I tell my children his story so that even the ones born after him will know that our family is not contained within the walls of our home but extends into eternity. And to this day, when I am taking a head count at the playground, I still look for one child too many. I don't suppose I'll ever shake the sense I have that someone is missing.

For us as for Rachel, there is nothing that can sweep away the pain, but some things do help us to bear it. For practical instructions, the Lost Innocents blog (https://lostinnocentsorthodox.blogspot.com/) is very helpful. Most importantly, we must not hesitate to honor the reality of the person we have lost. Mothers who have found a body can bury it with honor. Each of us can give our child a name and speak that name aloud. We can take photos and keepsakes of this time in life. We may be able to say prayers with our church community. We can reach out for support and accept offers of help, so that we'll know we're not alone. This experience is valid, and we are seen by God.

Our loss has far-reaching implications. If we have had a baby, whether living or dead, we should consider ourselves postpartum and treat ourselves accordingly. We can nourish our bodies with nutritious foods and our souls with time to rest. We may wish to try to conceive again right away, but often it is good to let ourselves grieve and heal for some months before becoming devoted to a new pregnancy. We can seek medical and spiritual advice about this. If and when another child comes, he will not take the place of the one who has died but will add new layers of loss and love to life.

In the coming years, surprising things may bring strong feelings to the surface, like going for an ultrasound during a new pregnancy, celebrating the birth of a friend's baby, or milestones throughout the year that remind us of what has happened and what might have been. At these times we can be gentle with ourselves. We are mother to these children, and both the loss and the relationship between us will always exist. Though the pilgrimage through this pregnancy has ended, our journey has not been for nothing—it has taken us over different holy ground. By the prayers of the Theotokos, may we all come at last to our final destination, and be united with our lost children "in a place of brightness, a place of refreshment, a place of repose, where all sickness, sighing, and sorrow have fled away."

Endnotes

1   Robert Macfarlane, *The Old Ways* (London and New York: Penguin, 2013), p. 249

2   Lisa Baraitser, *Maternal Encounters: The Ethics of Interruption* (New York and London: Routledge, 2009), p. 4

3   Ann Borders et al, "Chronic Stress and Low Birth Weight Neonates in a Low-Income Population of Women," *Obstetrics and Gynecology* 2007 Vol. 109(2), pp. 331–338

4   G. Persico et al, "Maternal singing of lullabies during pregnancy and after birth: Effects on mother-infant bonding and on newborns' behaviour," *Women Birth* Vol. 30(4), 2017, pp. e214–e220

5   One study found that traumatic experiences altered the sperm of male mice so that their offspring exhibited behavioral consequences of trauma they themselves had not suffered. See K. Gapp et al, "Implication of sperm RNAs in transgenerational inheritance of the effects of early trauma in mice," *Nature Neuroscience* 17, 2014, pp. 667–669

6   Met. Kallistos Ware, "In the Image and the Likeness of God: the Human Person in Orthodox Spirituality," talk given at Marquette University on March 7, 2016, https://law-media.marquette.edu/Mediasite/Play/f81907906ea84b2f9a247cd43fecb9211d (accessed May 15, 2019)

7   Ibid.

8   Alexander Schmemann, *For the Life of the World: Sacraments and Orthodoxy* (Crestwood: St Vladimir's Seminary Press, 2004), p. 37

9   Ina May Gaskin, *Spiritual Midwifery* (Summertown: Book Publishing Company, 2002), p. 271

10 Francis Cuthebert, *The Rule of St. Benedict with Expository* (Brandon: Revelation-Insight Publishing Co., 2015), ch. 53

11 Gustl Marlock, Halko Weiss, Courtenay Young, and Michael Soth (eds.), *The Handbook of Body Psychotherapy and Somatic Psychology* (Berkeley: North Atlantic Books, 2015), p. 336

12 Robert E. Sinkewicz (trans.), *Evagrius of Pontus: The Greek Ascetic Corpus* (Oxford: Oxford University Press, 2003), p. 51

13 Cuthebert, op. cit., ch. 53

14 Naomi Wolf, *Misconceptions: Truth, Lies and the Unexpected on the Journey to Motherhood* (London: Vintage, 2002), p. 53

15 Op. cit., p. 67

16 Met. Kallistos Ware, *The Inner Kingdom* (Crestwood, St. Vladimir's Seminary Press, 2001), p. 30

17 Ina May Gaskin, "Maternal Death in the United States: A Problem Solved

or a Problem Ignored?" *Journal of Perinatal Education* 17(2), Spring 2008, pp. 9–13

18 Naomi Stadlen, *What Mothers Do Especially When It Looks Like Nothing* (London: Piatkus Books Ltd, 2004), p. 183

19 Wolf, op. cit., p. 62

20 Holy Transfiguration Monastery (trans.), *St. Isaac the Syrian: The Ascetical Homilies* 8 (Boston: Holy Transfiguration Monastery, 1984), p. 67

21 BBC News, "Born Above the Floodwaters," http://news.bbc.co.uk/1/hi/world/africa/662472.stm (accessed May 13, 2019)

22 Ellen Hodnett, "Pain and women's satisfaction with the experience of childbirth: A systematic review," *American Journal of Obstetrics and Gynecology* 186, 2002, S160–172

23 See David Schwartz (ed.), *Maternal Death and Pregnancy-Related Morbidity Among Indigenous Women of Mexico and Central America: An Anthropological, Epidemiological and Biomedical Approach* (Cham: Springer Nature, 2018), p. 23

24 Frederica Mathewes-Green, *Welcome to the Orthodox Church: An Introduction to Eastern Christianity* (Brewster: Paraclete Press, 2015), p. 173

25 From the Akathist to the Mother of God and the Annunciation Kontakion, respectively

26 Penny Armstrong and Sheryl Feldman, *A Wise Birth* (London: Pinter & Martin, 2007), p. 15

27 Sam and Bethany Torode (eds.), *Aflame: Ancient Wisdom on Marriage* (Grand Rapids: Wm. B. Eerdmans Publishing Company, 2005), p. 102

28 "Three Methods of Prayer," attributed to St. Symeon the New Theologian, *Philokalia*

29 See Shannon Fischer, "What Lives in Your Belly Button?" https://news.nationalgeographic.com/news/2012/11/121114-belly-button-bacteria-science-health-dunn/ (accessed May 13, 2019)

30 As my mother, Barbara Smith, would say!

31 James Joyce, *Ulysses* (Oxford: Oxford University Press, 1998), p. 38

32 Catharine Roth and David Anderson (trans.), *St. John Chrysostom on Marriage and Family Life* (Crestwood: St. Vladimir's Seminary Press, 1997), p. 76

33 Frederica Mathewes-Green, *Gender: Men, Women, Sex, Feminism* (Ben Lomond: Conciliar Press, 2002), p. 36

34 Baraitser, op. cit., p. 38

35 Met. Kallistos Ware, *The Orthodox Way* (Crestwood: St Vladimir's Seminary Press, 1995), p. 33

36 See Morwenna Ludlow, *Gregory of Nyssa: Ancient and (Post)modern* (Oxford: Oxford University Press, 2007), p. 28

37 Ware, *The Orthodox Way*, p. 17

38 St. Augustine of Hippo, "On the Trinity" 12:5 http://www.newadvent.org/fathers/130112.htm (accessed May 15, 2019)

39 Julian Stead, "Perichoresis in the Christological Chapters of the De

Trinitate of Pseudo-Cyril of Alexandria," *Dominican Studies* Vol. 6, 1953, pp. 12–20

40 J.A. Mennella, C.P. Jagnow and G.K Beauchamp, "Prenatal and postnatal flavor learning by human infants," *Pediatrics* Vol. 107(6), June 2001, p. E88

41 Holy Transfiguration Monastery (trans.), op. cit., pp. 226–227

42 Dumitru Staniloae, *Orthodox Spirituality: A Practical Guide for the Faithful and a Definitive Manual for the Scholar* (South Canaan: St. Tikhon's Seminary Press, 2002), p. 38

43 L. Bricker, N. Medley and J. Pratt, "Routine Ultrasound in Late Pregnancy (After 24 Weeks' Gestation)," *Cochrane Database of Systematic Reviews* No. 6, 2015

44 Andrew Williams, "Masks and Veils," http://ftftl.org/2016/05/masks-and-veils/ (19 May 2016) (accessed August 28, 2019)

45 J.T. Jones et al, "How do I love thee? Let me count the Js: implicit egotism and interpersonal attraction," *Journal of Personality and Social Psychology* 87(5), 2004, pp. 665–683

46 B.W. Pelham, M.C. Mirenberg, and J.T. Jones, "Why Susie sells seashells by the seashore: implicit egoism and major life decisions," *Journal of Personality and Social Psychology* 82(4), 2002, pp. 469–487

47 Thomas Hopko, "Jesus—Name Above Every Name," https://www.ancientfaith.com/podcasts/namesofjesus/jesus_-_name_above_every_name (accessed May 13, 2019)

48 Stadlen, op. cit., p. 208

49 Nativity Troparion

50 Among others, St. Seraphim, St. Gregory Palamas, St. Symeon the New Theologian, Elder Sophrony, and St. Anthony the Great

51 All my observations about the cultural significance of the caul are drawn from Thomas Forbes, "The Social History of the Caul," *Yale Journal of Biology and Medicine* 25(6), 1953, pp. 495–508.

52 Ware, *The Inner Kingdom*, p. 27

53 T. S. Eliot, *Four Quartets* (New York: Harcourt, Brace and Company, 1943), p. 26

54 Jacques-Paul Migne (ed.), *Patrologiae cursus completus* (Paris: Migne, 1844–55), Vol. 75, col. 612

55 Pam England, *Birthing from Within* (Albuquerque: Partera Press, 1998), p. 6

56 Hodnett, op. cit., S160–172

57 Deering et al, "Patients Presenting with Birth Plans in a Military Tertiary Care Hospital: a Descriptive Study of Plans and Outcomes," *Military Medicine* 171(8), 2006, pp. 778–780

58 Gant et al, "Expert opinion vs. patient perception of obstetrical outcomes in laboring women with birth plans," *Journal of Reproductive Medicine* 55(1–2), 2010, pp. 31–35

59 Virginia Woolf, "On Being Ill," in T.S. Eliot, *The New Criterion* (London:

Faber, 1926), p. 34

60 Siri Leknes and Brock Bastian, "The Benefits of Pain," *Review of Philosophy and Psychology* Vol. 5(1), 2014, pp. 57–70

61 C.S. Lewis, *The Problem of Pain* (London: Fount, 1977), p. 76

62 E.g. ,N.I. Eisenberger et al, "Attachment figures activate a safety signal-related neural region and reduce pain experience," *Proceedings of the National Academy of Sciences of the United States of America* Vol. 108, 2011, pp. 11721–11726

63 B. Bastian et al, "Physical Pain and Guilty Pleasures," *Social Psychological and Personality Science* 4(2) 2012, pp. 215–219

64 Quoted in Philip Yancey and Paul Brand, *The Gift of Pain: Why We Hurt and What We Can Do About It* (Grand Rapids: Zondervan Publishing House, 1997), p. 300

65 "Kathy" in Ina May Gaskin, *Spiritual Midwifery*, p. 206

66 See Josiah Trenham, "Sexuality, Virginity and Marriage," https://www.ancientfaith.com/podcasts/aftoday/sexuality_virginity_and_marriage (accessed May 15, 2019)

67 Lewis, op. cit., p. 84

68 Georges Florovsky, "The Resurrection of Life," *Bulletin of Harvard University Divinity School* LXIX, 71 (1952)

69 Roth and Anderson (trans.), op. cit., p. 76

70 St. Ephrem the Syrian, Nativity Hymn 4:160–162, in: Kathleen McVey, "Ephrem the Syrian's Use of Female Metaphors to Describe the Deity," *Zeitschrift für Antikes Christentum* Vol. 5(2), 2001, p. 269

71 Torode (eds.), op. cit., p. 82

72 Ronald Hock (trans.), *The Infancy Gospels of James and Thomas* (Salem: Polebridge Press, 1996), p. 43

73 Wenda R. Trevathan, "An Evolutionary Perspective on Authoritative Knowledge about Birth," in Robbie E. Davis-Floyd and Carolyn F. Sargent (eds.), *Childbirth and Authoritative Knowledge* (Berkeley: University of California Press, 1997), p. 82

74 K.K.L. Chan & S. Paterson-Brown, "How do fathers feel after accompanying their partners in labour and delivery?" *Journal of Obstetrics and Gynaecology* 22:11–15 (2002)

75 For instance, scientists have found that when oxytocin is administered to a caged animal, the effects extend to its untreated cagemates. See G. Agren and T. Lundeberg, "Energy conservation in stressed rats exposed to an oxytocin-injected cage mate," *Neuroreport* 13(11), 2002, pp. 1453–7

76 M.A. Bohren et al, "Continuous support for women during childbirth," *Cochrane Database of Systematic Reviews* 7, 2017

77 Attributed to John Kennell

78 Such as Ss. Stylianos, Perpetua and Felicity, Elizabeth the New Martyr, and Irene Chrysovalontou

79 UNICEF, "Nearly 386,000 children will be born worldwide on New Year's Day, says UNICEF," 2018 https://www.unicef.org/rosa/press-releases/nearly-386000-children-will-be-born-worldwide-new-years-day-says-unicef (accessed May 15, 2019)

80 Benedicta Ward (trans.), *Sayings of the Desert Fathers* (Collegeville: Cistercian Publications, 1975), p. 131

81 St. Justin Martyr, *Second Apology*, Chapter 8 http://www.newadvent.org/fathers/0127.htm (accessed May 13, 2019)

82 N.S. Fink et al, "Relaxation during pregnancy: what are the benefits for mother, fetus, and the newborn? A systematic review of the literature," *Journal of Perinatal and Neonatal Nursing* 26(4), 2012, pp. 296–306

83 Frederica Mathewes-Green, *The Jesus Prayer: The Ancient Desert Prayer that Tunes the Heart to God* (Brewster: Paraclete Press, 2009), p. ix

84 George Sylvester Viereck, "What Life Means to Einstein," *The Saturday Evening Post*, October 26, 1929, p. 117

85 Ware, *The Inner Kingdom*, p. 183

86 A. Cagnacci et al, "Diurnal rhythms of labor and delivery in women: modulation by parity and seasons," *American Journal of Obstetric Gynecology* Vol. 178 (1 Pt 1), 1998, pp. 140–145

87 Research presented at the Society for Neuroscience meeting in New Orleans, October 2012, by Schirmer and Escoffier of the University of Singapore; see "The Power of Music: Mind Control by Rhythmic Sound," R. Douglas Fields 2012 https://blogs.scientificamerican.com/guest-blog/the-power-of-music-mind-control-by-rhythmic-sound/ (accessed May 15, 2019)

88 Ware, *The Inner Kingdom*, p. 30

89 St. John Cassian, Institutes 10:2 in Phillip Schaff and Henry Wace (eds.), Nicene and Post-Nicene Fathers, Second Series, Vol. 11 (Buffalo: Christian Literature Publishing Co., 1894), revised and edited for New Advent by Kevin Knight, http://newadvent.org/fathers/3507.htm (accessed May 13, 2019)

90 Peter Chamberas (trans.), *Nicodemos of the Holy Mountain: A Handbook of Spiritual Counsel* (New York: Paulist Press, 1989), p. 81

91 Ana Smiljanic (trans.), *Our Thoughts Determine Our Lives: The Life and Teachings of Elder Thaddeus of Vitovnica* (Platina: Saint Herman of Alaska Brotherhood, 2015), p. 63

92 Ibid., p. 69

93 Ina May Gaskin, *Ina May's Guide to Childbirth* (New York: Bantam Dell, 2003), pp. 136–137

94 Interview of Bethany Hayes, MD, on blogtalkradio.com

95 Gaskin, *Ina May's Guide to Childbirth*, pp. 140–141

96 Viktor E. Frankl, *Man's Search for Meaning* (New York: Pocket Books 1984), p. 86

97 G.E.H. Palmer, Philip Sherrard, and Kallistos Ware (eds. and trans.), *The Philokalia: The Complete Text*, Vol. 1 (New York: Faber and Faber, 1979), p. 539

98 Gaskin, *Ina May's Guide to Childbirth*, p. 162

99 Mathewes-Green, *The Jesus Prayer*, p. 150

100 W. Jardine Grisbrooke (ed.), *The Spiritual Counsels of Father John of Kronstadt* (Crestwood: St. Vladimir's Seminary Press, 1967), p. 59

101 This story from the life of St. Symeon of Emesa, Fool-for-Christ, is my retelling of material from *The Life of St. Symeon the Fool* by Bishop Leontius of Neapolis, https://publishing.cdlib.org/ucpressebooks/view?docId=ft6k4007sx&chunk.id=a1 (accessed May 15, 2019)

102 Dietrich Bonhoeffer, *Life Together* (San Francisco: HarperOne, 1954), pp. 99–100

103 Alexander Roberts, James Donaldson, Arthur Cleveland Coxe (eds.), The Ante-Nicene Fathers, Vol. 3 (New York: Cosimo Classics, 2007), p. 701

104 James McKenna et al, "Experimental Studies of Infant-Parent Co-Sleeping: Mutual Physiological and Behavioral Influences and their Relevance to SIDS (Sudden Infant Death Syndrome)," *Early Human Development* 38 (1994), pp. 187–201

105 Alicia Myers, Pater Nutrix, "Milk Metaphors and Character Formation in Hebrews and I Peter," chapter 6 in Beth Stovell (ed.), *Making Sense of Motherhood* (Eugene: Wipf & Stock, 2016), p. 81

106 H. Hausner et al., "Differential transfer of dietary flavour compounds into human breast milk," *Physiology and Behavior* 95(1–2), 2008, pp. 118–124

107 Philip Schaff and William Wilson (trans.), *The Sacred Writings of Clement of Alexandria*, Vol. 1 (Altenmünster: Jazzybee Verlag, 2017), p. 82

108 St. Ephrem the Syrian, Nativity Hymn 4:150–153, in Kathleen McVey, "Ephrem the Syrian's Use of Female Metaphors to Describe the Deity," *Zeitschrift für Antikes Christentum*, Vol. 5(2), 2001, p. 280

109 Elizabeth Spearing (trans.), *Revelations of Divine Love by Julian of Norwich* (London: Penguin Classics, 1998), p. 141

110 St. Ephrem the Syrian, Hymn 3, http://www.newadvent.org/fathers/3703.htm (accessed May 13, 2019)

111 National Center for Health Statistics, quoted in Kimberley Ann Johnson, *The Fourth Trimester* (Boulder: Shambhala Publications, 2017), p. 26

112 Margarita Kay, *Anthropology of Human Birth* (Philadelphia: F.A. Davis Co., 1982), p. 198

113 Julie Wray, "The Postnatal Period: An Ending or a Beginning?" *New Digest* 48, 2009, p. 28

114 Kimberley Ann Johnson, op. cit., p. 25

115 Michel Najim and Patrick O'Grady (eds.), *Services of Initiation* (La Verne: The Antiochian Orthodox Institute, 2017)

116 R.S. Rigda, I.C. McMillen, and P. Buckley, "Bed sharing patterns in a

cohort of Australian infants during the first six months after birth," *Journal of Paediatrics and Child Health* 36, 2000, pp. 117–121

117 Lia Amaral, "Mechanical Analysis of Infant Carrying in Hominoids," *Naturwissenschaften* 95(4), 2008, pp. 281–292

118 Britney Benoit et al, "The Power of Human Touch for Babies" https://static1.squarespace.com/static/50056474c4aa4387b4e629ea/t/5719260ac2ea517c03d5d582/1461265930827/The_Power_of_Human_Touch_for_Babies.pdf (undated) (accessed May 15, 2019)

119 McVey, op. cit., p. 268

120 Ibid., p. 268

121 Ibid., p. 269

122 Ibid., p. 263

123 Benedicta Ward (trans.), op. cit., p. 103

124 Lu Gao et al, "Steroid receptor coactivators 1 and 2 mediate fetal-to-maternal signaling that initiates parturition," *Journal of Clinical Investigation* 125(7), 2015, pp. 2808–2824

125 St. Paisios of Mount Athos, *Spiritual Counsels 4: Family Life* (Souroti: Monastery of John the Theologian, 2012), p. 4

126 Holy Transfiguration Monastery (trans.), *St. Isaac the Syrian: The Ascetical Homilies* 42 (Boston: Holy Transfiguration Monastery, 1984), p. 211

127 Oliver Davies (ed.), *Gateway to Paradise: Basil the Great* (Welwyn Garden City: New City, 1991), p. 39

128 Torode (eds.), op. cit., p. 103

129 Met. Philip Saliba and Joseph Allen, *Out of the Depths Have I Cried* (Brookline: Holy Cross Orthodox Press, 1979), p. 90

130 Lisa Baraitser, op. cit., p. 5

131 Hyder Rollins (ed.), *The Letters of John Keats, 1814–1821* (Cambridge: Harvard University Press, 1958), letter to George and Georgiana Keats on 21 April 1819, pp. 100–104

132 Elizabeth Leis-Newman, "Miscarriage and Loss," *Monitor on Psychology* Vol. 43(6), 2012, p. 56

aura S. Jansson is an Orthodox Christian doula, childbirth educator, and mother living and writing at the intersection of birth and faith. She earned her Masters degree in Theology and Philosophy from the University of Oxford, UK, and has also resided in the USA, Serbia, Germany, and Fiji. Since 2005 she has guided scores of expectant mothers on the path to parenthood, witnessing with wonder as bellies and souls grow along the way.

Ancient Faith Publishing hopes you have enjoyed and bene-fited from this book. The proceeds from the sales of our books only partially cover the costs of operating our nonprofit minis-try—which includes both the work of **Ancient Faith Publishing** and the work of **Ancient Faith Radio**. Your financial sup-port makes it possible to continue this ministry both in print and online. Donations are tax-deductible and can be made at **www.ancientfaith.com.**

To view our other publications,
please visit our website: **store.ancientfaith.com**

Bringing you Orthodox Christian music, readings,
prayers, teaching, and podcasts 24 hours a day since 2004 at
www.ancientfaith.com